Hopi Basket Weaving

ARTISTRY IN NATURAL FIBERS

With Photographs by the Author

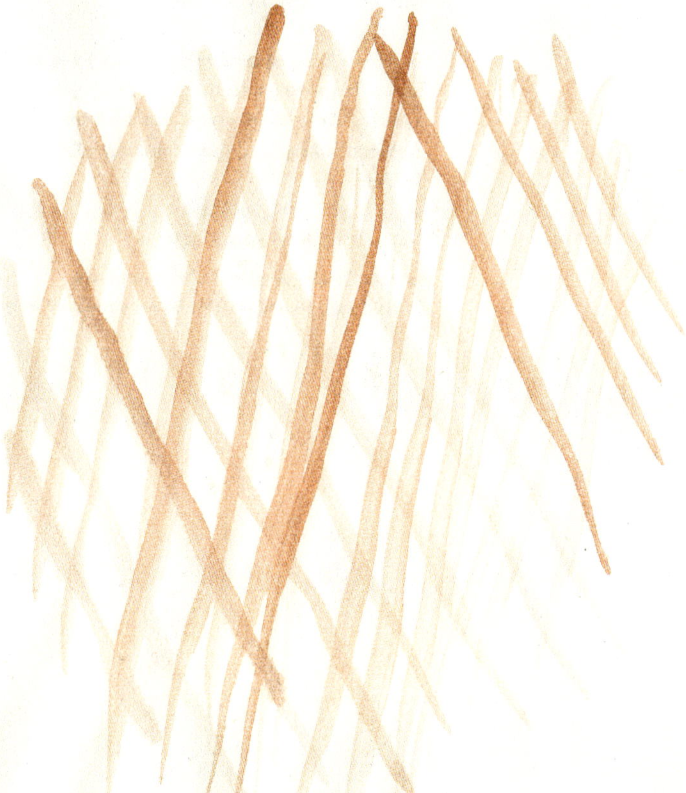

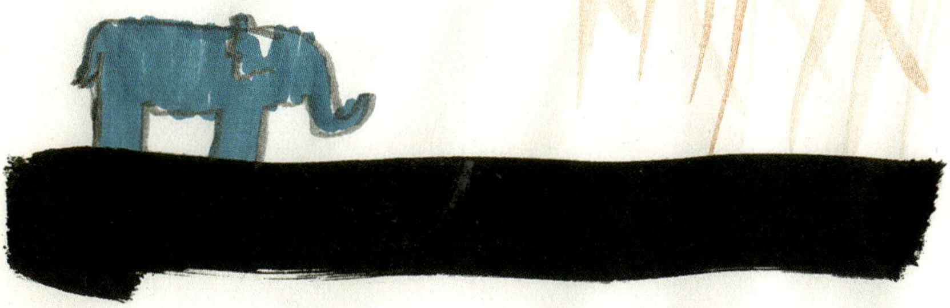

Published by:

Zach Feuer Gallery
530 West 24th Street
New York, NY 10011
T 212 989 7700
F 212 989 7720
www.zachfeuer.com

in conjunction with:

Sutton Lane Gallery
1 Sutton Lane
London EC1M 5PU
United Kingdom
T +44 20 7253 8580
F +44 20 7253 6580
www.suttonlane.com

Me.di.um
Rue du Roi Oscar II
Gustavia St. Barthélemy
97133 French West Indies
T +590 590 29 50 75
F +590 590 29 47 63
www.mediumstbarth.com

Allston Skirt Gallery
65 Thayer Street
Boston, MA 02118
T 617 482 3652
F 617 482 3654
www.allstonskirt.com

Kavi Gupta Gallery
835 West Washington
Chicago, IL 60607
T 312 432 0708
F 312 432 0709
www.kavigupta.com

Kantor / Feuer Gallery
7025 Melrose Avenue
Los Angeles, CA 90038
T 323 933 6976
F 323 933 8976
www.kantorfeuer.com

Produced osp catalogs © 2006
Edition of 1500
PRINTED IN CANADA
ISBN number 0-9768533-6-1

Dedicated to
A LITTLE BEAN

my friend and mentor,

who taught me to love the past and present

of the American Southwest

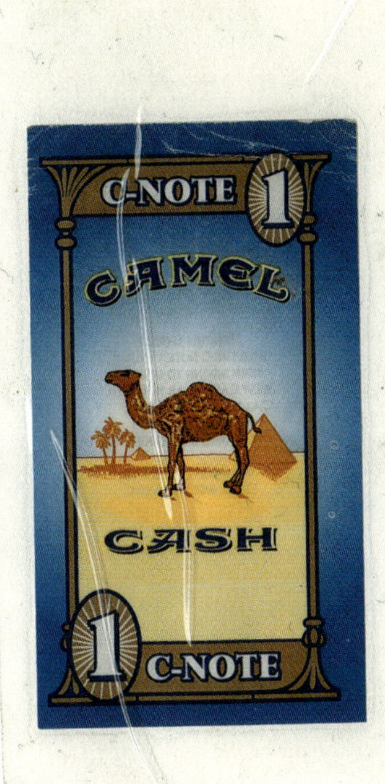

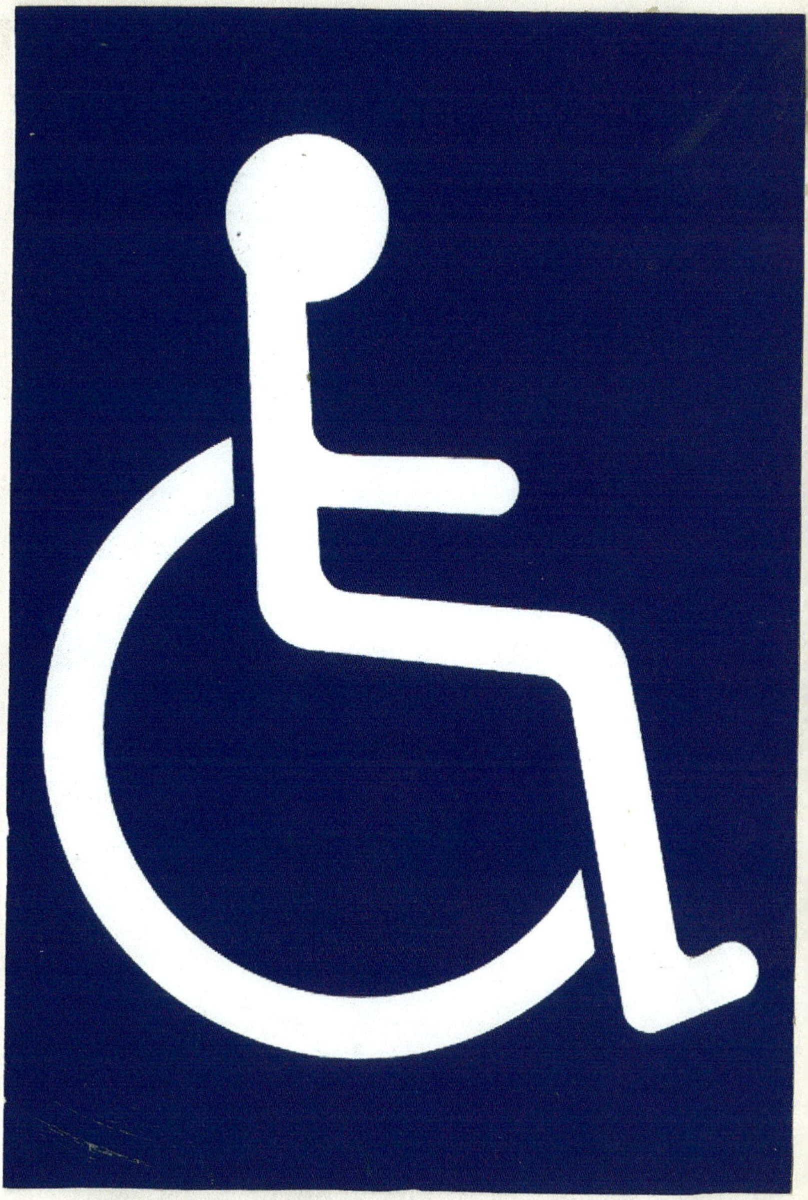

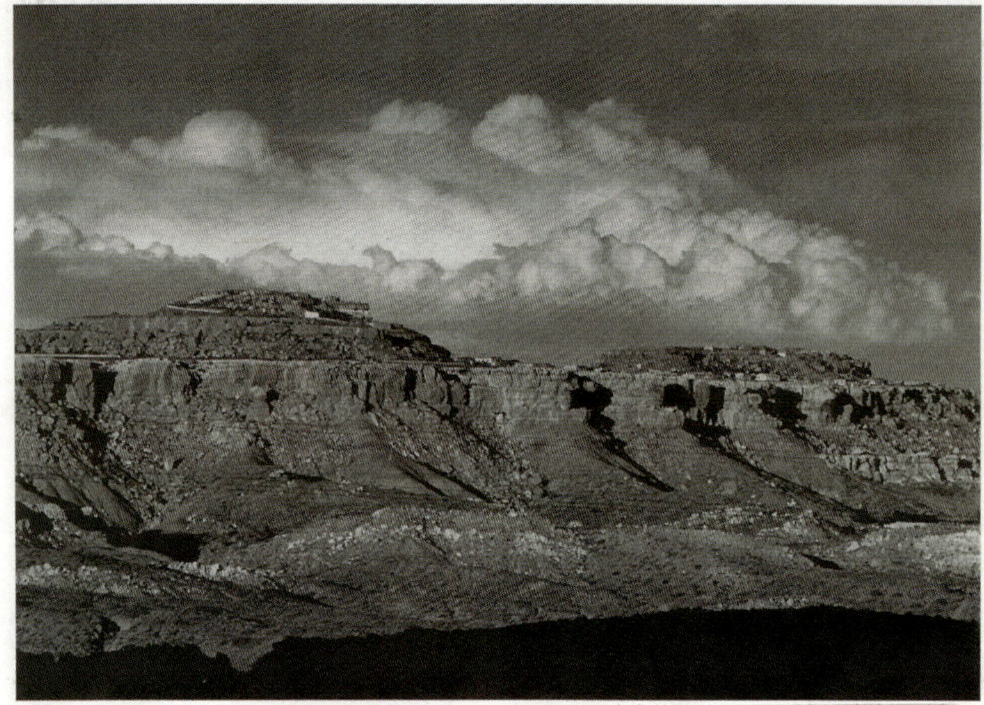

Few beings have ever been so impregnated, pierced to the core by the conviction of the absolute futility of human aspiration. The universe is nothing but a furtive arrangement of elementary particles. A figure in transition towards chaos. That is what will finally prevail. The human race will disappear. Other races in turn will appear and disappear. The skies will be glacial and empty, traversed by the feeble light of half-dead stars. These too will disappear. Everything will disappear. All human actions are as free and as stripped of meaning as the unfettered movement of the elementary

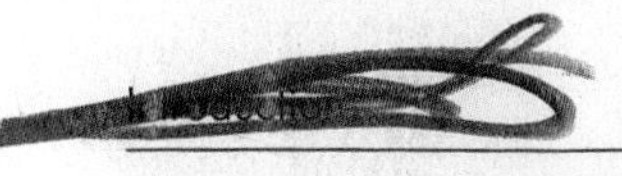

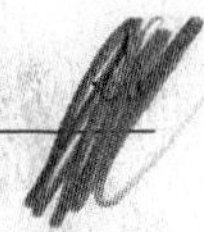

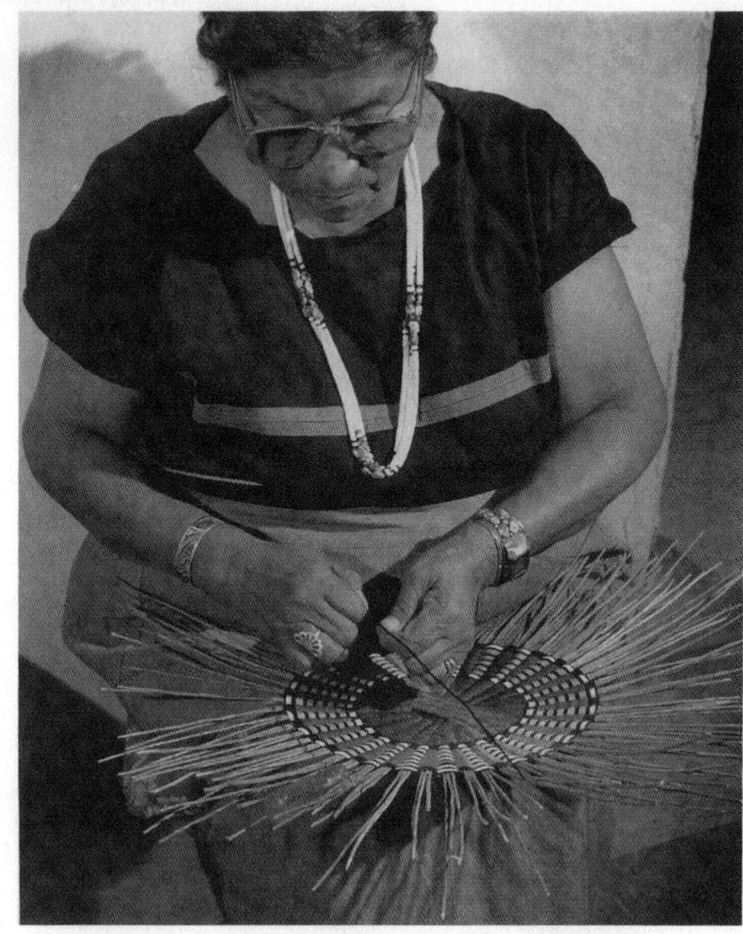

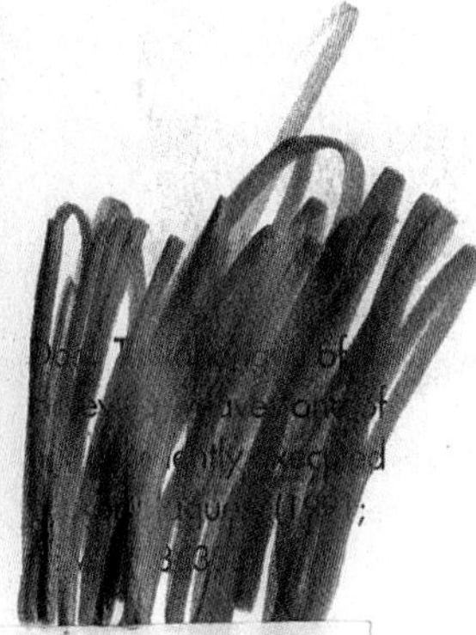

panticles. Good, Evil, Morality, Sentiments? Pure "Victorian Fictions." All that exists is egotism. Cold, Intact, and Radiant.

— Michel Houellebecq
Against the World, Against Life

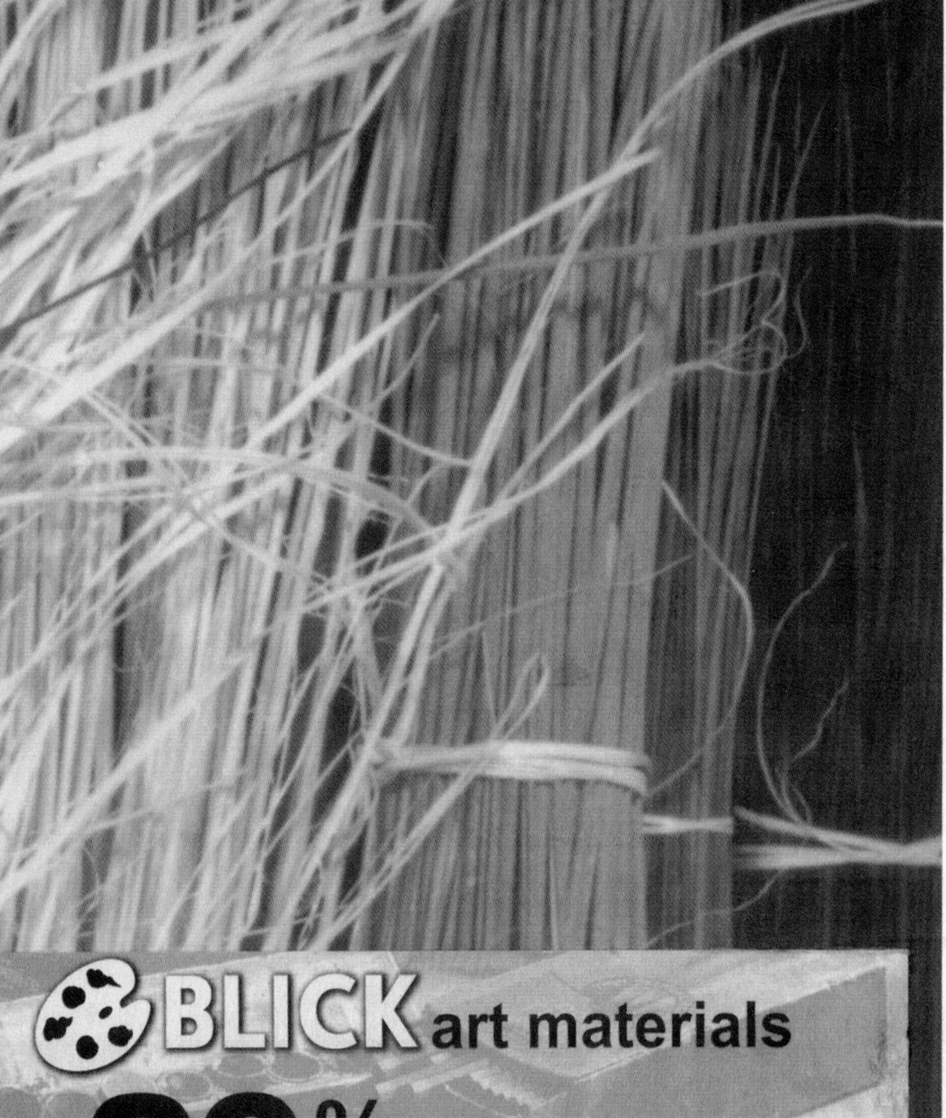

VALID 12/1 TO 12/31
BLICK art materials
20% OFF
one non-sale, in-stock item
see details on back
PREFERRED CUSTOMER PROGRAM

Plates

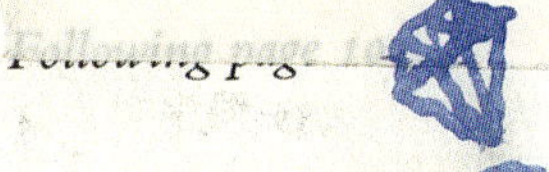

It's dark as a coal mine
up inside your pussy.
When I put my hand in your pussy
and I take it back out
It's covered in coal dust by
the gnomes that live inside.
When I chip off the pussy-coal
that's encrusted my hand
My fingernails have been transformed
into diamonds by your love.

— traditional

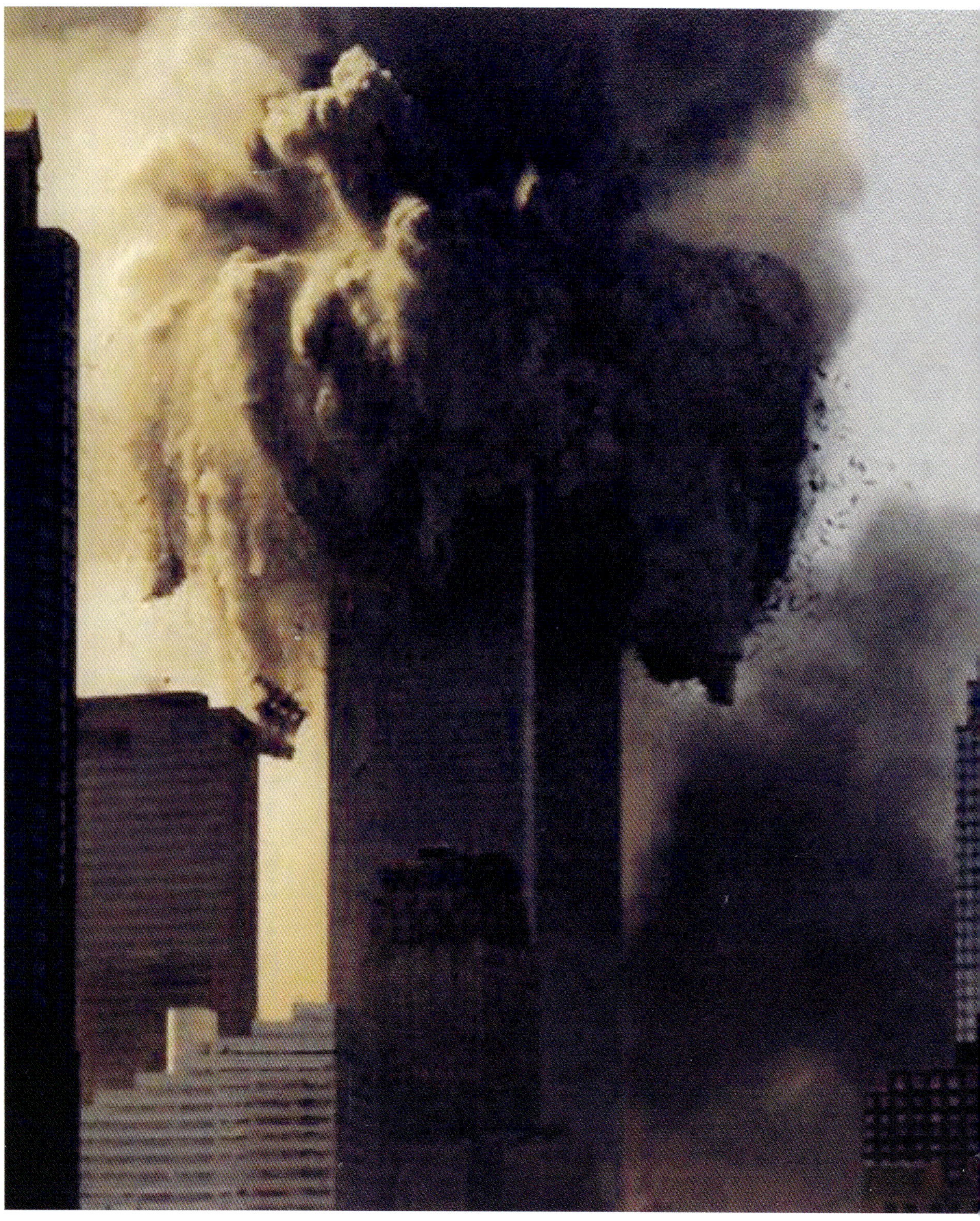

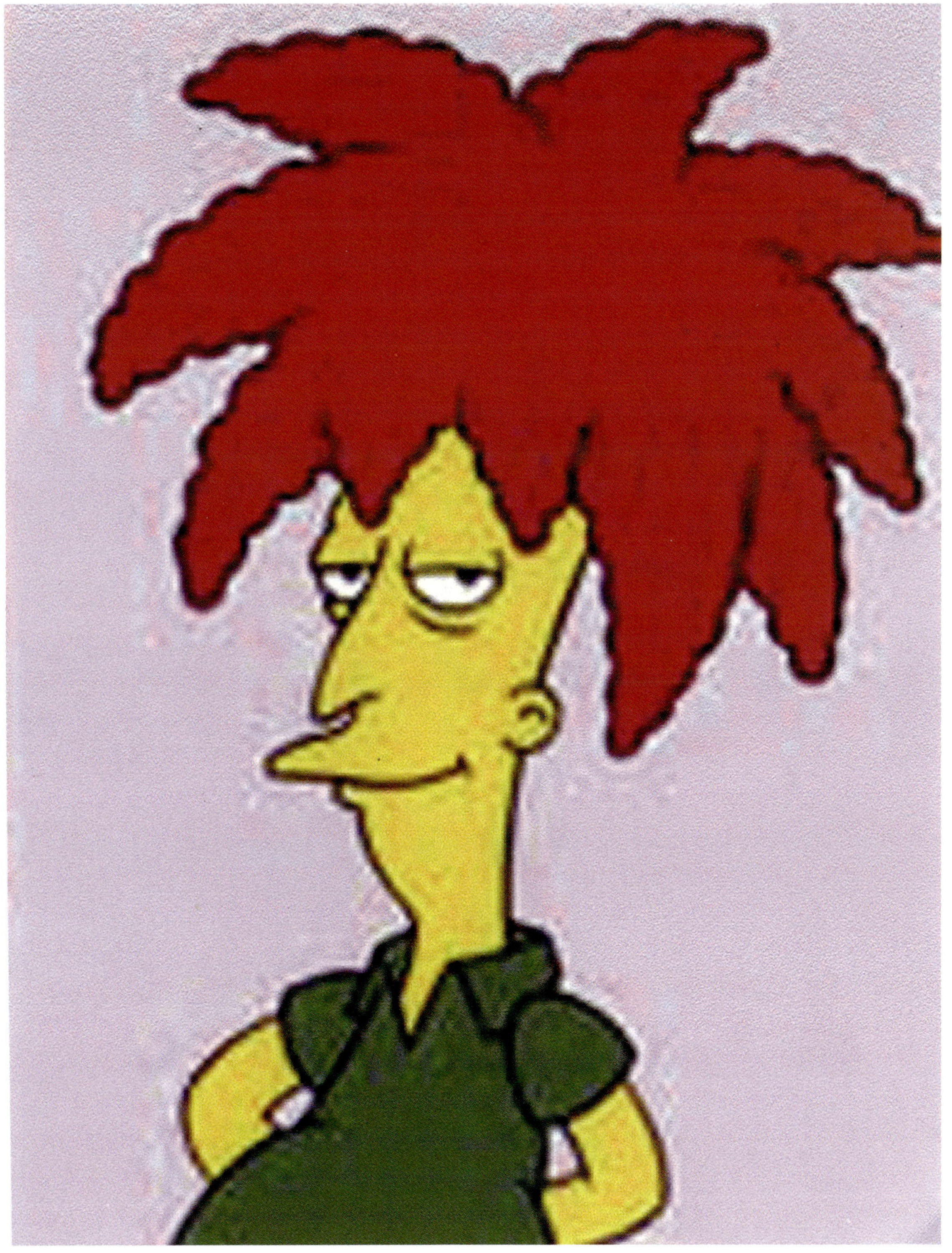

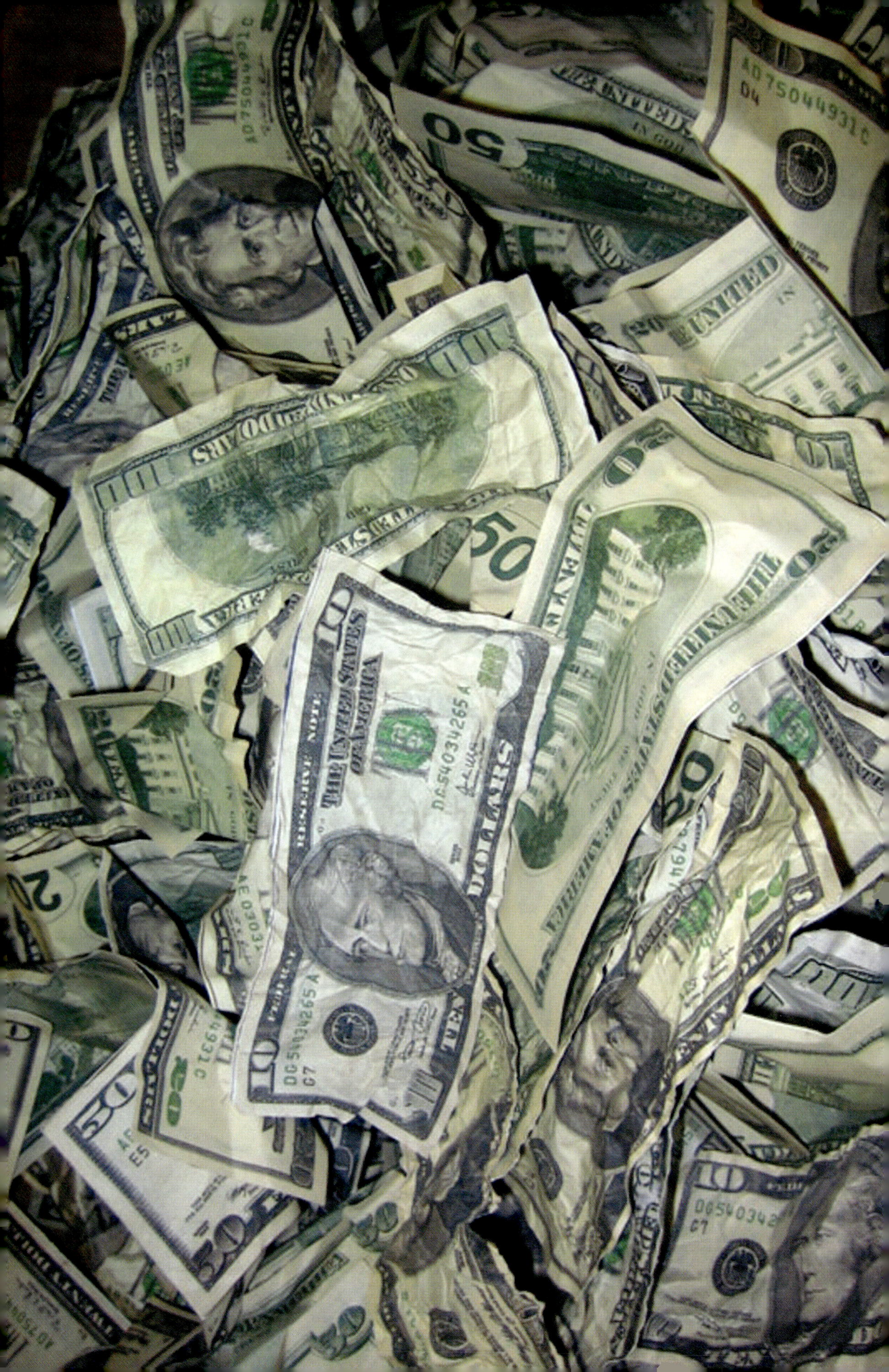

TIME AND MONEY

AN INSTALLATION

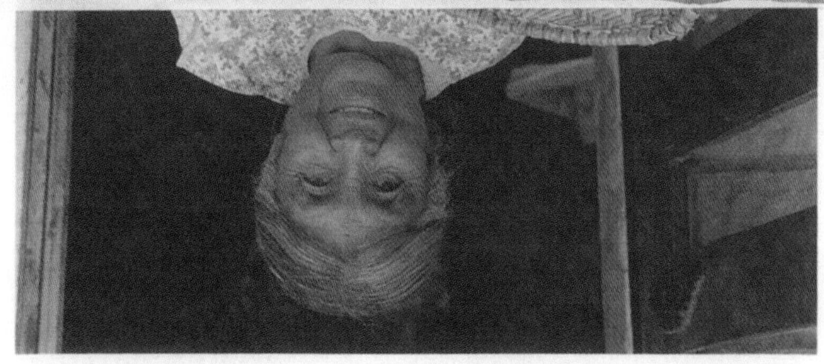

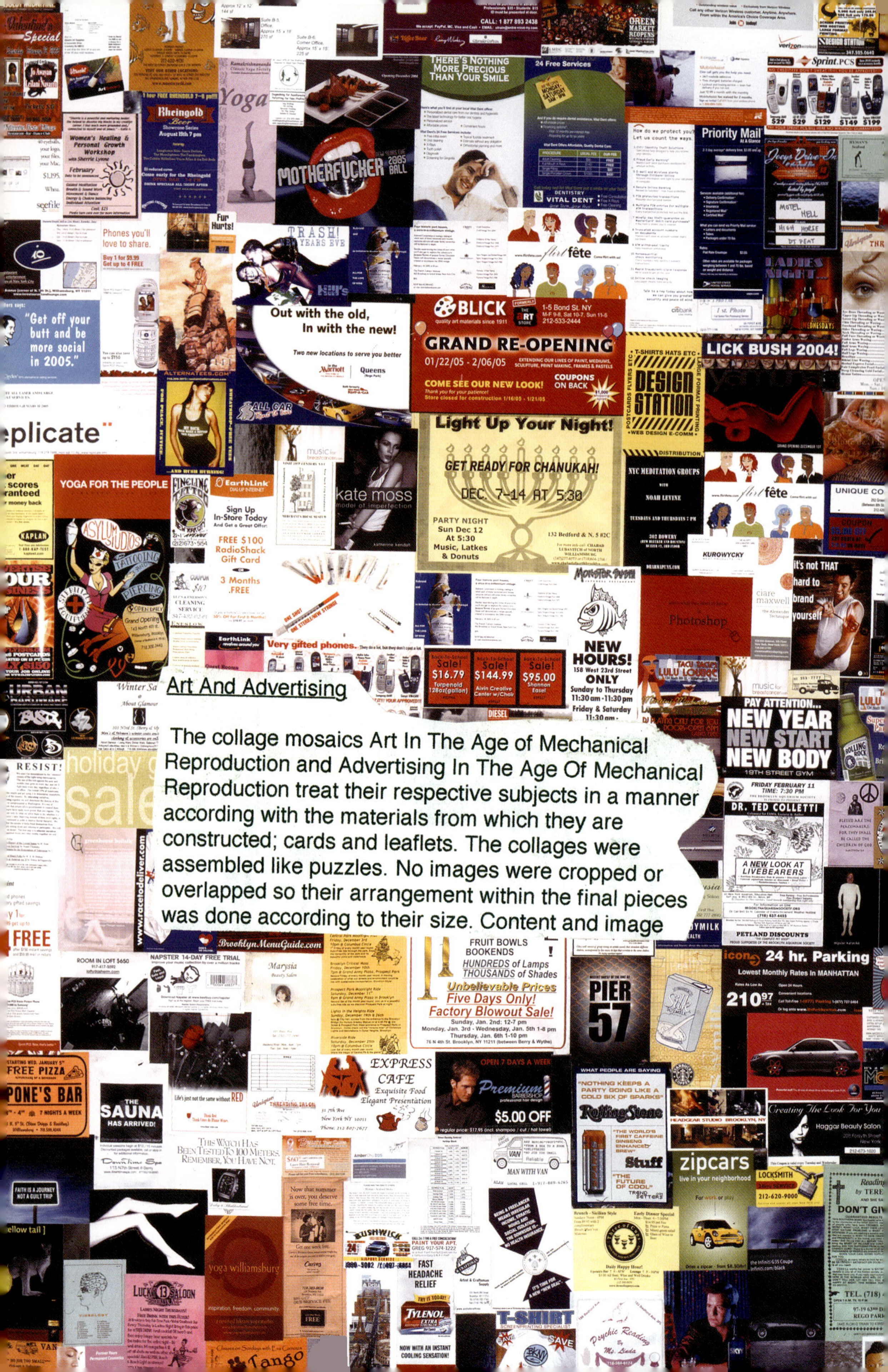

Art And Advertising

The collage mosaics Art In The Age of Mechanical Reproduction and Advertising In The Age Of Mechanical Reproduction treat their respective subjects in a manner according with the materials from which they are constructed; cards and leaflets. The collages were assembled like puzzles. No images were cropped or overlapped so their arrangement within the final pieces was done according to their size. Content and image

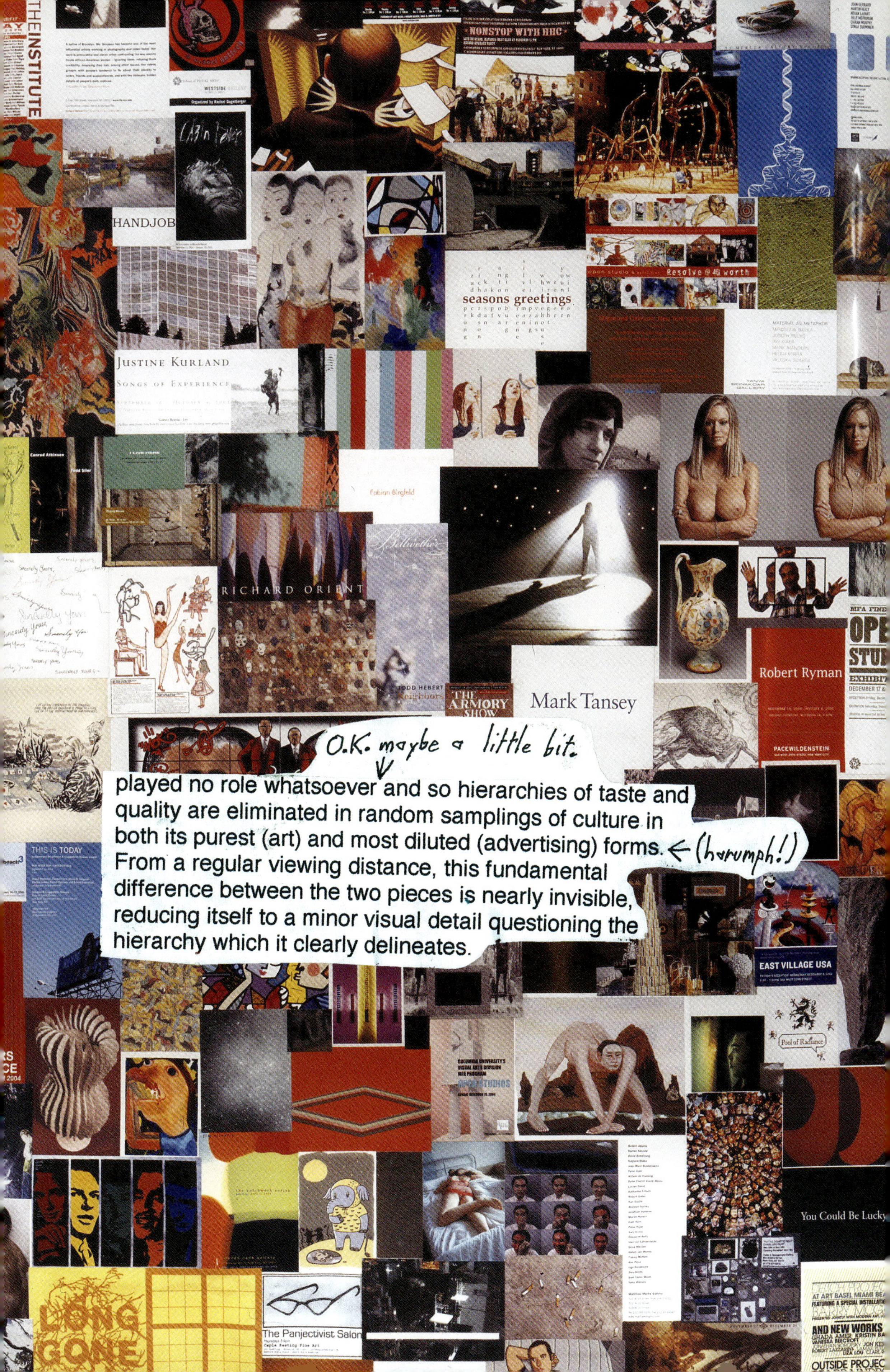
O.K. maybe a little bit.
played no role whatsoever and so hierarchies of taste and
quality are eliminated in random samplings of culture in
both its purest (art) and most diluted (advertising) forms. ← (harumph!)
From a regular viewing distance, this fundamental
difference between the two pieces is nearly invisible,
reducing itself to a minor visual detail questioning the
hierarchy which it clearly delineates.

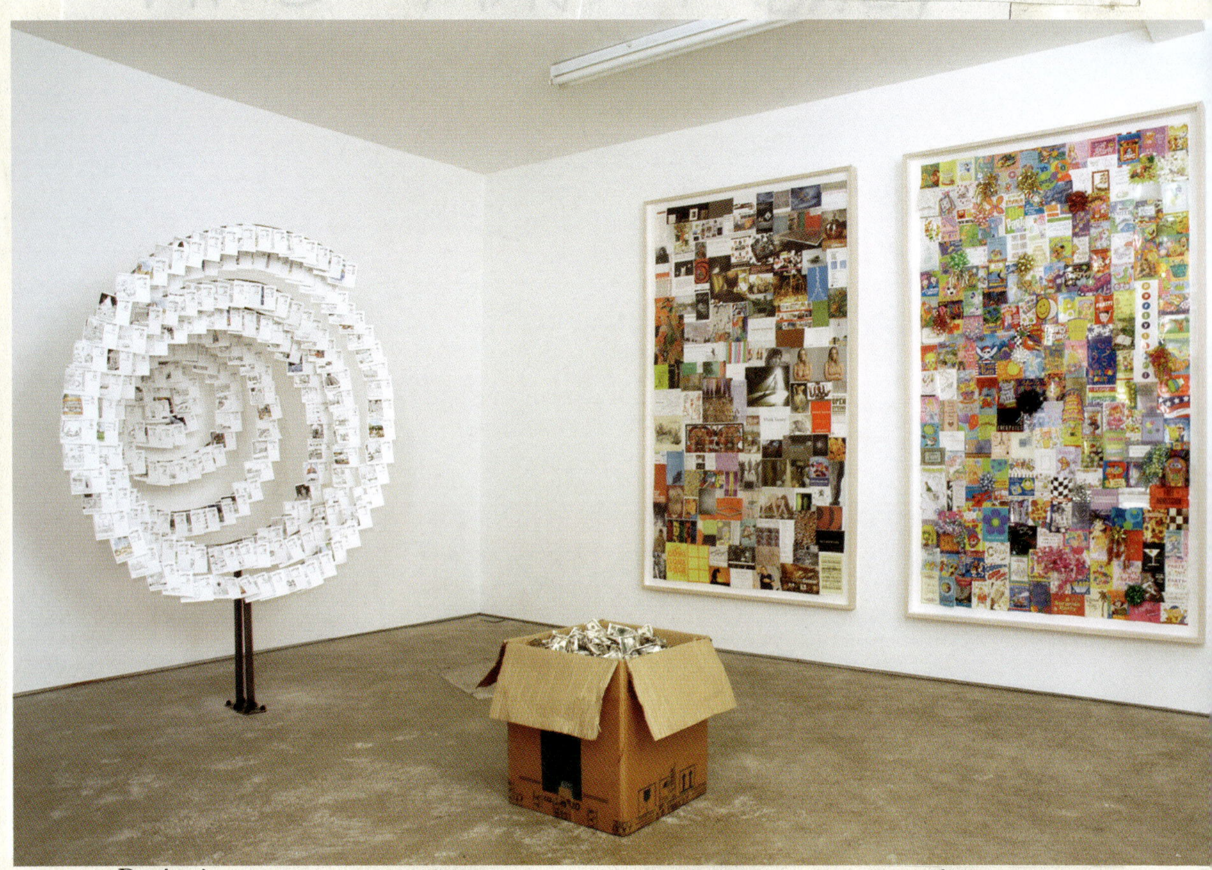

The installation is a work composed of discreet elements which relate to each other both spatially within the gallery and conceptually through a network of implied equivilancies, narratives and other more ephemeral associations. The ones which I outline here are but a few of them and the installation is by no means limited by this interpretation. Rather I think that these ideas might serve as a kind of guide to the thought processes that led to it's creation.

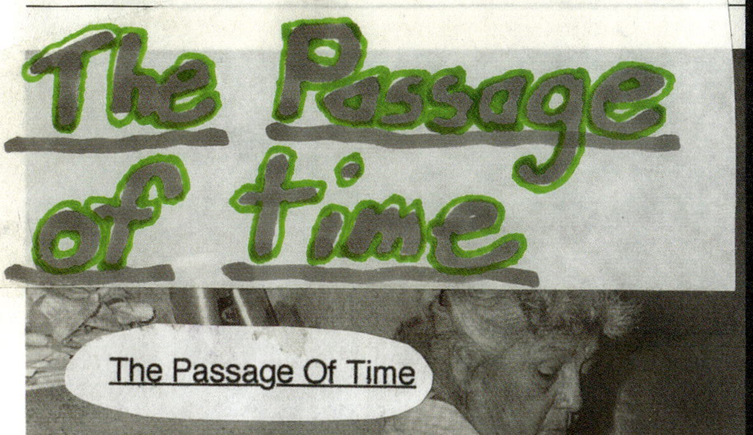

The Passage of time

The Passage Of Time

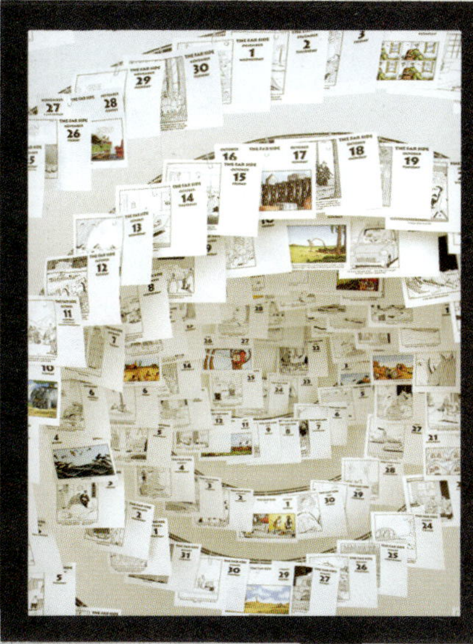

Memory and premonition come together and are depicted as equal forces within the context of The Far Side Calendar Time Machines. Meeting in the fleeting present represented by the exhibition itself, which takes place during the missing dates of March 23 (the opening of the exhibition) through April 23 (the last day of the show) and extending 1 year backwards and forwards of that span, these sculptures might be seen as a study in planned obsolesence. Even more so in that they are constructed from a combination of cultural artifacts and representational cliches whose time has already passed. The representation of memory, premonition, or time travel as a series of calendar pages spiraling into the distance is not without history. The image has been used frequently in film and television by Hitchcock, Rod Serling, and many others, as well as in comic books and science fiction illustration to the point of becoming an archetype of popular culture, a symbol of the concepts that resides within the collective unconscious. In a similar way, the Far Side Off-The-Wall calendar is an icon whose life was snuffed out by its creator, the brilliant cartoonist Gary Larson. For 17 years from 1985 through 2002 the Far Side calendar set the standard for the box calendar industry, whose sales took an enormous hit in 2002 when Larson retired his creation, which was by far the biggest selling calendar of all time. The ubiquity of this artifact made it a natural choice for the Time Machines. Day/date equivilancies were established matching Thursday, March 23rd 2005 to its match in 1994. The calendars from 1994, 1993, and 1995 were then procured from collectors on ebay in order to create a situation in which history's penchant for repeating itself literally illustrated. Even a broken watch tells the correct time twice a day.

Marcia
hot sto
sheets
ASM

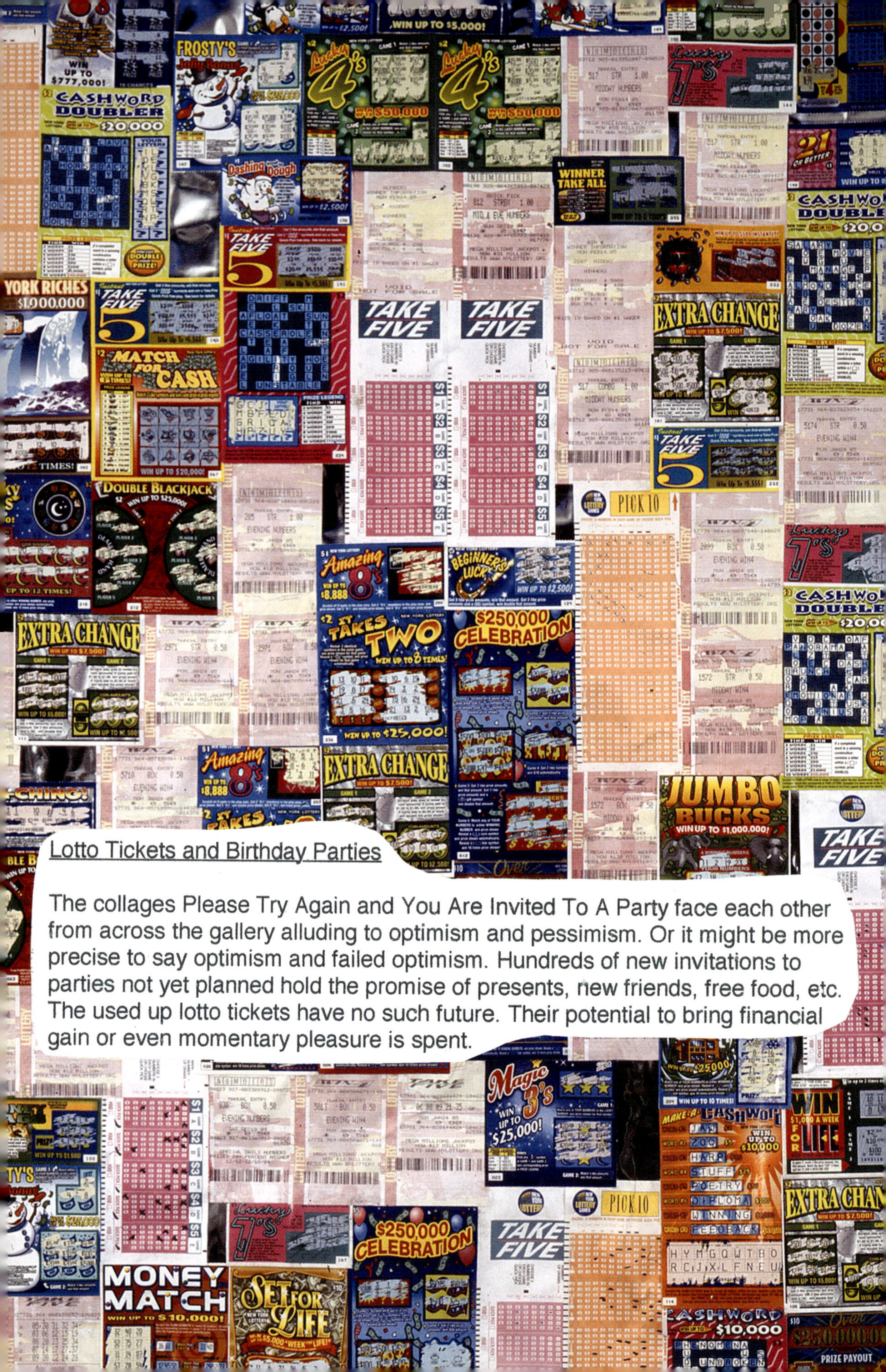

Lotto Tickets and Birthday Parties

The collages Please Try Again and You Are Invited To A Party face each other from across the gallery alluding to optimism and pessimism. Or it might be more precise to say optimism and failed optimism. Hundreds of new invitations to parties not yet planned hold the promise of presents, new friends, free food, etc. The used up lotto tickets have no such future. Their potential to bring financial gain or even momentary pleasure is spent.

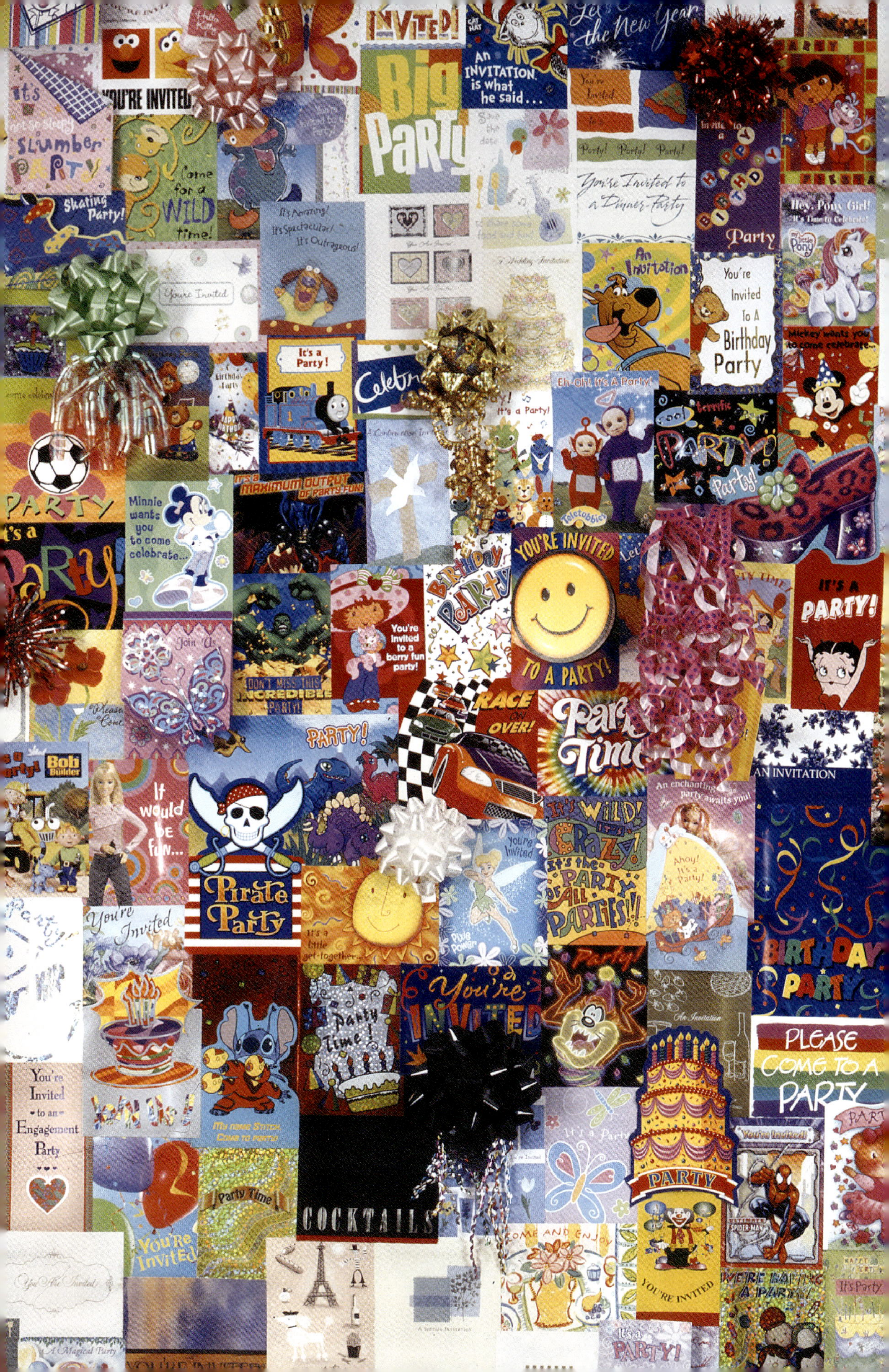

Contemporary Hopi Basket Weaving Techniques

The calendar pages themselves are taken from the Far Side Off-The-Wall Calendar from the years 1993, 1994, and 1995. The day/date correspondences of these years match those for the years 2004, 2005, and 2006 and the pages themselves are unmarked concerning the year that they are from. This creates a scenario in which the sculptures are specific to the time and place exploring the possible origins of contemporary Hopi basket weaving techniques. of the exhibition, however sometimes even intriguing, readings of Hopi oral history, as well as reports of dis- between march 23 of 2009 and the same date of 2011 the sculptures will again in more detail in the appendix, but they can be at least outlined come into their own in terms of synchronicity with the christian calendar. Zeroing in Contemporary Hopi plaited basket weaving is a continuation even more closely, we find that the days between March 23 some time before the first century A.D. and April 23 are missing and wicker basketry is not from the two year period described by techniques. the time machines. This missing time—the Mogollon, the Hohokam, and the Anasazi— constitutes the duration of the exhibition in which they were first presented and to which they will always in part be tied. The convoluted logic of these day/date correspondences mirrors in many ways the convoluted logic of time travel itself with that some Hopi clans brought their coiling tech all its inherent paradoxes. tions from southern locations sometime during the fourteenth and Concerning the use of the Far Side Calendar : The exact origin of Hopi wicker weaving remains a mystery, Created by Gary Larson in 1983, The Far Side Off-The-Wall Calendar quickly became the most popular desk calendar in America and possibly the world. Larson's humor also contained quite a bit of pretzel logic and consequently made an indelible mark on the popular unconscious. The Time Machines take Larson's

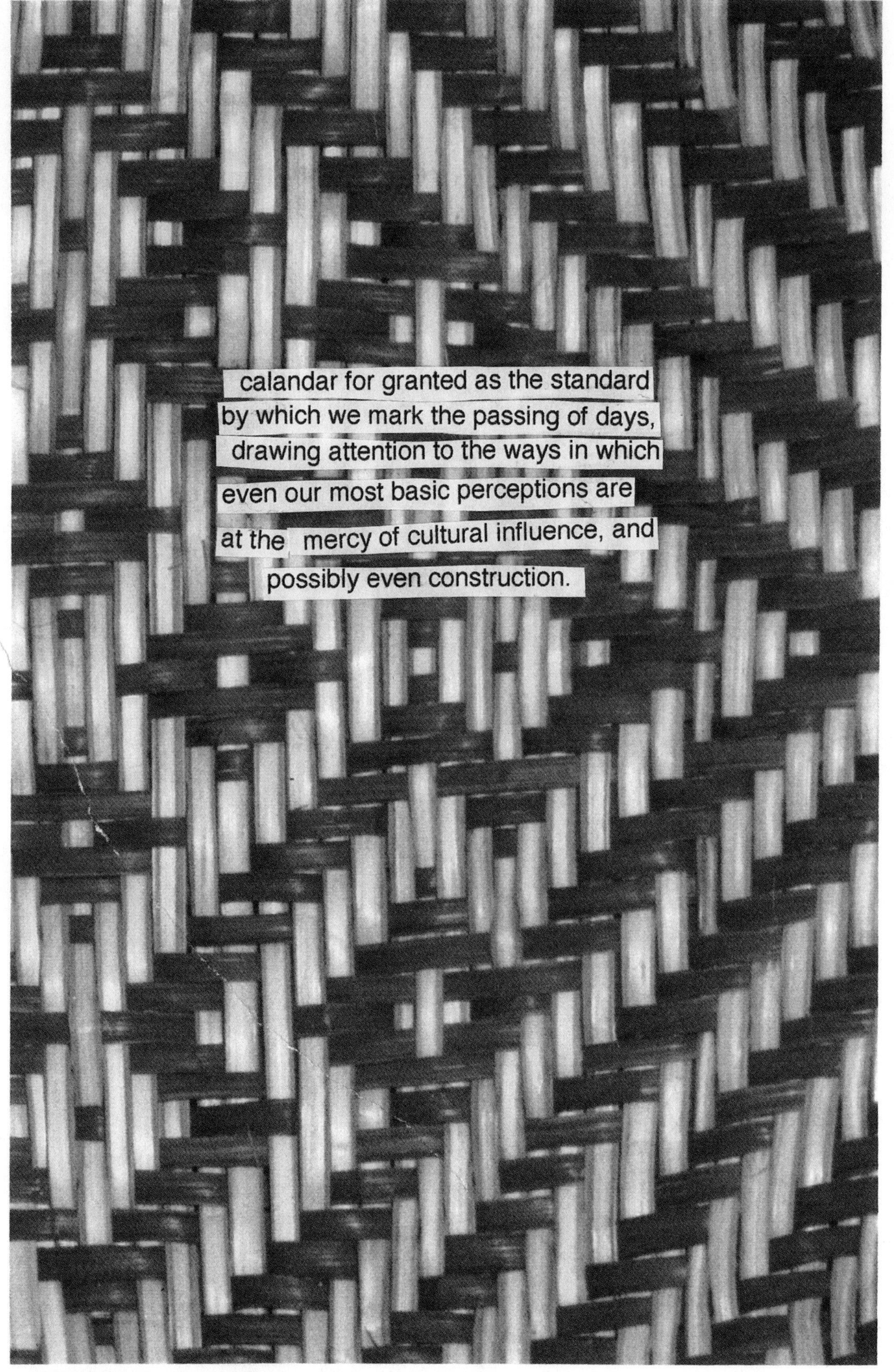

calandar for granted as the standard
by which we mark the passing of days,
drawing attention to the ways in which
even our most basic perceptions are
at the   mercy of cultural influence, and
possibly even construction.

BOX OF MONEY

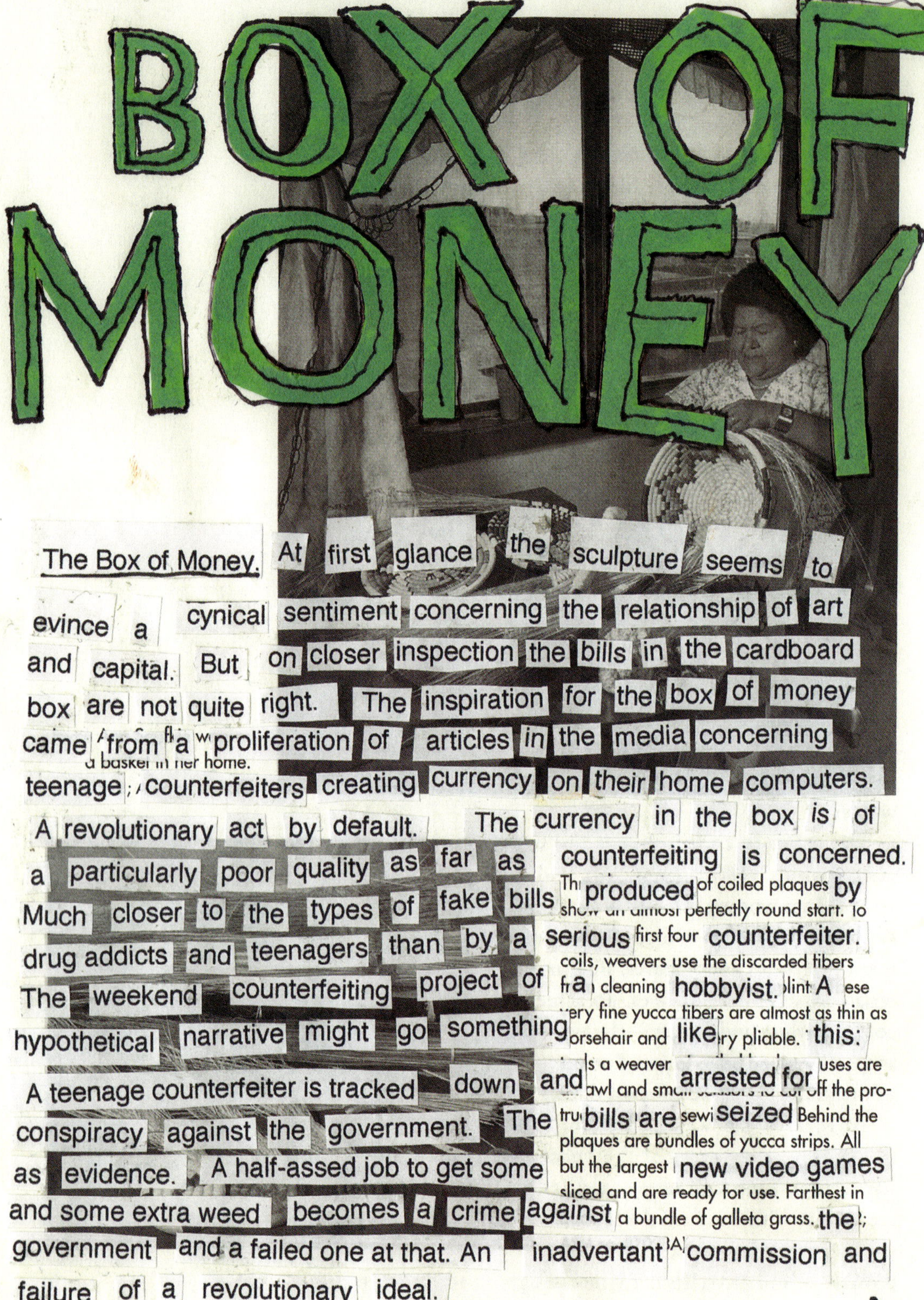

The Box of Money. At first glance the sculpture seems to evince a cynical sentiment concerning the relationship of art and capital. But on closer inspection the bills in the cardboard box are not quite right. The inspiration for the box of money came from a proliferation of articles in the media concerning teenage counterfeiters creating currency on their home computers.

A revolutionary act by default. The currency in the box is of a particularly poor quality as far as counterfeiting is concerned. Much closer to the types of fake bills produced by drug addicts and teenagers than by a serious counterfeiter. The weekend counterfeiting project of a hobbyist. hypothetical narrative might go something like this:

A teenage counterfeiter is tracked down and arrested for conspiracy against the government. The bills are seized as evidence. A half-assed job to get some new video games and some extra weed becomes a crime against the government and a failed one at that. An inadvertant commission and failure of a revolutionary ideal.

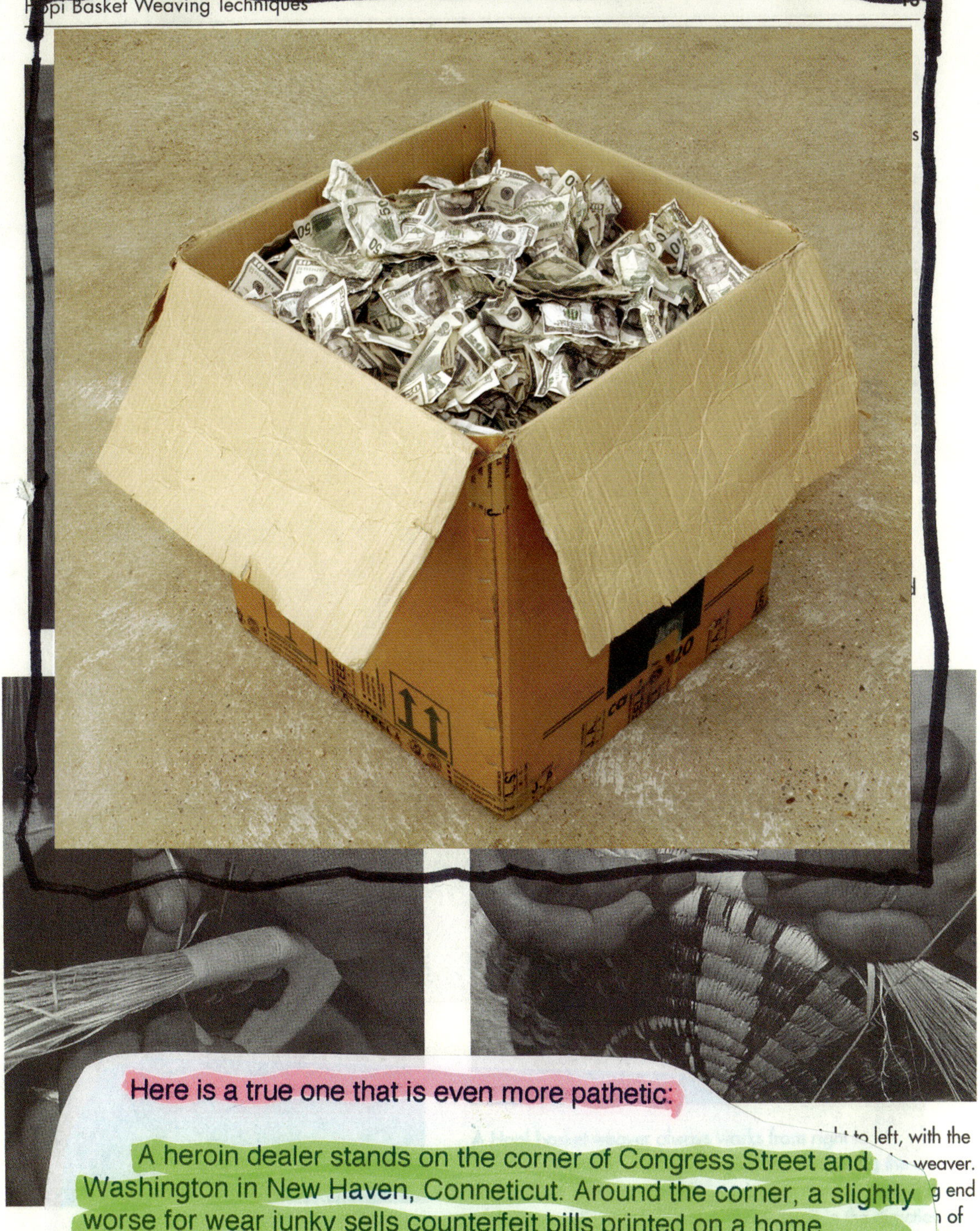

Here is a true one that is even more pathetic:

A heroin dealer stands on the corner of Congress Street and Washington in New Haven, Conneticut. Around the corner, a slightly worse for wear junky sells counterfeit bills printed on a home computer, then painstakingly stained and crumpled to give a realistic effect, twenties for five, to even worse for wear junkies who then try to pass them off to the dealer for dope. The dealer is of course familiar with this trick and the poor junky almost always gets a beating for even attempting it, not to mention losing his original five.

THE APPENDECTOMY BENEFIT

Gathering Yucca Leaves

The group of paintings Because I live collectively titled The Appendectomy Benefit
were inspired by the so-called or "traces" there when on many friends of the paintings
of Jackson Pollock. These traces, were pertinent cigarette butts, basket weaving. I
clumps of paint brush bristles, partial footprints on re the surfaces of yucca leaves the
paintings were an affectation of lassez faire example by the artist process deliberately
placed to give a macho impression of women meeting in the morning, not caring about
the finer,"unimportant" gasoline money, piling details of presentation and above all to
avoid treating the painting known to one of them as "precious". These yucca plants
elements of the paintings have become famous below Second Mesa. as well for the
problem of conservation By tradition, that they present. ed baskets A familiar and
comic scene is that of the group during the period of museum conservators by the
gathered around a cigarette butt This means that has fallen off not of done one of
the paintings with magnifying Niman ceremony, glasses and tweezers dance in hand,
bent on it's preservation. e departure of the Katsinam. Niman is held from mid to late

In the 9 paintings in the One woman show my intention was now to isolate this
particular idea by Niman, creating a group of traditional works in which there
was no paint at all, only "traces". cannot find suitable Debris from my studio floor
as well as the area surrounding the garbage near Santa Fe cans visit to outside my
building which I would apply in Santo Domingo Pueblo. by emptying my shop-vac
onto a sheet of paper as far as Kaibito, prepared with glue. This brings to mind
emptying was concieved of questions, If basket weavers as a cingular gesture that
would define the image. But after emptying the vacuum coiled basket weaving bag
I found that it was impossible now? to resist the urge to spread would the large,
debris around in order deep baskets be to create a more pleasing composition.
And so the formalism that The willingness and cooperation I had intended to mock
with my gesture ultimately made it possible had the last word.

On July 24, 1991, I drove Joyce and our
Nequatewa for many miles until we reached the place where Joyce

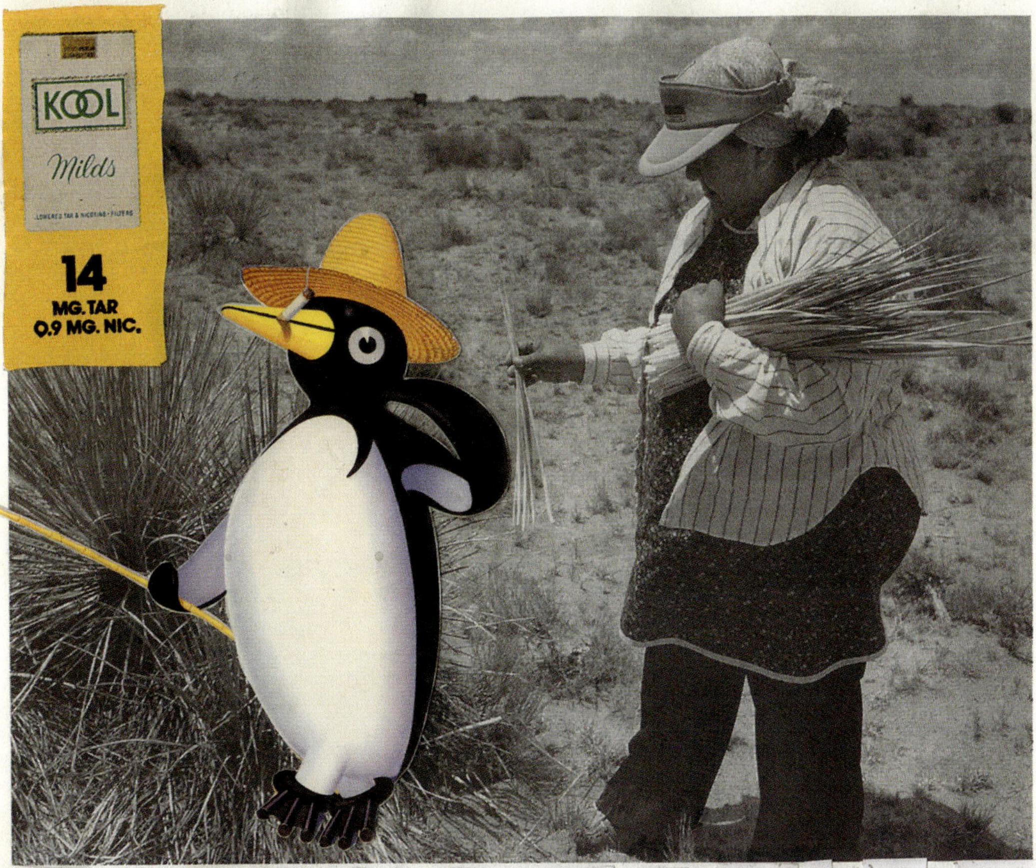

As for the "precious" aspect of the work, a frilly colored
yucca leaves, and at the same time they have fun and delight in white yucca leaves. (1991;
cut paper border frames each painting. These borders also serve
When we arrived at our destination, we were in a big field of
to differentiate the otherwise similar works through color as well
as introducing a minimal seriality to their installation. The borders
also provide the starting point for the puffy white titles of the individual
works : each one is named after the emotion ~~traditionally~~ *commonly*
below Second Mesa. She and Annabelle did not waste any time
associated with the color of its border. carefully to
I have accounted for the conservation of the paintings in advance
by providing a metal trough with each one
Guided by long experience, they either pulled out a handful of
(except for Envy, which has a matching broom)
leaves of selected only single that
to collect the bits and pieces which will inevitably drop off
with time.

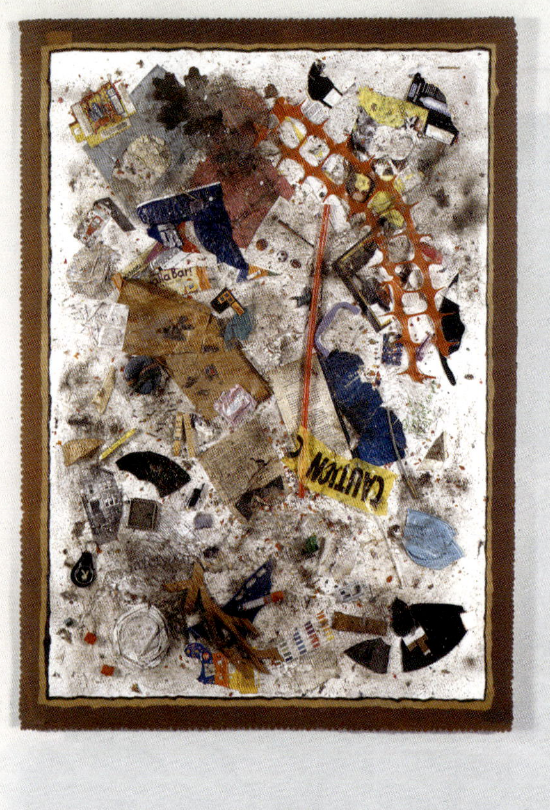

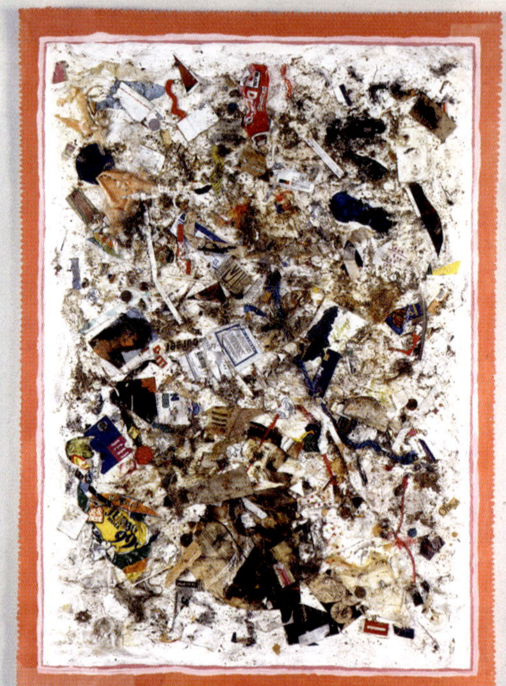

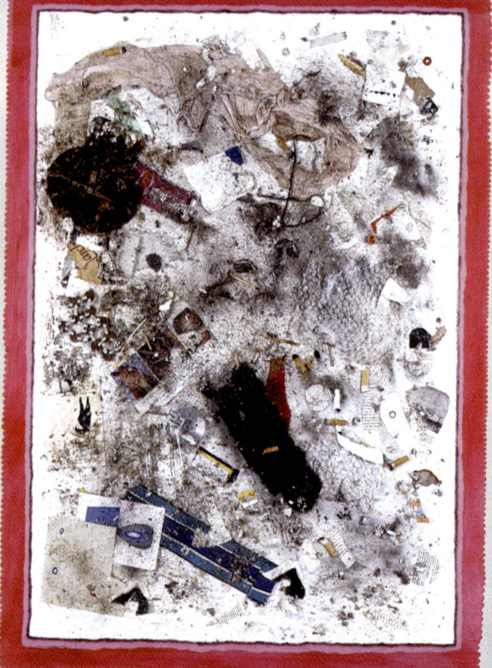

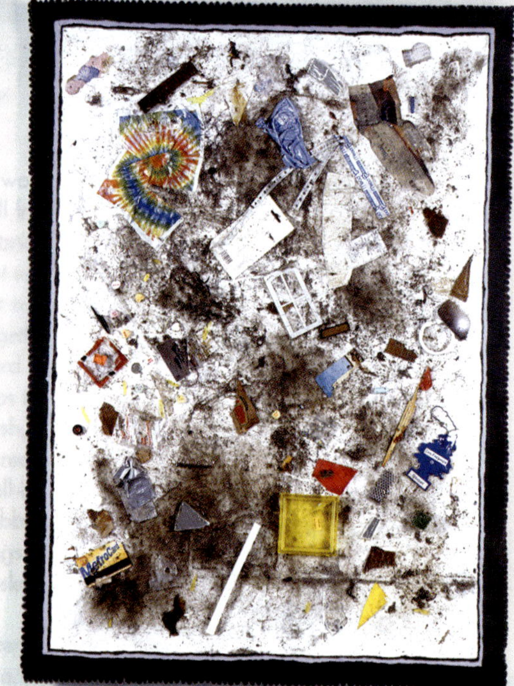

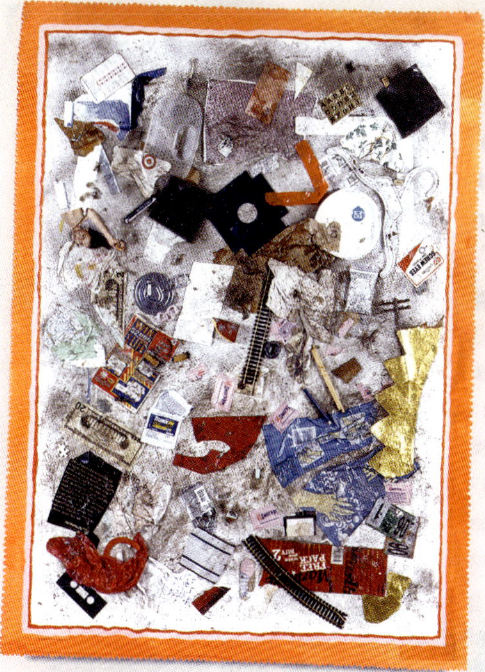

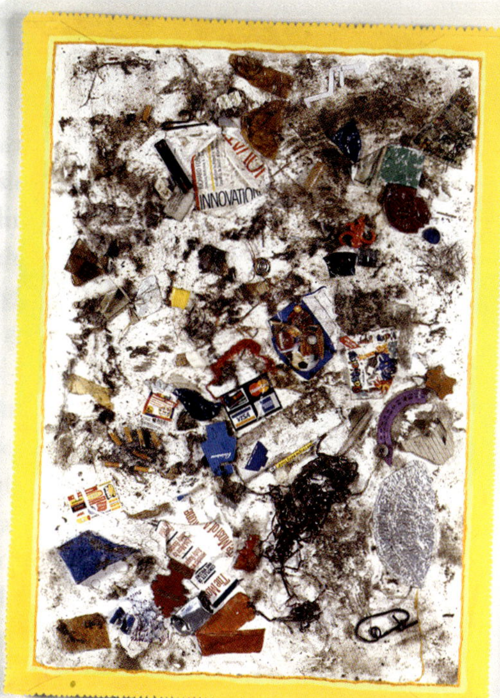

INNOVATION

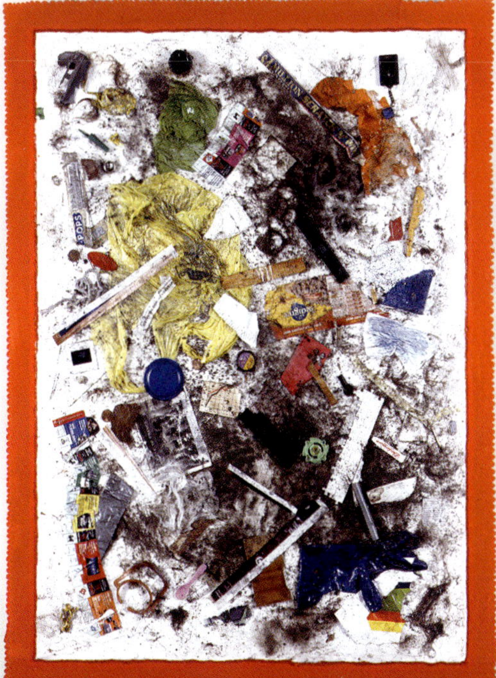

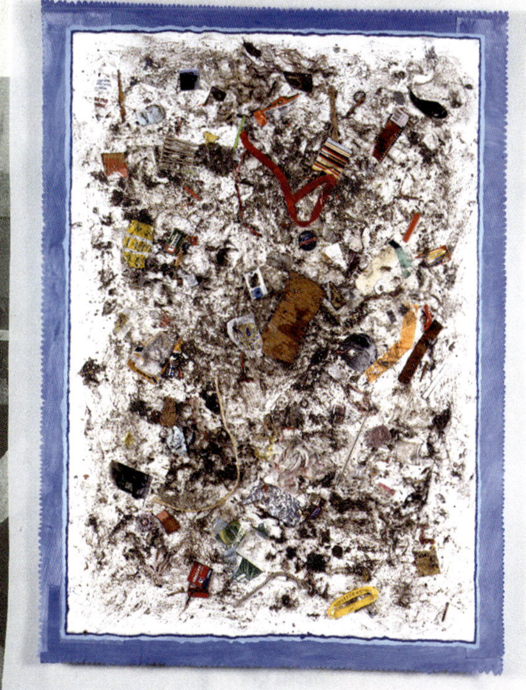

their dyeing in Treva's peach orchard. Many of her peach trees

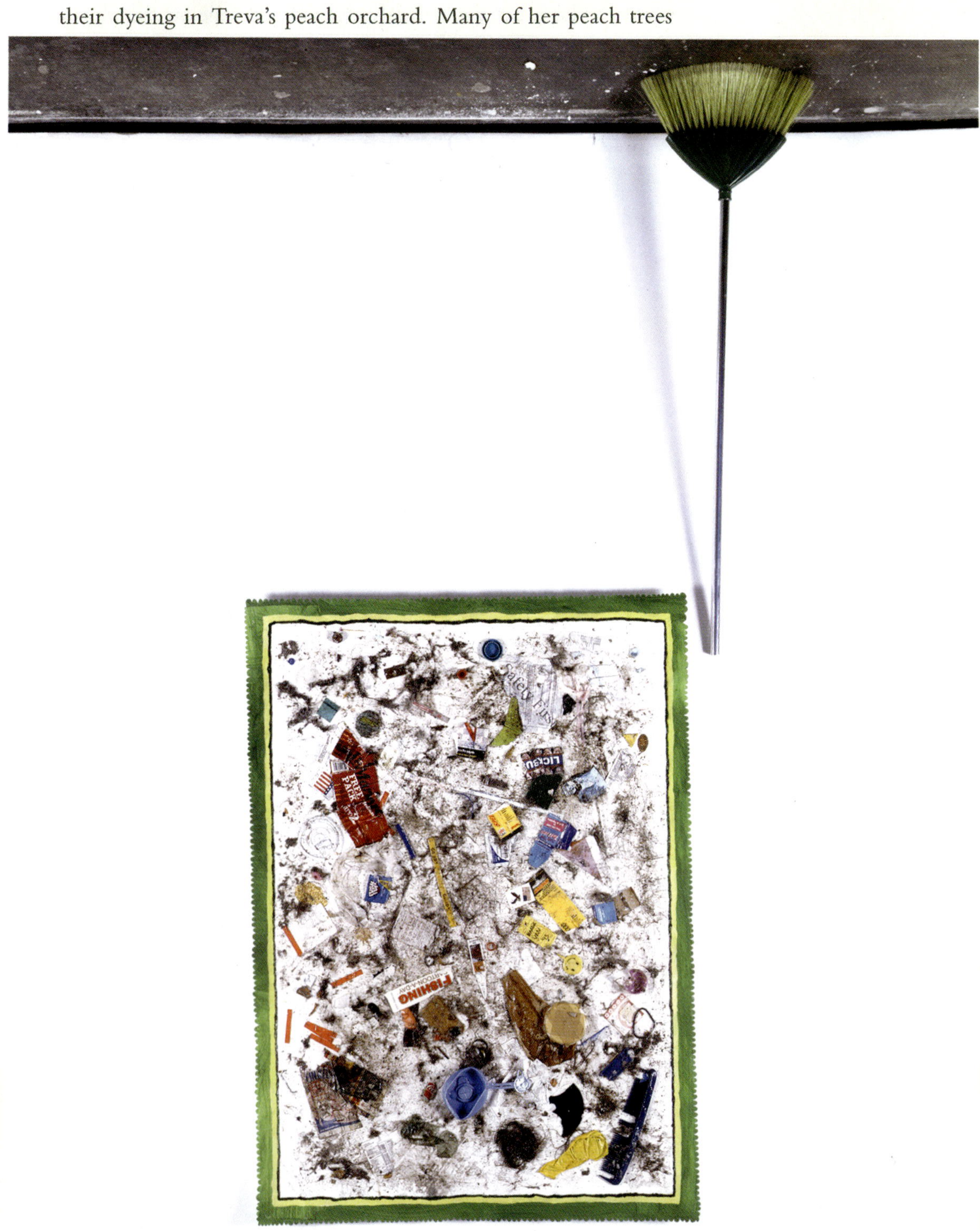

FINE FURNITURE

THE COFFEE TABLES

grass stem has to be still a bit green to be right for picking. Other basket weavers told me that galleta grass can be collected from August through December as long as no snow had covered it.

Annabelle Nequatewa and Joyce Ann Soufkie collect galleta grass (sōhö), the bundle foundation material for coiled basketry. (1991; ASM no. 35732)

And respond to

The coffee tables are white and green objects which identify their location again during critically process in just a number of ways. The support for the glass yucca fibers used for the surface of the red table is in each case the three-dimenional to be carefully cleaned, rendition of a particular punk rock logo. be removed For these I have chosen Dead Kennedys, The Germs, and Black Flag for family and community the iconic quality and cultural status of both the bands or relatives and the emblems. use to carry out For the creation of the emblems I together while chatting, used exotic hardwoods, Sandy Oak for the Dead Kennedys, powder-coated aluminum for the Germs, and Brazillian Wenge for Black Flag because it's naturally dark color closely matches Plants for the traditional Dyeing Process color of the Black Flag logo itself. The more Hopi basket weavers use common location one might find these emblems would be as a Third Mesa villages homemade patch sewn on to be collected easily, the leater or denim jacket of a 14-17 year old who might just as well have it tatooed taste pleasantly on or carved into a himself somewhere. There Navajo tea (siita) was a time school desk, or spray- commonly called Hopi tea (hohoisi), when the DK or the painted under an over- Black Flag bars symbolized Native Americans solidarity pass. with a radical youth culture whose only consistent ideological stance was a dissent from mainstream weaver culture. Through their transformation into she prefers. bourgeoisie Second Mesa luxury items, the ultimate failure of this once siita, radical ideology is, Mesa work in a way, eulogized. The origonal meaning more abundant. of the symbol favor is contradicted, betrayed, and ultimately degraded. In a gallery context, this is not all that It was at the end is degraded. Much like Annabelle Scott Burton's chairs of Nequatewa the 1970's the notion of sculpture itself is betrayed through it's presentation as a chance to photograph this useful object, a piece of furniture. To quote had told Gerhard son Edward Richter, "When art becomes useful it renounces it's status as such and and a very good basket becomes merely design. What, you might ask, quickly agreed prevents these drove tables from being seen as well-designed furniture, Mesa, classic modern with a theme? I would propose that siita plants the failure This year, of radical ideology has long been the domain of art, winter rains, and the plants we found not furniture design, which like higher than two architecture though they has a utopian belief system at it's core. Through Annabelle concluded this particular had thematization the tables there collecting already. remain in dark the and realm of degraded sculpture and avoid the idea of cling close to the elavated design. Their proper context is the gallery or clipping it off at ground level. possibly the collector's home. Imagine a record company executive which I thought was good, who in his youth was a assured renewed growth. punk through collecting, and through. Like Jerry Rubin, upon than a pound and a half reaching forty he renounces his antagonistic

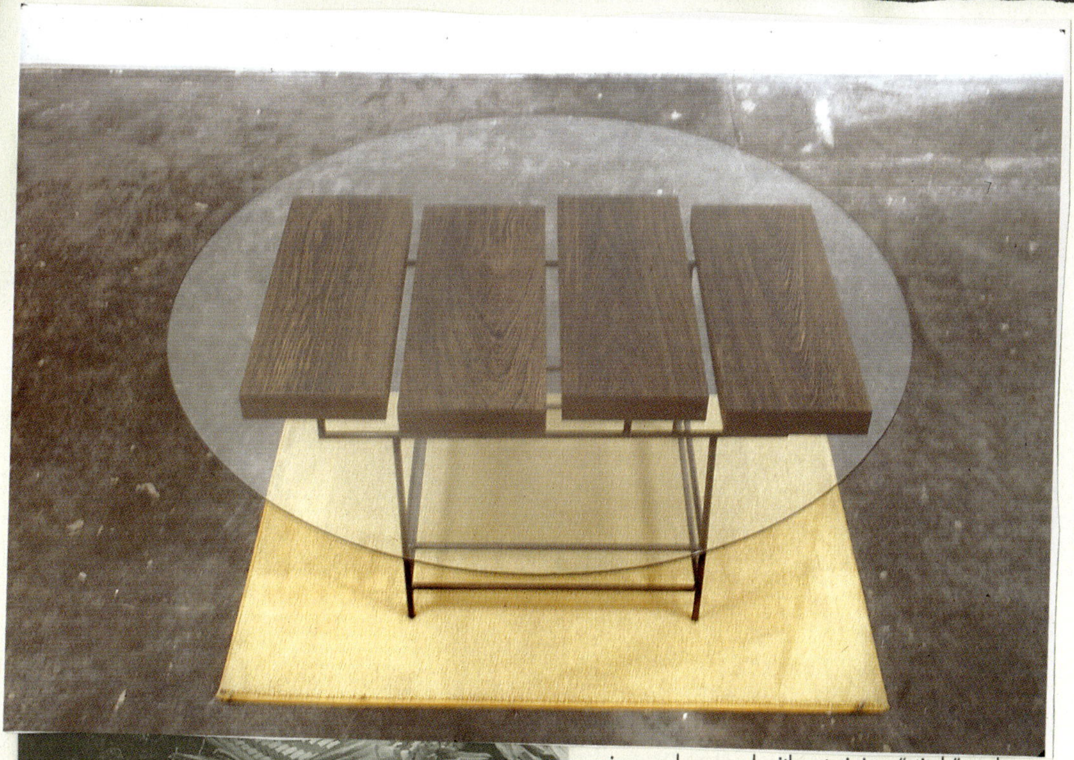

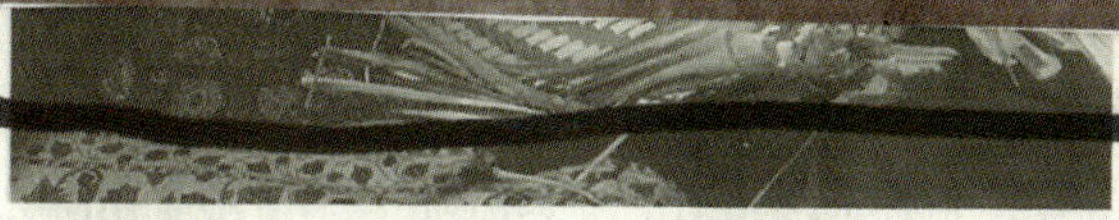

ring and secured with a twining "stitch" to the
basket. Annabelle is using split sea leaves as
"thread." (1991; ASM no. 86274)

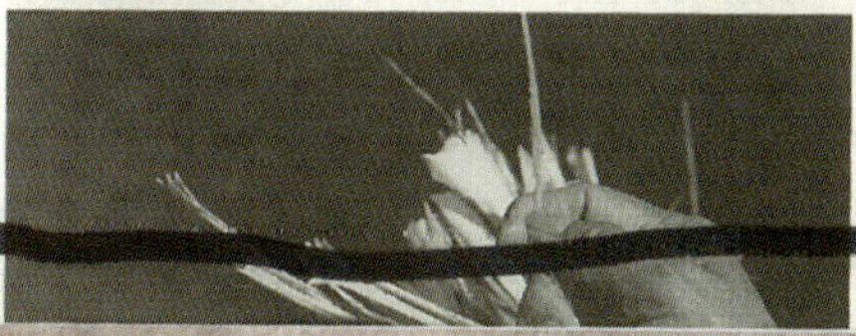

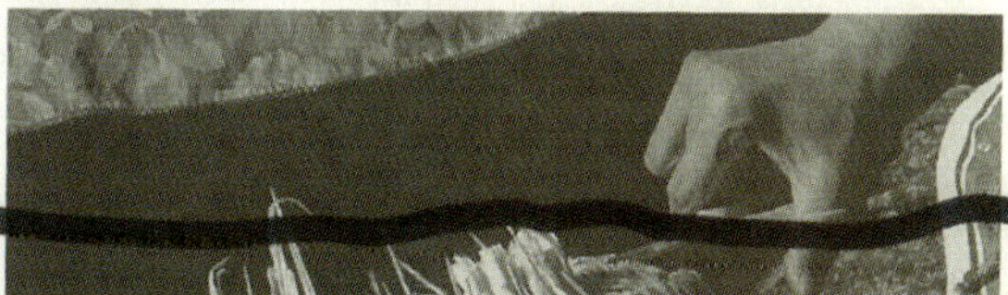

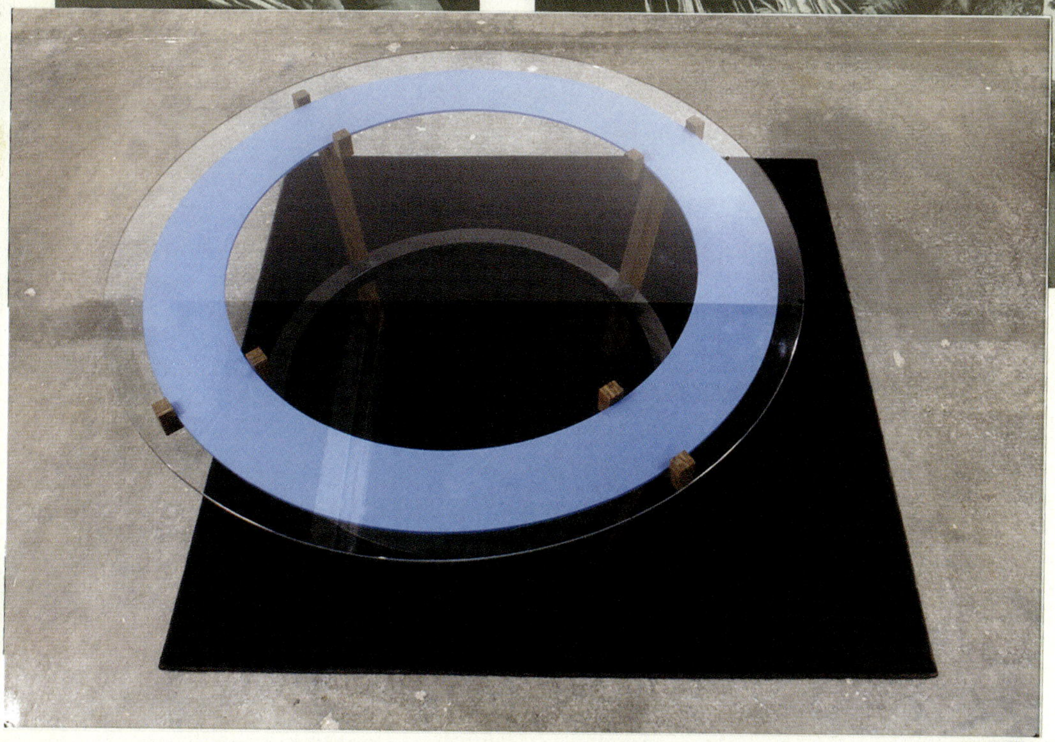

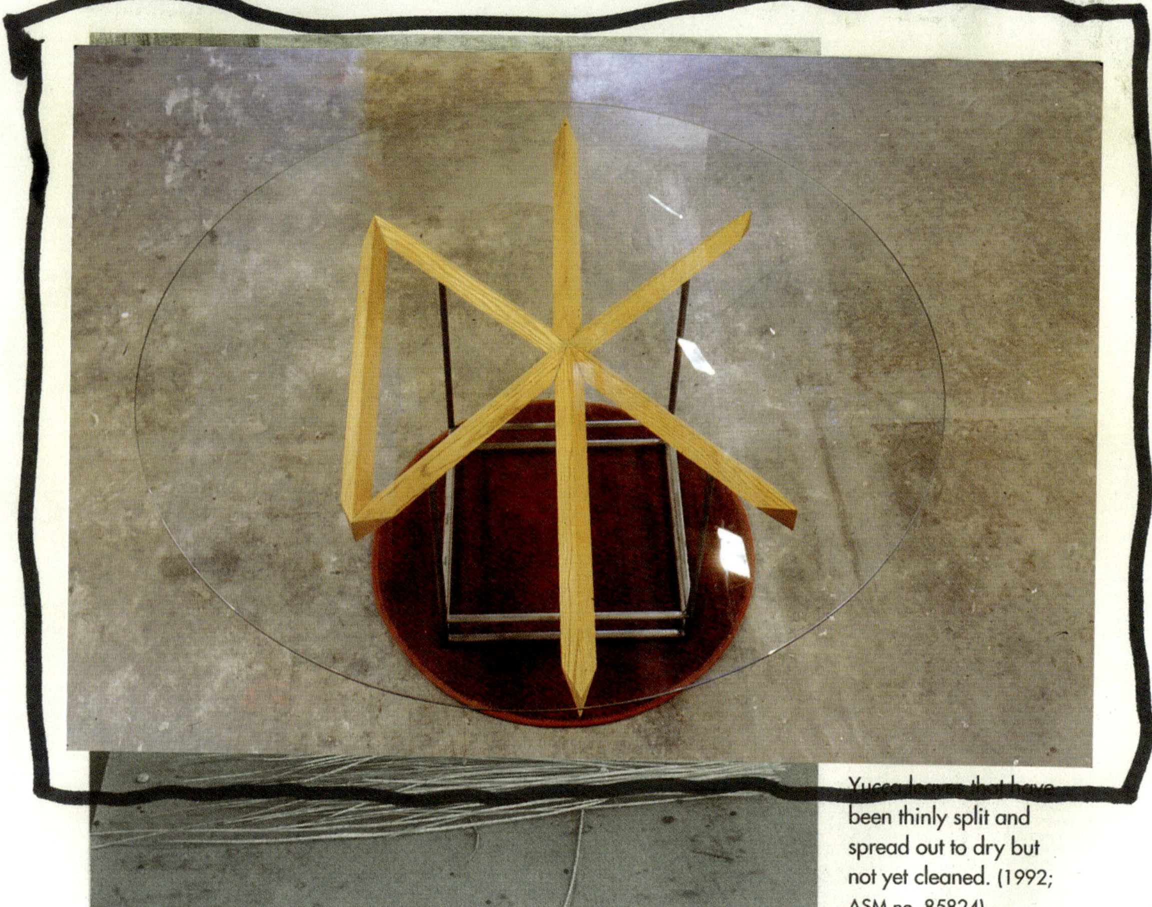

Yucca leaves that have been thinly split and spread out to dry but not yet cleaned. (1992; ASM no. 85824)

material. The sliced–off pieces **stance in** **relation** are not **to the culture and** wasted **instead looks** the galleta grass in **to his knowledge of it for some way** **of attaining** thinned yucca splint **financial stability.** times, **He begins to co-opt** **his** making each splint **own revolution, selling** it **The back to the younger** **generations of** a weaver **followers** a yucca leaf **in his footsteps. With the money** **he makes** width of **he begins** skill of the weaver, **an art collection. I wonder, in his** **home would** Of course, **the piece be** on what she **a nostalgic reminder of his** **mis-spent youth,** yucca strips. A miniature plaque **or a bitter ironic comment on the** **failure of his ideals?**

Abigail Kaursgowva holds one of her beautiful plaques with a Katsina face in the center. She is ready to prepare the rim for coiling. From each warp element, only one stem is retained; the others are broken off. The remaining siwi stems are bent to the left and loosely tucked under each other, then coiled and held securely with a yucca splint, which is usually dyed black. (1992; ASM no. 86479)

[...] August, [...] blossoms [...] green leaves grow [...] this signal the right [...] Another sign is that the [...] ish brown to a [...] very [...] stem, and it has to be [...] s time to pick the siwi. [...] et weaver to see this. [...] their search for stems with [...] also have to be very straight.

...bends the warps to the side so she
...ult it is for her to reach across it.
...is done more in the winter than
...causing it to break when bent
...he piece in progress will be rendered
...re-soaked in water. Therefore, great
...moist sand, which the weaver usually
...The sand, which comes from special
...re, and a special moisture-retaining co
...sand is changed about every three
week...

The weft ...
warp element...
with the awl th...
invisible. In most ...
element consist...
increase the radius, more ...
to the warp elements that they ...
this point the weaver divides each ...
into two, thus having two stems t...
which is arranged in four as ...
plaque grows. This two-divide...
elements usually coincides with ...
white band toward the center of ...
band symbolizes clouds and is rep...
rim. A geometric design on a pl...
enclosed by two cloud designs.

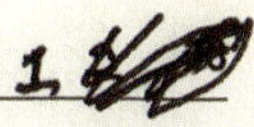

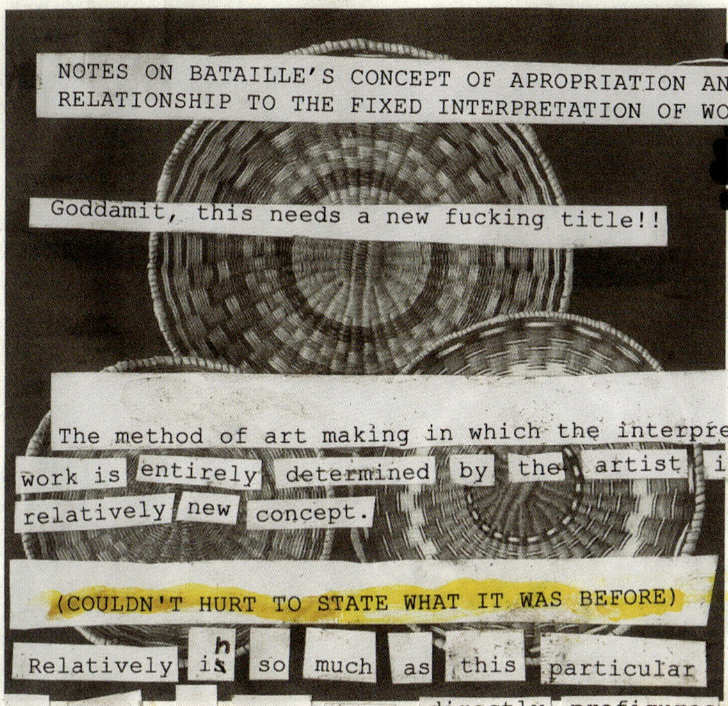

NOTES ON BATAILLE'S CONCEPT OF APROPRIATION AND EXCRETION, and ITS
RELATIONSHIP TO THE FIXED INTERPRETATION OF WORKS OF ART

Goddamit, this needs a new fucking title!!

The method of art making in which the interpretation of the Hopi
work is entirely determined by the artist is wicker plaques from Third a
Mesa. These three plaques
relatively new concept. were woven by Bessie
Monongye of Oraibi, who
used ... dyed in vegetal
(COULDN'T HURT TO STATE WHAT IT WAS BEFORE) dyes. or of love
und by only a
Relatively is so much as this particular approach weavers today. may
be seen as one that directly prefigures modernism", 60)

lik   nique,
(DO YOU HAVE SOME SPECIFIC ERA IN MIND?
Ho   g from
OTHERWISE IT'S HARD TO USE "PREFIGURES")
the

which has experts on basket weaving dominated the entire
field technique as either a form of visual culture for of its well over a hundred
years. At the indisputable point in women time when artists were no longer deemed
wicker technique into an art form. craftsmen, whose duty it was to live up to
the expectations of their viewing public, but visionaries or geniuses whose

powers of Materials for Wicker Plaques and Baskets perception extended far beyond

those In wicker basketry of relatively rigid normal people, with the possibility of artist
and the fairly supple viewer standing as equals before a work of art became ever
more *Parryella filifolia*, which has no remote. name and is called Abstraction in painting
and in Hopi. fractured narrative of the stems in literature present the best
possible examples. spp.; in Hopi, *siváapi*). Using As in literature, painting entered
into the collecting crisis around the turn of the at the same century

(was that the time when Manet was painting and Joyce was writing?)

James Joyce's siwi writing sought not to be collected until a description of the
four days after Niman, when the world by way of Hopi narrative storytelling
but a THING year in the world through it's use of fractured language. And

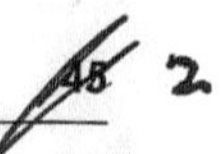

the hoisi on hand for her orange color, the reading of it unique experience that
reflected prevented us from makingits creation. documentation Painting mirrored this
transformation time-consuming throughprocess has to the advent of impressionism,
expressionism, and ultimately, abstraction. In this way painting became like
sculpture Considering the rather complex tasks involved since it was no longer a window to
see into another room or perhaps little wonder that Hopi women outside but an object in
and of itself, again reflectingachieve their the manner for of its creation. At the
center wicker weaving. It is, how of the ethos behind knowledgethis work was the conceit
of the rich artist available astheir plant god himself, incapable not only of mere
imitationforeseeable future, but of divine creation. The world is no longer the
subject Leora Kayquoptewa of Hotevilla of the work, the artist himself has taken its
place. To establish using aniline dyes in his creation as utterly unique the artist
must first purge directions on the package, the work of all dye signs of the existing
world. By not in the right amount of relying on an the liquid to existing pre-ordained
set of boiling on the stove. signs she put in order to make and a statement (in the
sense that language stems looselydoes) the work She used a separates itself from and
declares red dye, and her pan was large itself independent of the existing world.
Modernism as it persists in art wooden stick in each hand today is not so extreme as
its predecessor. Signs of thethe boiling dye. existing world are now permisible

(ALLOWED OR REQUIRED? YOUR SOLUTION TO THE PROBLEM INVOLVES SIGNS, MAKING
IT SEEM LIKE WE'RE DOOMED TO THEM. IF SO, WHY?)
(IF NOTHING ELSE, WHY WEREN'T THEY ALLOWED BEFORE?),

(IT WOULD MAKE SENSE TO DISCUSS POSTMODERNISM FIRST, IF THAT'S THE REASON
(OR A MORE CLEAR MAINFESTATION OF SOME LARGER REASON) WHY SIGNS HAVE COME
INTO EXTANT MODERNISM.)

provided (or possibly they remain depending on the indistinct and/or divorced from
their commonly perceived additional time and work are meanings. This separation of
sign and smoke the meaning order to set the desired shade allows the work to maintain
its autonomy siwi and siváapi and timelessnesswicker plaques and (,) allowing for endless
interpretations, a wicker tray or deep basket, all equally correct. This is the work's
ambiguity. It's traditional basketry value lies in baskets, which the artist's use of it
to claim all on the interpretations of piiki trays; and of the work as a result of his
universal vision of baby cradles.

(I'M STILL NOT SURE WHY ORIGINAL MODERNISM ISN'T AMBIGUITY. EVEN IF
IT'S NOT DEALING WITH SIGNS, THERE'S STILL THE SAME ISSUE OF MULTIPLE
INTERPRETATIONS. MAYBE YOU NEED TO MAKE IT CLEAR THAT AMBIGUITY IS
THE AMBIGUITY OF SIGNS, NOT MEANING IN GENERAL),

The work's (and November. It can be collected concurrently in the artist's) ambiguity attributed by , leaving the blossoms on those who submit that to a belief system in which the women of Third Mesa use the origins dyeing the yellow of the many meanings ascribed come from the work alone. And this is Modernism's core: A belief system relying on the later I was back presumption of the my visit universality of all human experience Eva Honyungva, a great lady of wisdom and knowledge. (,) in certain absolutes (CUT that is) from Oraibi and contingent on faith in was the idea of a center (god, Eva's house too, science, the artist) I brought my

(ARE THESE THE CERTAIN ABSOLUTES? IF NOT THE STRUCTURE OF THE SYSTEM GETS A LITTLE MURKY).

Such a method blooms too early of art making can never smell dwell

(I DON'T THINK "DWELL" DOES IT HERE. COULD SOUND A LITTLE LIKE YOU'RE CONTRADICTING THE STATEMENT THAT IT'S AN OBJECT, NOT A REFLECTION OF ONE, I.E. MORE REAL.)

Bessie stripped the peel off one stem in the concrete reality that is the world.

(I THINK THIS DEFINITION OF MODERNISM NEEDS TO GO WITH THE FIRST MENTION OF IT, SINCE IT APPLIES MORE OBVIOUSLY TO THAT PART)

In what has been Hotevilla has no electricity; deemed post-modernism in art, ambiguity is still houses are powered by solar panels, present and seen as valuable

(WAIT, I THOUGHT AMBIGUITY ONLY OCCURED IN TODAY'S MODERNISM, AND THAT IT WASN'T THE VALUABLE THING IN THIS DISCUSSION, AND THAT IT WASN'T SO MUCH VALUABLE AS NOT BAD),

but for stripped off peels and entirely different reasons. Since post-modernism rejects the idea of a universal center from which to use the peels and everything else is derived , the separation making her yellow dye of signs from their she meanings in the work serves a different At least my harvest could be used for something! purpose; it is used as a metaphor Later on, for the lack of certainty as she too to the truth of commonly agreed upon the two kinds of meanings said that the gray one is attributed to signs or symbols not suitable for weaving. However, if the few wicker basket we examine closely the motives behind Hotevilla who still use this separation, it is becomes apparent that the meaninglessness of basket weavers and signs is itself taken to be a kind of universal truth. outstanding in execution and Superficially, the artist abandons his design and form. ownership of the ideas in the work but his goal of producing an object capable of variations in how the individual speaking to the widest possible audience remains the dyeing process. same. *The artist vegetal gives over the role of center to the siita and smoke it. Others work itself. They boil Post-modernism's assumption that communication for a very long time is impossible smoke it, fails to recognize the reality though I know of one who does. of the discourse through which we understand ideas hoisi plant and blossom, boiled and smoked as they are presented to us

*In a way, not unlike contemporary demographic marketing strategy

(I THINK THIS SENTENCE IS THE BEGINNING OF A NEW IDEA, ONE THAT WOULD LEAD AWAY FROM POSTMODERNISM, NOT EXPLAIN HOW IT IS MISINTERPRETED)

Both of these ideas of Hopi Basketry (WHAT TWO? I'M NOT CLEAR) are reliant on a
belief system of art's role in society as a purveyor of mystic truths. These
truths may keep it and hang it in his home, give it to his mother so may be metaphysical, social,
and cultural. have a plaque handy should Both (SEE ABOVE) bastardize the clarity of
their message through one of his unmarried sisters to use in the meaningless valorization
of ambiguity (WHO IS VALORIZING IT MEANINGLESSLY? ARE ANY OF THE CATEGORIES
DOING SO MEANINGFULLY?). As in a social dance. meaning ceases to become ambiguous
(IS THIS REALLY A PROCESS?) , the idea or he can sell it of a center (god,
for money.

science, the artist), between aunt and nephew is driven from the work.
(OKAY, SO UMABIGUOUSNESS MEANS NO UNVERSALITY) societies, Before the dawn of
Modernity and O'waqölt. in the arts ambiguity held no all such status. God or the
King dances was finished and all the center of the work.

(SO THE CENTER WAS PRESENT BEFORE, BUT NOT THE AMBIGUITY) (THIS SOUNDS
LIKE YOU'RE CONTRADICTING WHAT YOU JUST SAID, ABOUT HOW UMABIGUOUSNESS
DRIVES OUT THE CENTER.) (IF THE IDEA IS THAT THE CERTAINTY IS SOMEHOW
LOCAL IN NATURE, "CENTER" ISN'T GOING TO WORK)

and this was communicated from plaques. These coveted prizes artist to viewer through a
system of visual cues," with the first winner receiving and storytelling. Signs that were
recognized most beautifully decorated to mean specific three runners things were used
accordingly receiving ever smaller plaques to convey a message. So may a work of art today
fix its interpretation size and decoration
(WAIT, I THOUGHT THE FIXED INTERPRETATION WAS MODERN; HERE YOU'RE
EQUATING IT WITH PRE-MODERN)
small plaques, so-called baby plaques, to infant girls and thus attain clarity by utilizing
come to be understood only to little girls by a particular audience w/o altering their
meaning. Then re-presenting only girls receive these small signs to said audience in
combination. given as gifts increase in size as the girl grows, and by the

1. WHEN WASN'T INTERPRETATION FIXED?
2. WHY ISN'T THIS ABOUT DRIVING OUT THE CENTER TO ACHIEVE SPECIFICITY, NOT
FIXING INTERPRETATION?
3. THERE CAN BE NO UNIVERSAL WITHOUT AMBIGUITY, OR NO AMBIGUITY WITHOUT
UNIVERSAL? I.E. IS THE "SOLUTION" YOU PROPOSE INCAPABLE OF AMBIGUITY BECAUSE
IT ESCHEWS THE UNIVERSAL, OR NOT UNIVERSAL BECAUSE IT IS UAMBIGUOUS?
4. HOW DOES THE "SOLUTION" NOT LEAD AGAIN TO ONTOLOGICALLY AMBIGOUS ART?)

If, By far the most important compensatory as Bataille proposes, the two dominant
modes of wedding payback. After the human interaction bride are indeed appropriation
and excretion, (1) to the bride by her in-laws, then artists in order to communicate
or represent the world with a substantial payback of plaques in which they live must
acknowledge this and act accordingly. Taking signs whole and unaltered into a
work When a young Hopi man and woman agree to marry, is appropriation. The
re-presentation of gifts to the bride's family in the form of these signs is excretion.
The sacks of flour, meat, groceries, and shawls and artist After who presumes to create
original artworks has been performed, is doomed to a series of mute,

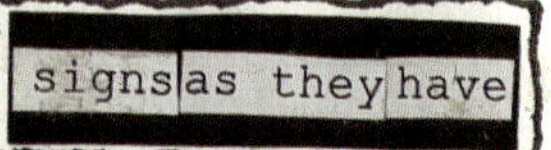

incommunicative gesticulations, weaving plaques for the various wedding paybacks of
their daughters. like one who has suddenly lost his voice.
These are the gesticulations working on of the artist who is middle-aged and her attempts
to communicate broad children are all universal truths can delay a payback because
(MOVE THIS TO THE END OF THE PARAGRAPH) . The viewer has to be sold for recognizes
this attempt and unconsciously needed cash. This substitutes his reason for own ideas for
the ones the artist has intended. Thus, often years pass by before Two deaf old women
conversing with each other make ritual of compensatory gift giving is all the gestures,
little nods of understanding, left to the bride's discretion pauses in speech, and signs of
recognition that people makes for the who understand the amount one another do, but
it is merely the hollow shell of she received at a conversation that her wedding they
are carrying out. (WHAT ABOUT UNIVERSAL TRUTH WITHOUT SIGNS? IS THAT IRRELEVANT
OR IMPOSSIBLE?) (THIS ALL GOES BACK TO HOW SIGNS BECAME SO IMPORTANT)
(EXPLAIN HOW TRANSGRESSION FOLLOWS) In the 1960's the group of goods artists
known as the Vienna Actionists a payback has seemed executed a series of Some
performances that carried women the idea of transgression in art to extremes,
which had yet to be even hinted making at, paybacks ever more generous. by the art that
preceded them. The artists hoeoma of Shipaulovi Gunter Brus, Hermann Nitsch, Rudolf
Schwarzkogler, and Otto Muhl used blood, she was given six or self-painting, animal
sacrifice, self-mutilation, filled with groceries, fifty sacks of flour, and sex in an
iconoclastic and self-destructive way she made twenty-three plaques that was often
ironic and humorous (particularly one of her daughters in the cases of Brus and Muhl)
rather than spiritual in its larger number of gifts from her husband's family and associations
The extremity of their transgressions have made Frieda said that it is quite subsequent
attempts at transgression today for a bride in an art context sacks of flour seem pithy by
comparison. For the contemporary artist, fifty blankets the creation of work that relies
on physical or sexual violence for large its transgression is no longer viable, as
these are everywhere in our Third Mesa culture and have ceased to now include
constitute a transgression up to a hundred wicker plaques at all. new garbage cans filled
previous to the Actionists, the artist had ground cornmeal, fifty to a hundred sacks of
traditionally played a role flour, and many cakes and pies, in society of transgressor,
but this is a role that had gone numerous pots and pans. I never had more or less
unacknowledged by both witness artist and viewer. It was simply of the groom's taken
or granted that the artist mother, live in the gutter, was visiting the family and report
back to the wealthy, kachina-doll carver in Shungopovi, a art-buying elite on its
(predictable) conditions. baskets and tubs heaped high with piiki Among other things, the
actionist's art attempted to implicate the large amounts involved in viewer by creating
a situation in which delivery is done in stages. At other times audiences are made more
keenly aware of the expectations of wheat flour they bring to an artwork It was by
placing them in extremely close sight. Two proximity to images for Frieda's sister and
occurrences of the abject and Shipaulovi and was chaotic. inside her house. In the
(WHAT ARE THESE EXPECTATIONS?) women were busy preparing stews and other festive

It is that coiled basketry storage jars precisely the viewer's recognition of this dynamic (THE DYNAMIC BETWEEN ARTIST AND AUDIENCE, PRE-ACTIONIST? OR THE DYNAMIC OF RECOGNITION THAT THE ACTIONISTS HATH WROUGHT?) that purpose. ultimately resulted in the strain of art we now recognize as abject. The Actionists introduction of trading posts in themselves fostered this recognition. Their performances helped metal, wood, glass, and stoneware jars to clear a space in whi the abject could exist through tubs that were more its demystification of the artist's role in rodents and insects, society. probably were used less

(STICK THIS SOMEWHERE IN THE PRECEDING PARAGRAPH. IT EXPLAINS THE RESULT OF THE ACTIONISTS) (YOU SHOULD REITERATE THAT THEY MADE TRANSGRESSION IMPOSSIBLE. THIS IS THE KEY POINT, THIS IS HOW THE ARTIST WAS DEMYSTIFIED) (BUT WHY MUST THIS LEAD TO THE ABJECT? IF ANYTHING, IT WOULD SEEM THAT THE IMPOSSIBILITY OF TRANSGRESSION WOUDL OUTMODE THE ABJECT)

However, the needs of, Anglo society. actionists making coiled were not the only ones dealing with baskets in the form of wastebaskets, which these Issues (A LITTLE VAGUE) at the time. readily bought for just that purpose. Many gay male artists and writers found their un-Hopi form, but it was produced for voices through the expression and use of abject quantity and with increasingly colorful or transgressive material early on. Jack Smith and William Burroughs made medium-sized bowl- and were among the first to position their work in (particularly seed jars) this particular adversarial stance. Fittingly so, since at the time as seen in photographs from that time homosexuality itself was seen by the majority of the Arizona State Museum. Americans as a state of abjection in and of itself. constriction toward the rim, (SWITCH THE ORDER OF THE NEXT TWO PARAGRAPHS) When deployed though a queer usually coiled, focal point, abjection takes on a decidedly tighter weave and is different (IN WHAT SENSE?) tone (THAN?) . An example of difference I have not seen between hetero and several years, homo sexual viewpoints of the relationship of abjection by metal and plastic containers. to the depiction of homosexual signifiers shapes in coiled baskets, but art lies in the ((FAILED)) romantic quality wider rim and no lid attached to these signifiers, non- failed or otherwise. The sweet Hopi market. comedy of failed romance in the queer work of art is an elusive and sometimes coiled deep baskets made for collectors today subtle marker of this difference. A heterosexual usage of homosexuality toward the top in (abject) art,

(ON THE OTHER HAND) (THAT WAY WE KNOW THAT THIS IS BEING RAISE AS A CONTRAST, TO LIKEN IT TO THE MORE LIMITED QUEER ABJECT RATHER THAN IMPLY THAT HOMO SIGNIFIERS ARE AN ESSENTIAL PART OF ALL ABJECT) (OR ARE THEY?)

rarely large baskets are made only for the collector market, makes use of this type of romantic anti-idealism. by only a few of the Second Mesa basket weavers. The difference is analagous to the Even fewer wicker basket weavers still make difference between a heterosexual female The Forms and Functions of impersonator who is doing a deliberately poor job of it (a jock at a frat party dressed as a cheerleader) and a drag queen who is doing a similarly deliberate poor job (one who wears a beard). Although the difference between these two might at first seem to be as simple as the fact that one is gay while the other is not I do not believe that the philisophical inquiries underlying the abjection in these example of expression can be explained so easily. The fact of the matter is that the female impersonator has no stake in his impersonation. For the drag queen it is an act loaded with personal meaning.

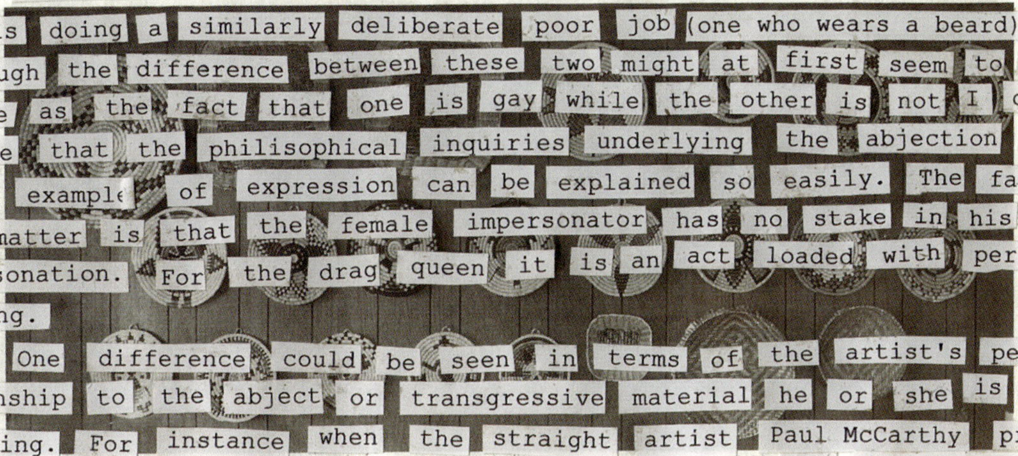

One difference could be seen in terms of the artist's personal relationship to the abject or transgressive material he or she is presenting. For instance when the straight artist Paul McCarthy presents an image of the abject, it bespeaks his view on the degradation of the culture to feed in groom's which who he lives. When the queer payback author William Burroughs that Rita was preparing for presents an image of abjection, we are inclined to believe that in the adjacent living room, it bespeaks his own the house self-loathing. (OKAY, SO NOW WE RETURN TO THE ORIGINAL POINT) each more beautiful than the last. After the death of art ASM no. 86213) (WHEN DID IT DIE IN THIS ESSAY?), overwhelmed. (was it ever alive?) have been at least eighty coiled plaques on that wall. (CUT THAT IT'S TOO CUTESY) what options in front of the wall are open to meal, and the artist that he may continue his practice? It was not the right time for photography, as wonderful as I suggest the one-liner as a possible solution for my documentation. to this problem. The one-liner makes use of both appropriation and Frieda's third sister, excretion simultaneously as it evades the essentialism inherent in the grand plaques idea. In its combination of appropriated on a wall in her elements, the one-liner for one of her functions as a stepladder to it's daughters who had own implications, years, and which can be manifold. Each erson's back was a reaction for both mother and reveals something of both the joke and hemselves. plaques for a wedding So, in the same way the bride's that a joke provokes different reactions for the groom's family based on The guests are the context in which it s told, welcomed with a warm meal so does the artwork display of whose interpretation is fixed reflect The next day back each goods are delivered to the viewer's particular perception of mother, it. distributes plaques and food In this way the object asserts tself and may stand in the bride's robes and contributed the judgment even as it is being udged. (DID YOU PLAGIARIZE THIS FROM A MIKE KELLEY ESSAY? TELL THE TRUTH...) However, there is a problem with this mandatory. game-like system of art-making and the so-called art criticism which is the largest in which the shuffling of variables s of primary and which belongs to the concern. the rest of his life. Herbert Read, in his essay 'Psycho-analysis is delivered heaped high and the problem of aesthetic value' (2) attacks the somewhat smaller Freudian psychoanalytic filled view of art as reductive, placing too much cornmeal and importance on the sweet cornmeal subject of a work of art and not enough on its formal piiki tray loaded with piiki. The qualities, which he sees as art's primary concern. In a way, this is true insomuch as an art with no formal

qualities would be little shape. They produced more than a game and this style has itself,
a useless diversion. Art must bear great favor among collectors. some relationship to real
lived everyday experience Weavers of miniature coiled plaques and baskets have refined

(WHY? WHAT ART IN THIS ESSAY DOESN'T? IS THIS THE "CONCRETE REALITY" ISSUE?)

(IF THIS IS THE MOTIVATION BEHIND THE WHOLE ESSAY, THIS SHOULD COME OUT SOONER.

LIKE ACCUSE SOMEONE OF NOT DOING IT INT HE EARLYGOING)

. But how? The experience of art should not be confused with calls into question
any notion of the real four to five inches in diameter that are made for newborn babies
to begin with. In our suspension of disbelief have thicker coils than miniatures before a
work of art, what had once seemed colors and designs. Miniature concrete reality
begins to crumble. Bataille says, depending on the skill of the weaver of poetry:
"...starting from the moment when this unreality immediately
constitutes itself as a superior reality, whose mission is to eliminate
(or degrade) inferior TRADITIONAL UTILITARIAN vulgar reality, poetry is
reduced to playing the standard role of things..." (3)
I believe there is yet another among the utilitarian forms solution to the problem of
ambiguous meaning, and this is of yucca, which is described to expand our definition
of art to include utilitarian basketry forms used by the objects made which have
no meaning at all. Specifically, technique or, like the piiki tray (*pik'inpi*), objects that were
not created with the intention of becoming wicker works of art. basket, Art piiki tray that
serves a purpose, i.e.; is not the most used basketry item today useless, renounces its status
as art and becomes merely applied either rolled up or as unrolled art (4) in certain

(ISN'T IT ART ONLY THROUGH A PARTICULAR KIND OF APPLICATION, NOT ART TO BE
APPLIED?). Although it by twenty inches, which does not necessarily piiki sheet. follow
that all useless things are art, I believe somewhat smaller than the that the on
intention to create a real cornmeal mush is thinly spread by a thing and its subsequent
failure could also constitute a work of the hand of art. I refer to piiki stone a real
thing in the sense that art heated by a piñon fire and real things are thinly spread often
identical in appearance (5) Heidigger (HEIDEGGER) referred to the sheet these failed
pieces of equipment as present-at-hand, times in each direction, and rolled meaning that they
made (HAVING MADE. THIS ISN'T THE DEF. OF PRESENT-AT-HAND) wide, and themselves
ostentatious through the frustration A piiki tray can hold a pile of experienced at their
attempted use. (6) Heidigger found this tray, ostentatious-ness houses and kivas. to be
bland and boring, but is The center section of art so different? one of The object
in question would possess stepped designs. The material for a number of interesting
qualities. In some sumac (*suuvi*), ways it would resemble a siwi kitsch
object by carrying with it the history of thinner branches of it's own debasement. But
performative in that this preferably the longest ones, and they would be split down a
compressed physical history of The outer side of debasement rather the inner side than a
cultural one. It differs from alternately, the readymade in to the variation that it is
not a functioning real thing design. The border is made useless wicker technique, by its

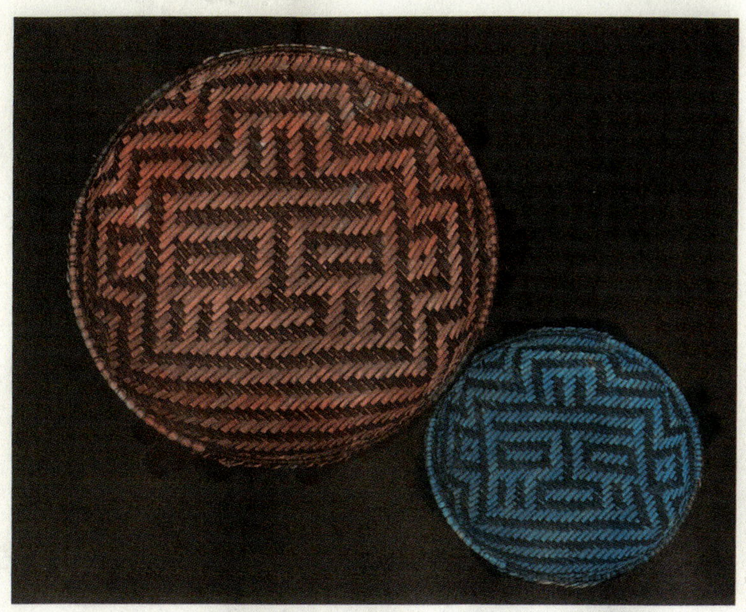

Two sifter baskets with Mudhead Katsina faces, created by Kevin Navasie of First Mesa with red-dyed yucca leaves. (Photographed at McGees Indian Art Gallery, Keams Canyon, 1994)

declared form. The plaited sifter basket, however, has status as art. More likely it was made useless and today it is by poor design or utilitarian craftsmanship. Whereas the readymade by the Hopis could be put back into use with little effort, the new type of object is By splitting the yucca leaf, dead to the two colors old world of useful things and may only with—the green outer side go on living in the almost white its artificial zombie-like state inside. By using both plaiting elements as a work of art. It differs from a camp object, or diagonal, in that it is not beautiful a failed work of art. It possesses no patterns and variations thereof such glamour. As a failed real thing it is difficult to surpass in its banality which is beyond intention. Broken machines and crumbling sifter baskets (also called ring baskets) architecture are like blind spots in our vision. in Hopi households. Memory glosses all kinds of food: over them as if they weren't there. apples, ears of corn and shelled corn, brown beans, Because of their invisibility, they are the lima beans, wild spinach, and haunt of crime and this makes their banality ominous. The laughter that accompanies used according to the failed real thing is a cold and heartless one.

create patterns... leav... doing they achieve stunning geometric de... very stylistically sophisticated Katsina faces. These colorful plaited sifter baskets are used as gifts, are sometimes submitted to juried shows, or are used in the basket dance by young girls who have not yet mastered the art of making coiled or wicker plaques. Plaited sifter baskets are still made by most women of all three

1.Bataille, Georges. "The Use Value of D.A.F. de Sade (An Open Letter to my Current Comrades) (1929-30)", in Allan Stoekl (Ed.), Bataille, Georges. Visions of Excess: Selected Writings, 1927-1939, Minneapolis: University of Minnesota Press, pg. 91

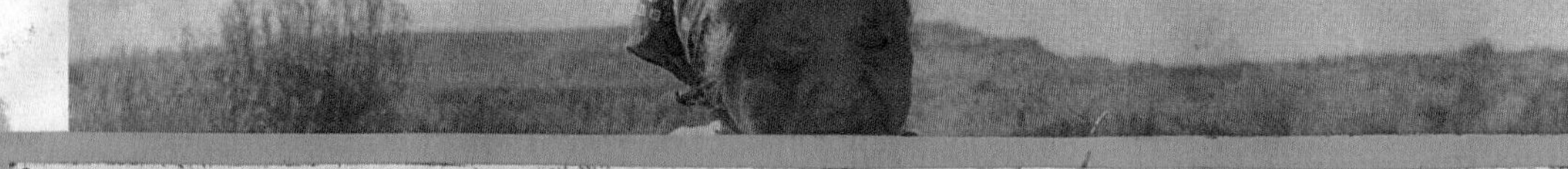

2.Read, Herbert. (1950), "Psycho-analysis and the Problem of Aesthetic Value". The Forms of Things Unknown: Essays Toward an Aesthetic Philosophy. New York: Faber and Faber, pg. 76-93.

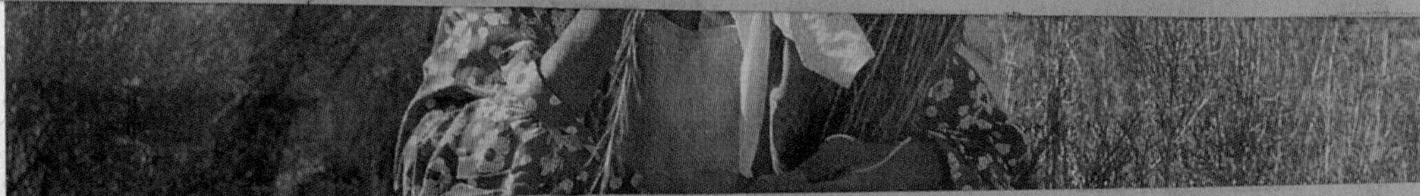

3.Bataille, Georges. "The Use Value of D.A.F. de Sade (An Open Letter to my Current Comrades) (1929-30)", in Allan Stoekl (Ed.), Bataille, Georges. Visions of Excess: Selected Writings, 1927-1939, Minneapolis: University of Minnesota Press, pg.97

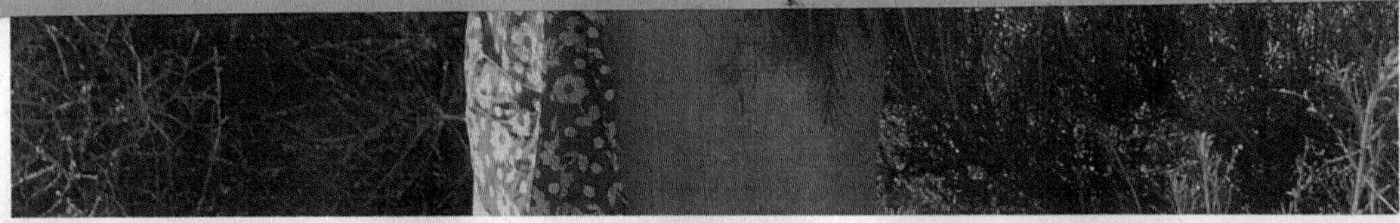

4.Richter, Gerhard. "Notes, 1988". The Daily Practice of Painting: Writings 1962-1993. Cambridge, Massachusetts: The MIT Press, pg.170 Here, Richter is referring specifically to art objects that function in a practical way, be it socially, politically or even culturally. Graphic Design for example.

holding this lower part with their teeth, they stripped off the peel and leaves with one quick downward pull. If siváapi is not cleaned right away, or is collected later than October, the outer peel gets

5.Danto, Arthur. "Works of Art and Mere Real Things". The Transfiguration of The Commonplace: A Philosophy of Art. Cambridge, Massachusetts: Harvard University Press, pg.3

is collected in great quantity between August and October to be stored for future use. Its leaves have to be stripped off before storing. The stems have a tendency to dry out fast, and if not used right away, will have to be soaked in water for three to four days

6.Heidigger, Martin. The Origin of the Work of Art

green. To bleach them lighter, the weavers spread them out under the sun, turning them frequently. Should it threaten to rain,

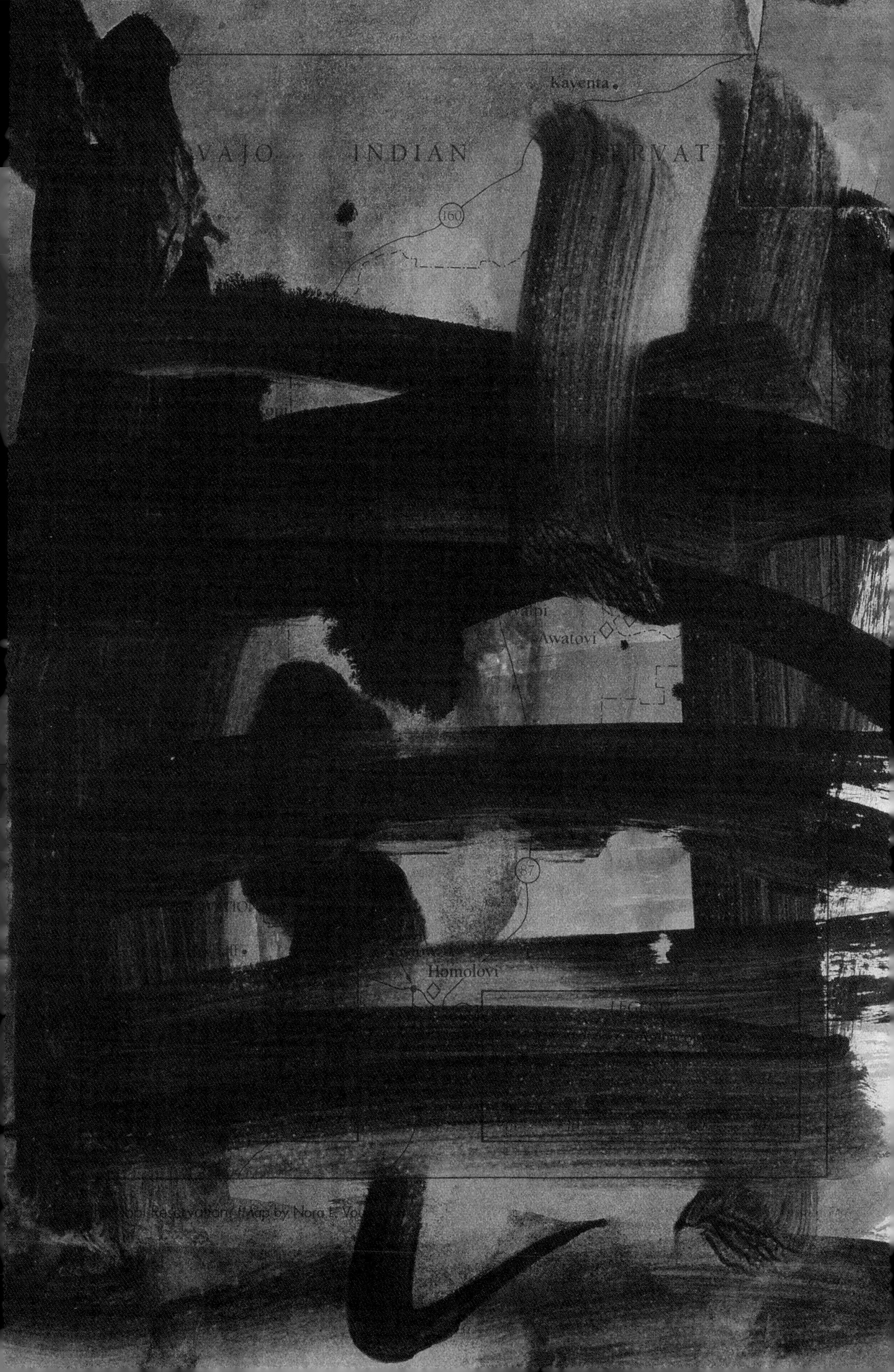

Kayenta
NAVAJO INDIAN RESERVATION
160
Walpi
Awatovi
87
Homolovi
Reservation. Map by Nora E. Vo

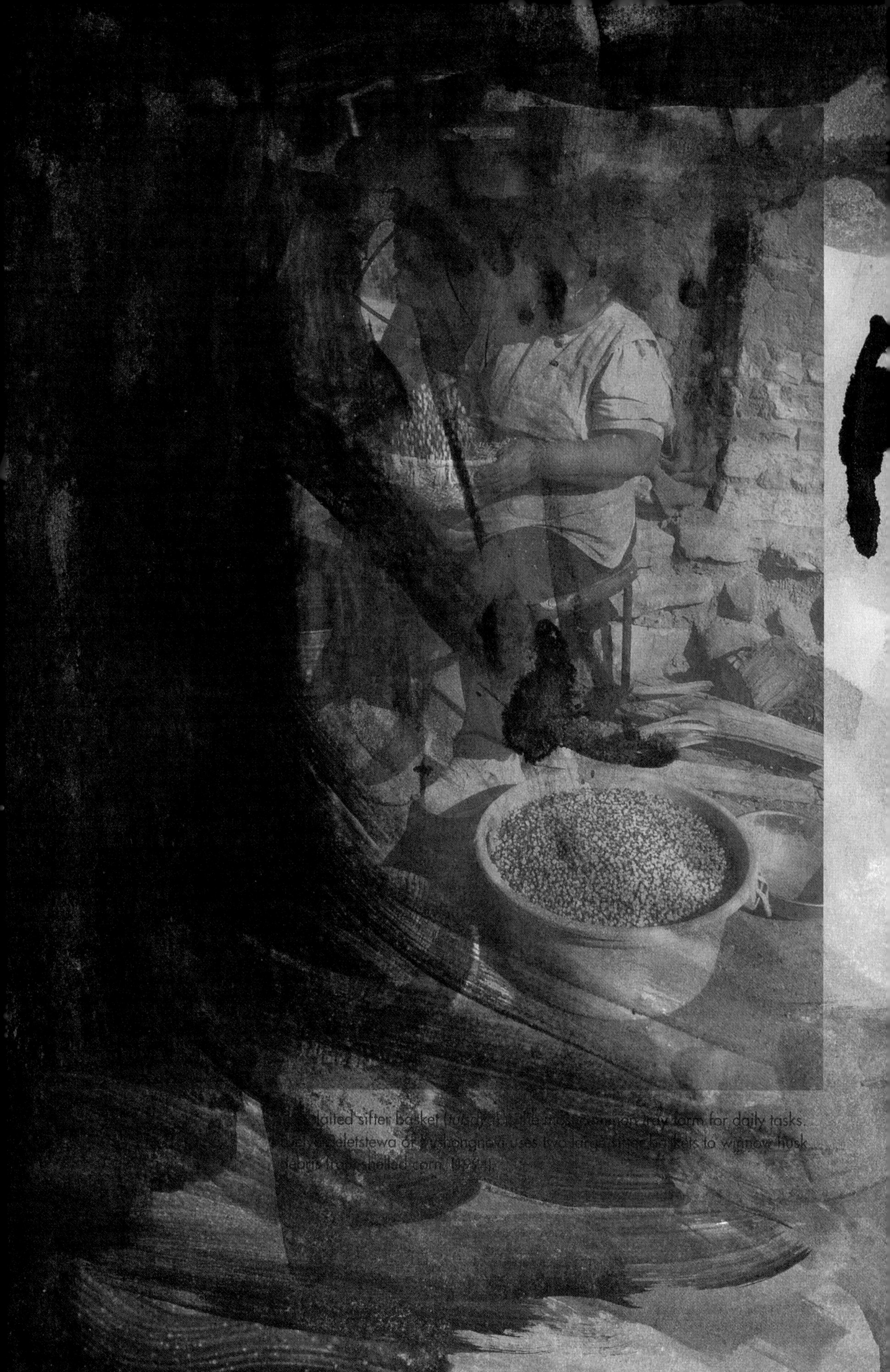

The plaited sifter basket (tutsaya) is the most common tray form for daily tasks. ...eletstewa of Shongnovi uses two large sifter baskets to winnow husk debris from shelled corn (1992).

they bring them inside. When the siváapi stems have turned to a
pale beige, they have bleached long enough and are in the best

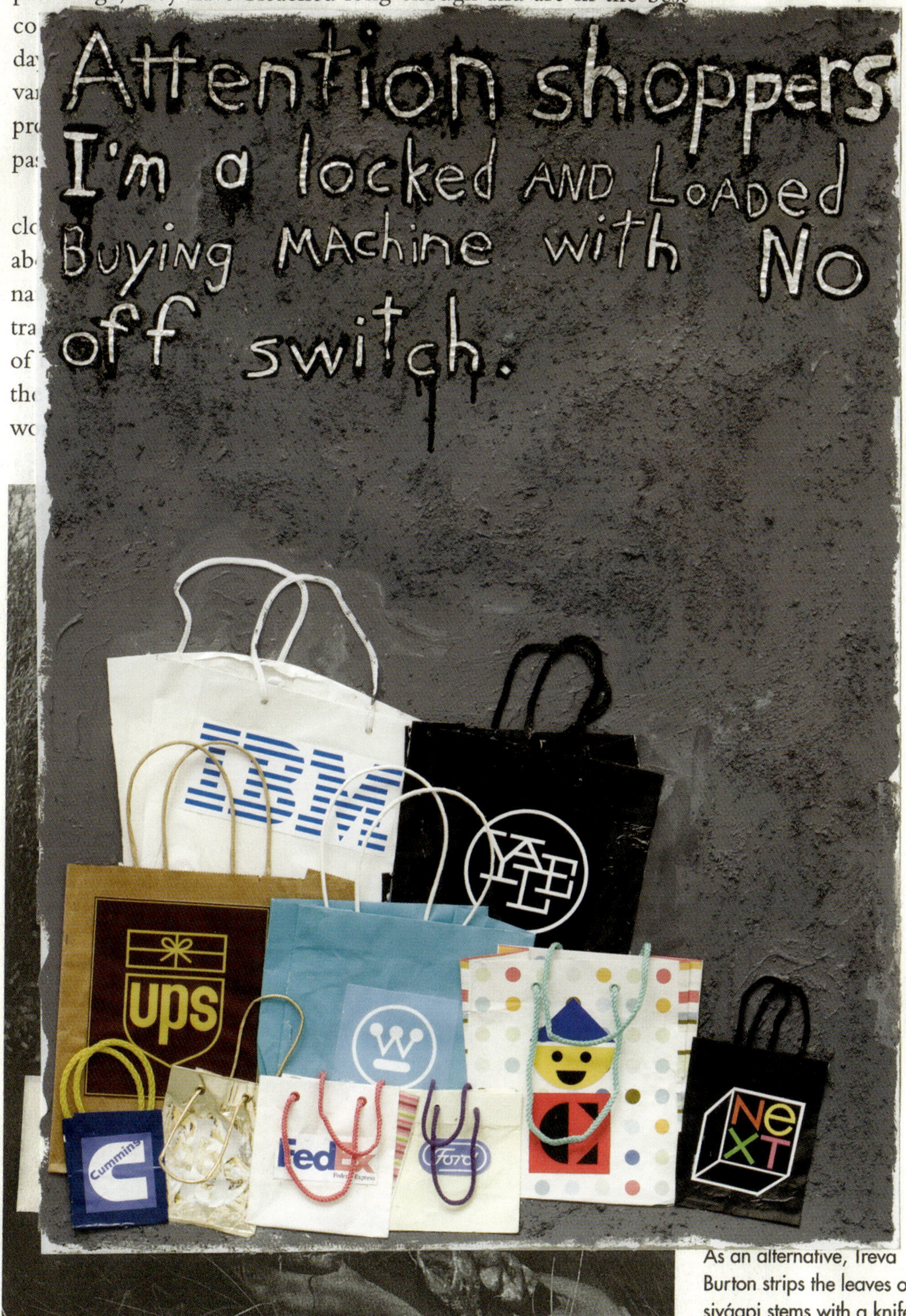

As an alternative, Treva
Burton strips the leaves off
siváapi stems with a knife.
(1991; ASM no. 85869)

Homage to Paul Rand

The Rules of Attraction

THREE

The Forms and Functions of Hopi Basketry

Considered
dates potter
basketry iter
used as food
utensils. Bag
forms of bas
back into an

With the
were sugges
pottery, part
vent of potte
bowls were
the cooking
into the time

Like any i
new forms w
perpetuated
erences of t
used them.
and form, a

PLAQUES

The flat, pe
because of it
ond Mesa ar
common for
lages, plaque
Many are ma
them enter t

However,
reservation,
serve to reaf

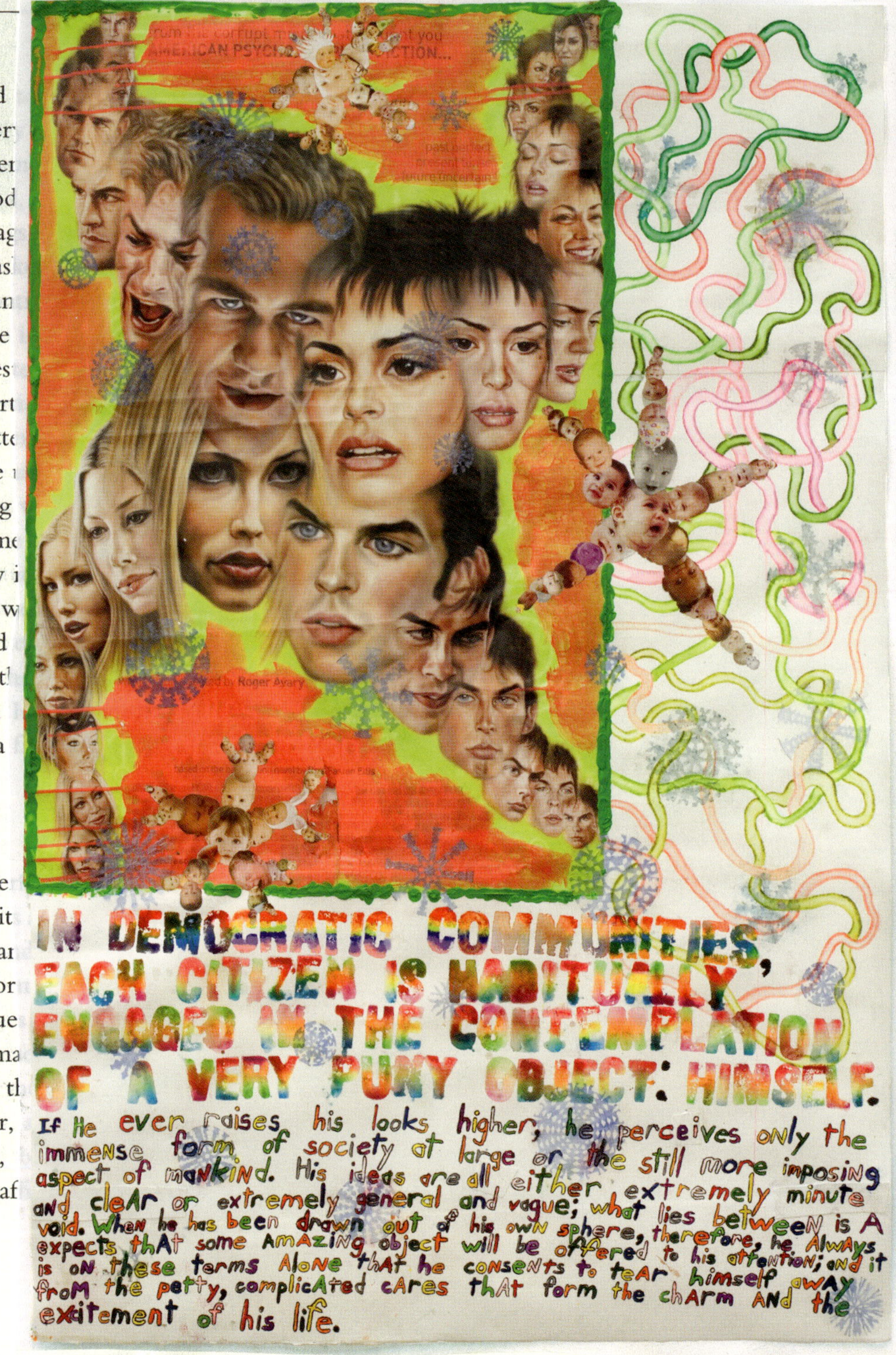

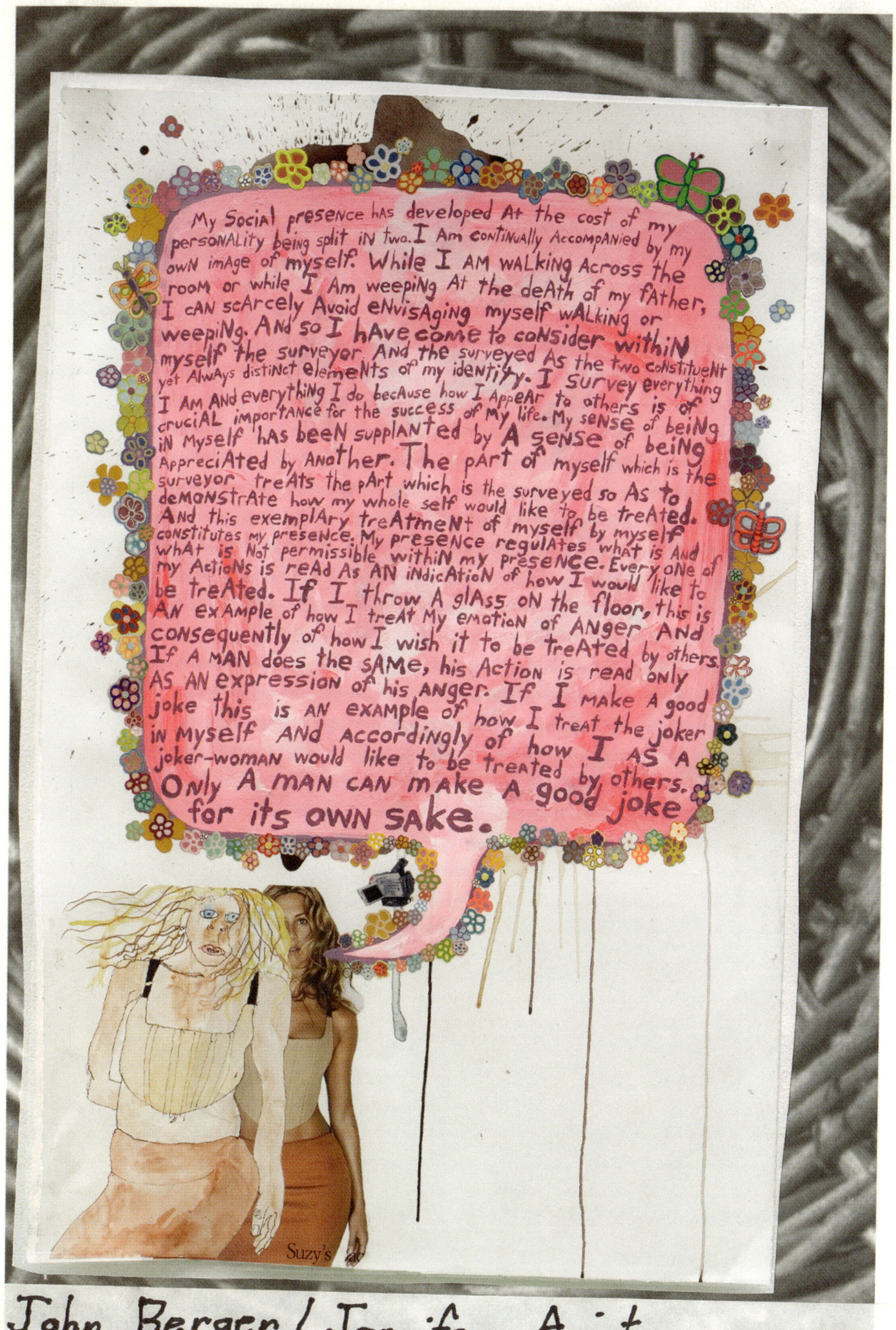

John Berger / Jennifer Aniston
Feminine Revision / Reclamation

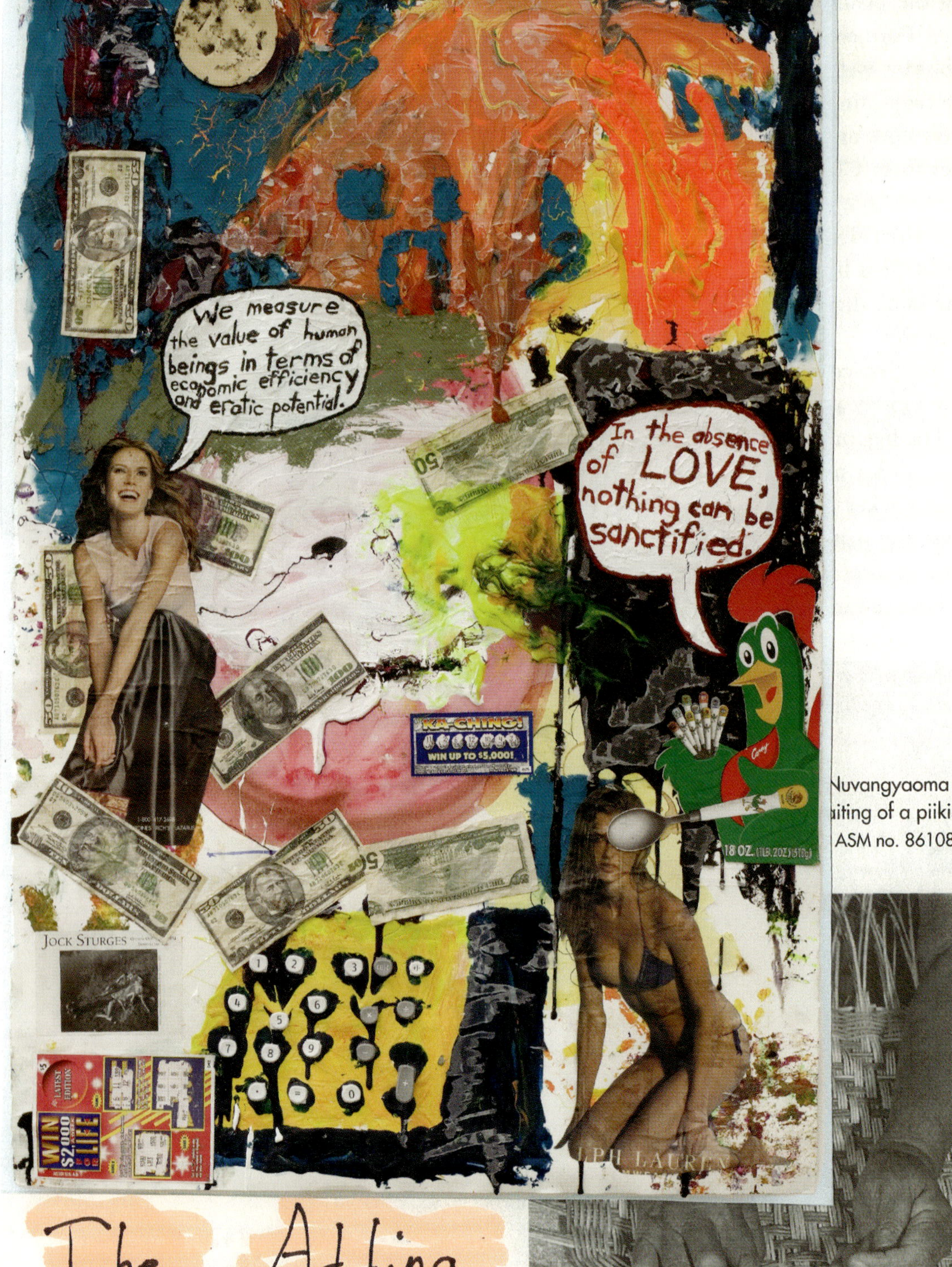

Nuvangyaoma starts plaiting of a piiki tray. (ASM no. 86108)

The Adding Machine

She uses the wicker technique in weaving the border. (1991; ASM no. 86142)

...Not from the written, but from the spoken word

takes its title from a statement by Adolf Hitler *Attesting to the location from which* all great movements take there cues. The first part of the painting's text is Theodore Adorno's famous "anti-feminist" remark from an early essay on the nature of recorded speech. The second part is a combination of a similarly themed quote from Jacques Lacan and another from his popular disciple Slavoj Zizek. In this part all speech is deemed "disembodied and spectral". The painting is accompanied by a tape recorder which plays a "cut-up" pieced together from 50 or so of Rod Serling's introductions to various episodes of The Twilight Zone. These fragments of speech are excerpted and assembled in a way which eliminates the specific subject of Serling's monologue save for a vague reference to "the dimension you are entering". A spectral and disembodied speech if there ever was one.

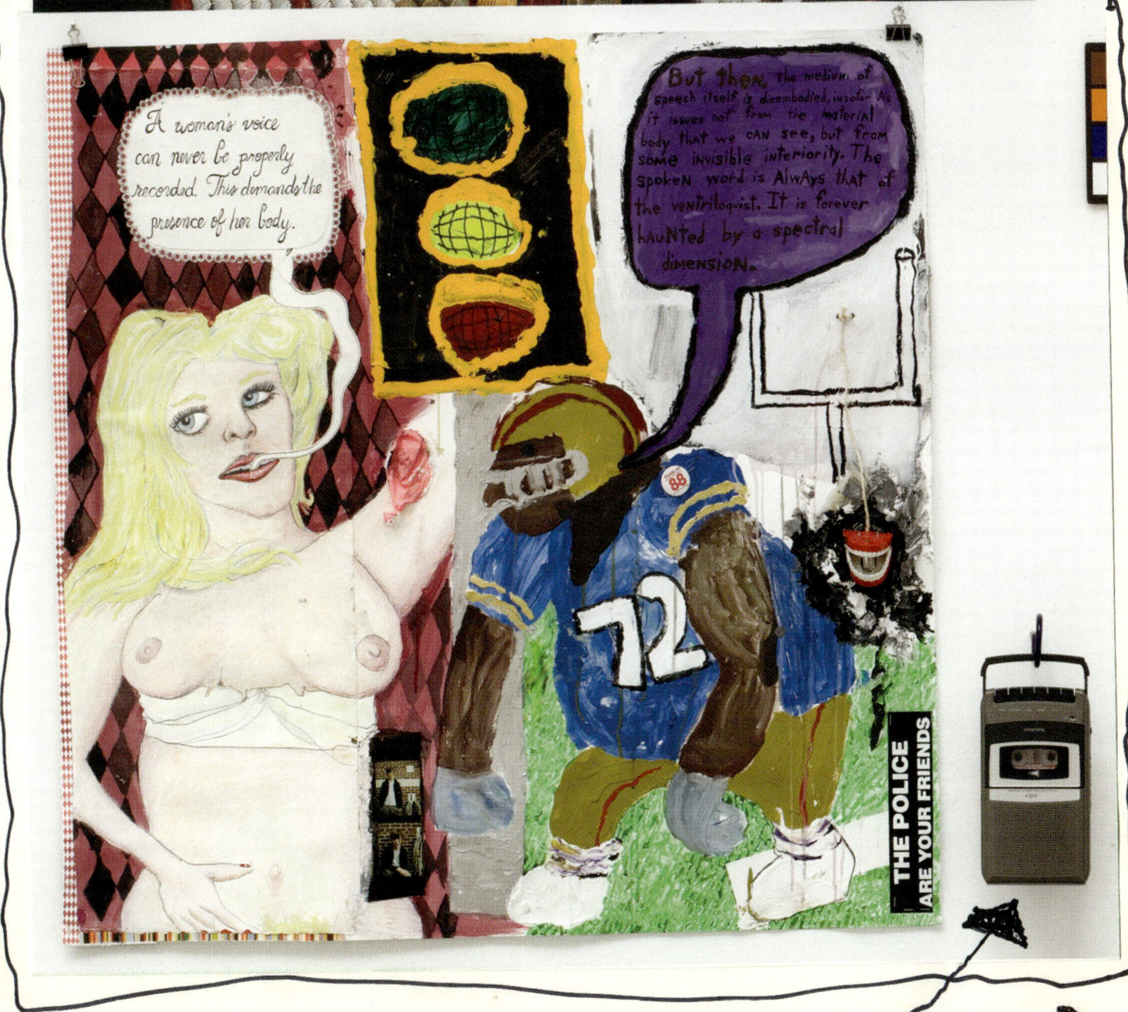

You're traveling through another dimension, a dimension not only of sight and sound but of mind; a journey into a wondrous land whose boundaries are that of imagination. There is a fifth dimension beyond that which is known to man. It is a dimension as vast as space and timeless as infinity. It is the middle ground between light and shadow, between science and superstition, and it lies between the pit of man's fears and the summit of his knowledge. Witness if you will a dungeon, made out of mountains, salt flats and sand that stretch to infinity. An old touring car that squats in the sun and goes nowhere— for there is nowhere to go. Confinement in this case stretches as far as the eye can see, because this particular dungeon is on an asteroid nine million miles from the Earth. There's a saying, 'Every man is put on Earth condemned to die, time and method of execution unknown.' Perhaps this is as it should be. Some wisp of memory not too important really, some laughing ghosts that cross a man's mind, a long, agonizing route through a maze of bottles. Because, you see, Fate *can* work that way. Life is a treadmill built out of sidewalks. Age: indeterminate. Duly recorded is the course to destination, weather conditions, temperature, longitude and latitude. But what is never recorded is the fear that washes over a deck like fog and ocean spray. Fear like the throbbing strokes of engine pistons, each like a heartbeat, parceling out every hour into breathless minutes of watching, waiting and dreading. It travels alone like an aged blind thing grouping through the unfriendly dark, stalked by unseen periscopes of steel killers. This is what is meant by paying the fiddler. This is the comeuppance awaiting every man when the ledger of his life is opened and examined, the tally made, and then the reward or the penalty paid. This is the penalty. This is the justice meted out. A man can be lost not only in terms of maps and miles, but also in *time*— and time in this case can be measured in eternities. The shrouds that cover mysteries are not always made out of a tarpaulin. They used to exist, but don't any longer. Someone—or something—took them somewhere. At least they are no longer a part of the memory of man. This too does not exist. The best-laid plans of mice and men who wanted nothing but time. Now just a part of a smashed landscape, just a piece of the rubble, just a fragment of what man has deeded to himself. You're looking at a species of flimsy little two-legged animal with extremely small heads whose name is Man. Man unshackling himself and sending his tiny, groping fingers up into the unknown. Time for supper now. Time for families. Time for a cool drink on a porch. Time for the quiet rustle of leaf-laden trees that

An Eagle
weaver us
tion at the
Dove Meh

time a
an's Exhibi-
Margo

screen out the moon. And underneath is all, behind the eyes of the
men, hanging invisible over the summer night, is a horror without
words. For this is the stillness before storm. This is the eve of the end.
A doomed planet on the verge of suicide. An ordinary scene, an
ordinary city. Lunchtime for thousands of ordinary people. To most of
them, this hour will be a rest, a pleasant break in the day's routine. To
most, but not all. Time is an enemy, and the hour to come is a matter of
life and death. They say a dream takes only a second or so, and yet in
that second a man can live a lifetime. He can suffer and die, and who's
to say which is the greater reality: the one we know or the one in
dreams, between heaven, the sky, the earth. Once-brilliant star in a
firmament no longer a part of the sky, eclipsed by the movement of
earth and time. Whose world is a projection room, whose dreams are
made out of celluloid. Struck down by hit-and-run years and lying on
the unhappy pavement, trying desperately to get the license number of
fleeting fame. To the wishes that come true, to the strange, mystic
strength of the human animal, who can take a wishful dream and give it
a dimension of its own. What you're looking at is a ghost, once alive
but no deceased. Now it houses nothing but memories and a wind that
stirs in the high grass, a wind that sometimes bears a faint, ghostly
resemblance to the roar of a crowd that once sat here. We're back in
time now. A cheapness of mind, a cheapness of taste, a tawdry little
shine on the seat of conscience, and a dark-room squint at a world
whose sunlight has never gotten through.

As if some omniscient painter had mixed a tube of oils that were at one
time earth brown, dust gray, blood red, beard black, and fear— yellow
white. For this is the province of combat and these are the faces of war.
A tree-lined little road of front porch gliders, barbecues, the laughter of
children, and the bell of an ice-cream vendor. At the sound of the roar
and the flash of light on a late Saturday afternoon, in the last calm and
reflective moment—before the monsters came. The tools of conquest
do not necessarily come with bombs and explosions and fallout. There
are weapons that are simply thoughts, attitudes, prejudices—to be
found only in the minds of men. For the record, prejudices can kill and
suspicion can destroy, and a thoughtless, frightened search for a
scapegoat has a fallout all is own—for the children, and the children yet
unborn. And the pity of it is that these things cannot be confined.
You're looking at Act One, Scene One, of a nightmare, one not
restricted to witching hours or dark, rainswept nights. Last stop on a
long journey, as yet another human being returns to the vast

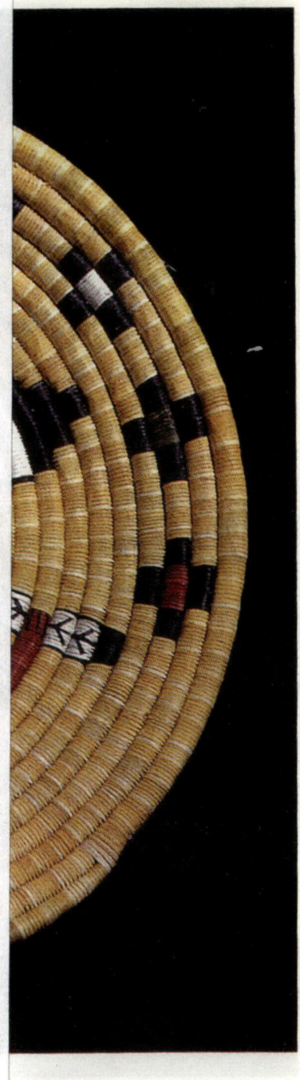

...Best of Division award at the Hopi
...er: 19.5")

nothingness that is the beginning and into the dust that is always the
end. Four and a half years of planning, preparation and training, and a
thousand years of science and mathematics and the projected dreams
and hopes of not only a nation but a world. And this is the countdown,
the last five seconds before man shot an arrow into the air. Practical
joke perpetrated by Mother Nature and a combination of improbable
events. Practical joke wearing the trappings of nightmare, of terror, of
desperation. A small human drama played out in a desert. You're
looking at a tableau of reality, things of substance, of physical material:
a desk, a window, a light. These things exist and have dimension.
Flesh and blood, muscle and mind. But in just a moment we will see
how thin a line separates that which we assume to be real with that
manufactured inside of a mind. The *modus operandi* for the departure
from life is usually a pine box of such and such dimensions, and this sis
the ultimate in reality. But there are other ways for a man to exit from
life. Along a highway there is an exit sign that reads: 'This way to
escape.' A most inoperative, deadly, life-shattering affliction known as
an inanimate metal machine variously described as a monster with a
will all is own.

A wicker plaque made by [...]
Keams Canyon, Arizona. (

Picture For
Chiltren 2
—2005

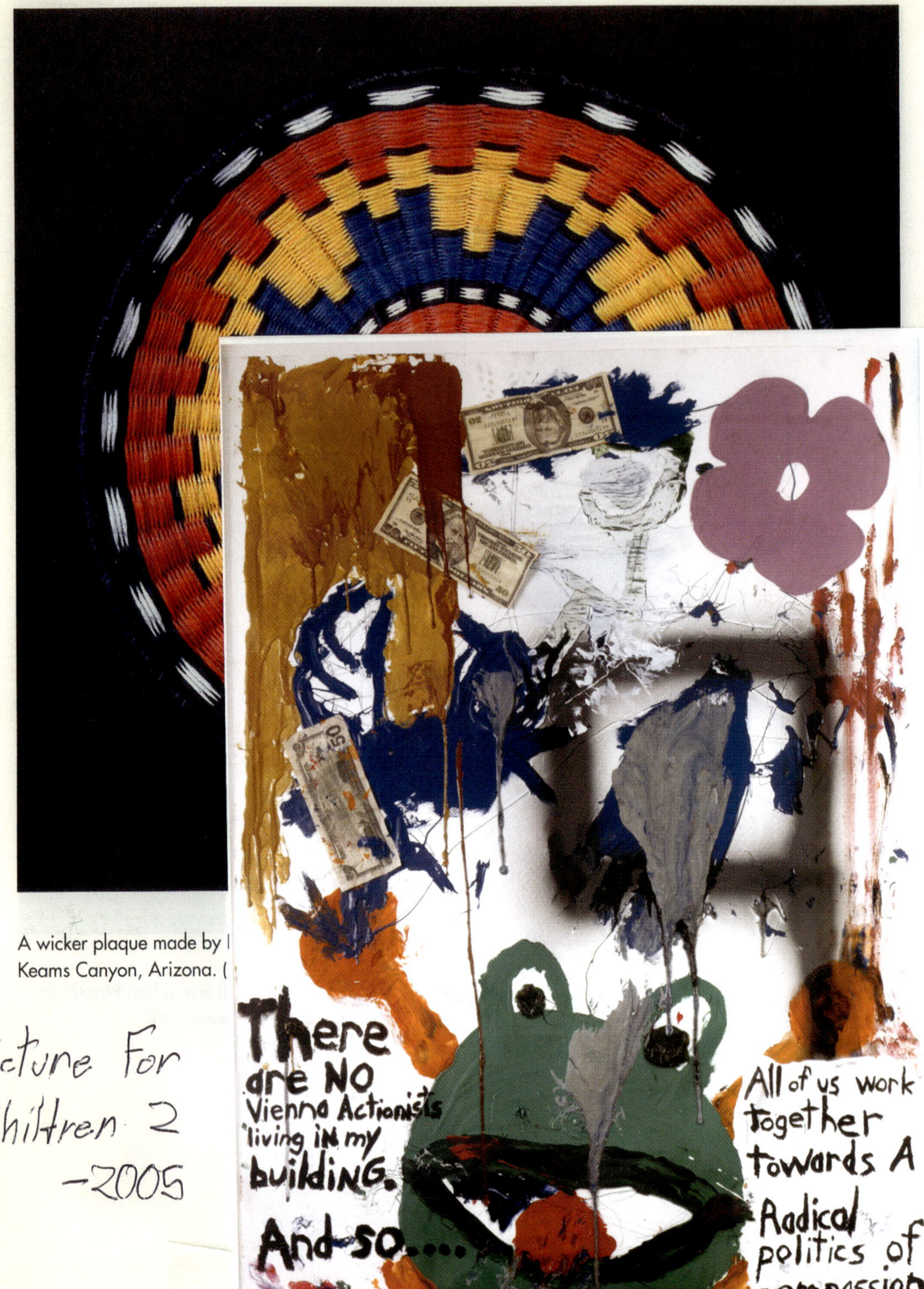

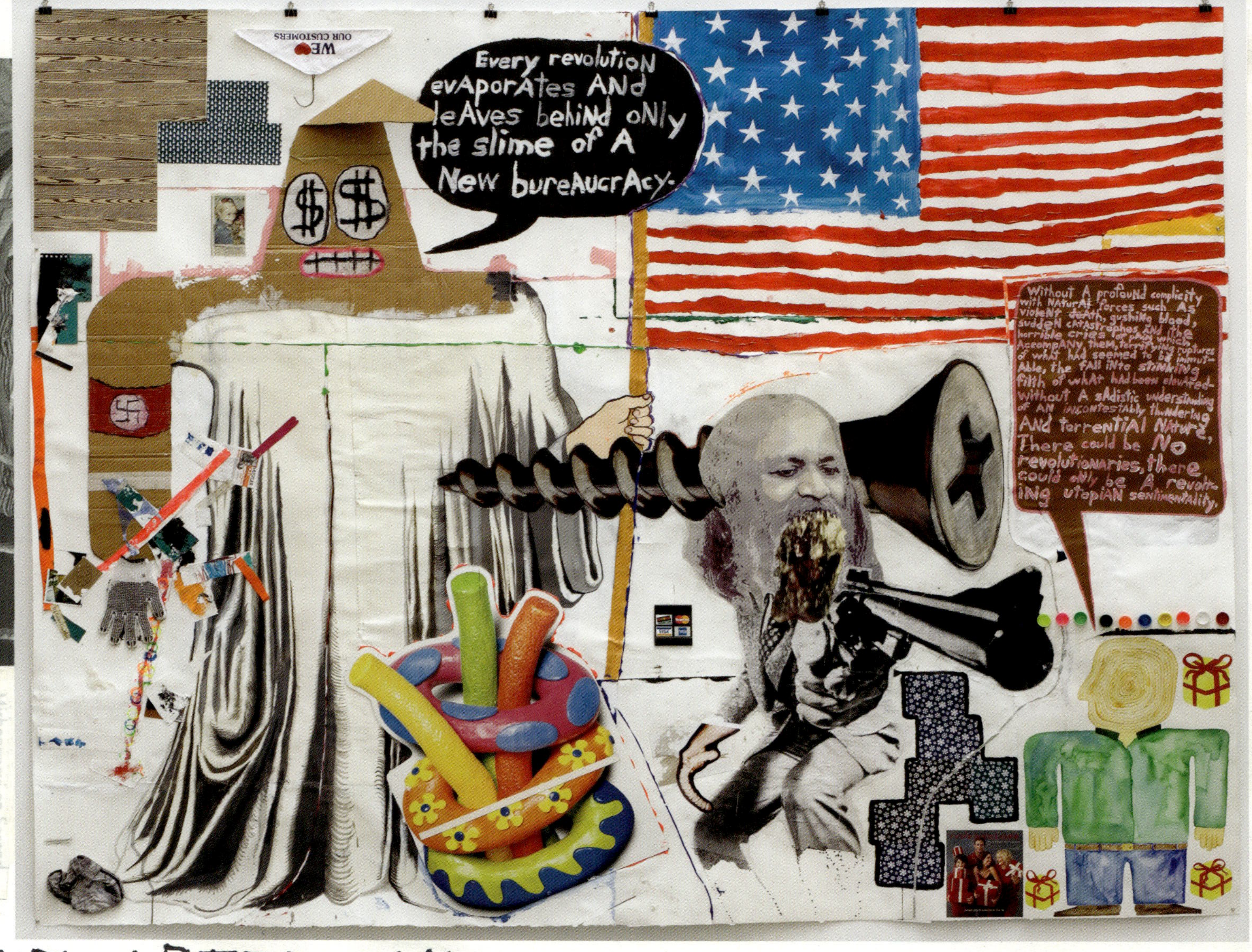

Mishongnovi on Second Mesa uses scrub sumac

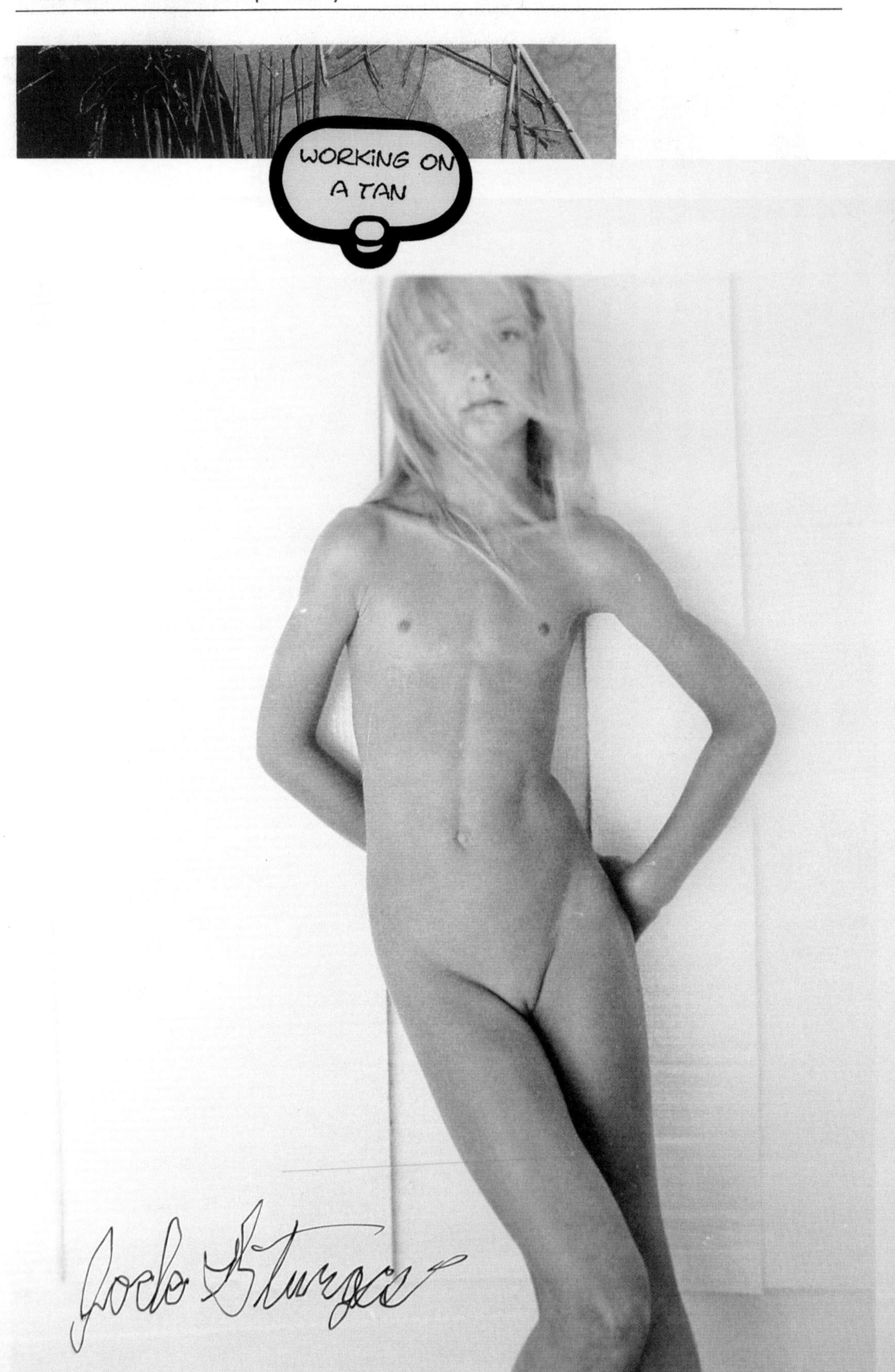
WORKING ON
A TAN

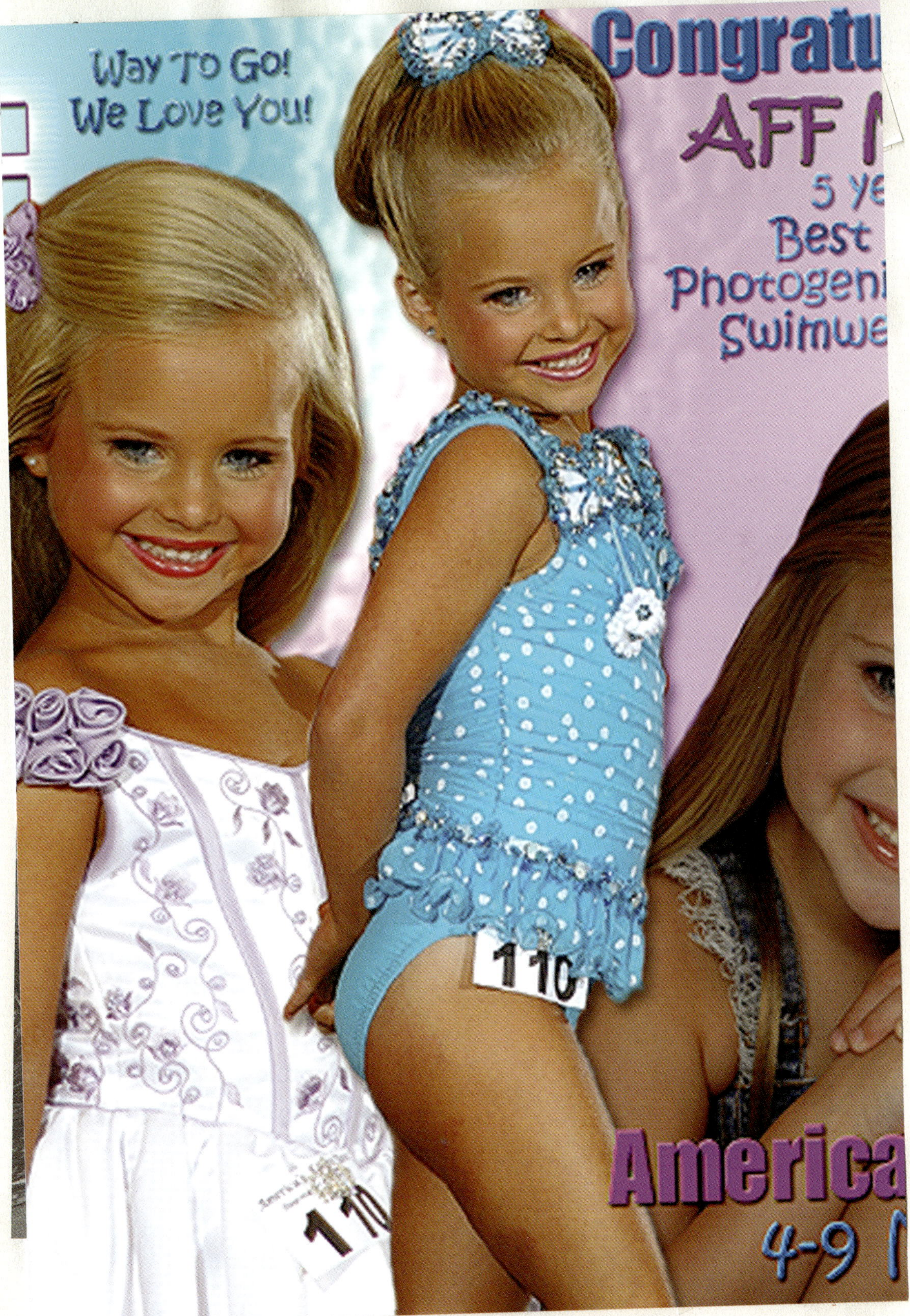
Way To Go!
We Love You!
Congratu
AFF
5 ye
Best
Photogeni
Swimwe
America
4-9
1 10

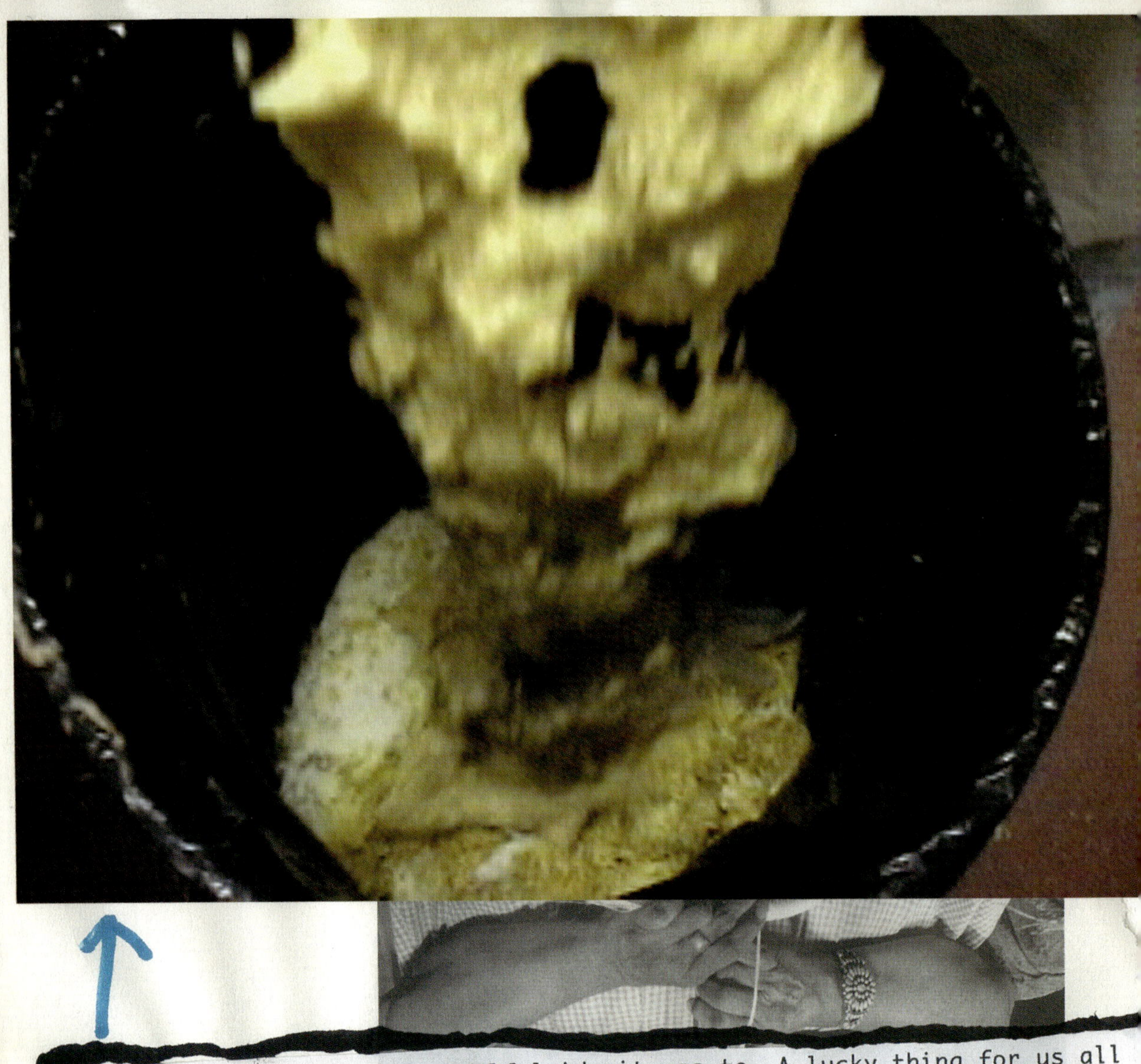

Here is a spectere that I myself laid witness to. A lucky thing for us all that I was able to capture his image. You may say to yourself, "Surely he will haunt your dreams as vengence for this tresspass!", but don't worry, I shall not fear him. Crossing this astral plane once took as much energy as such a low level spirit could possibly muster.

THE DISH-
WASHERS
SONG

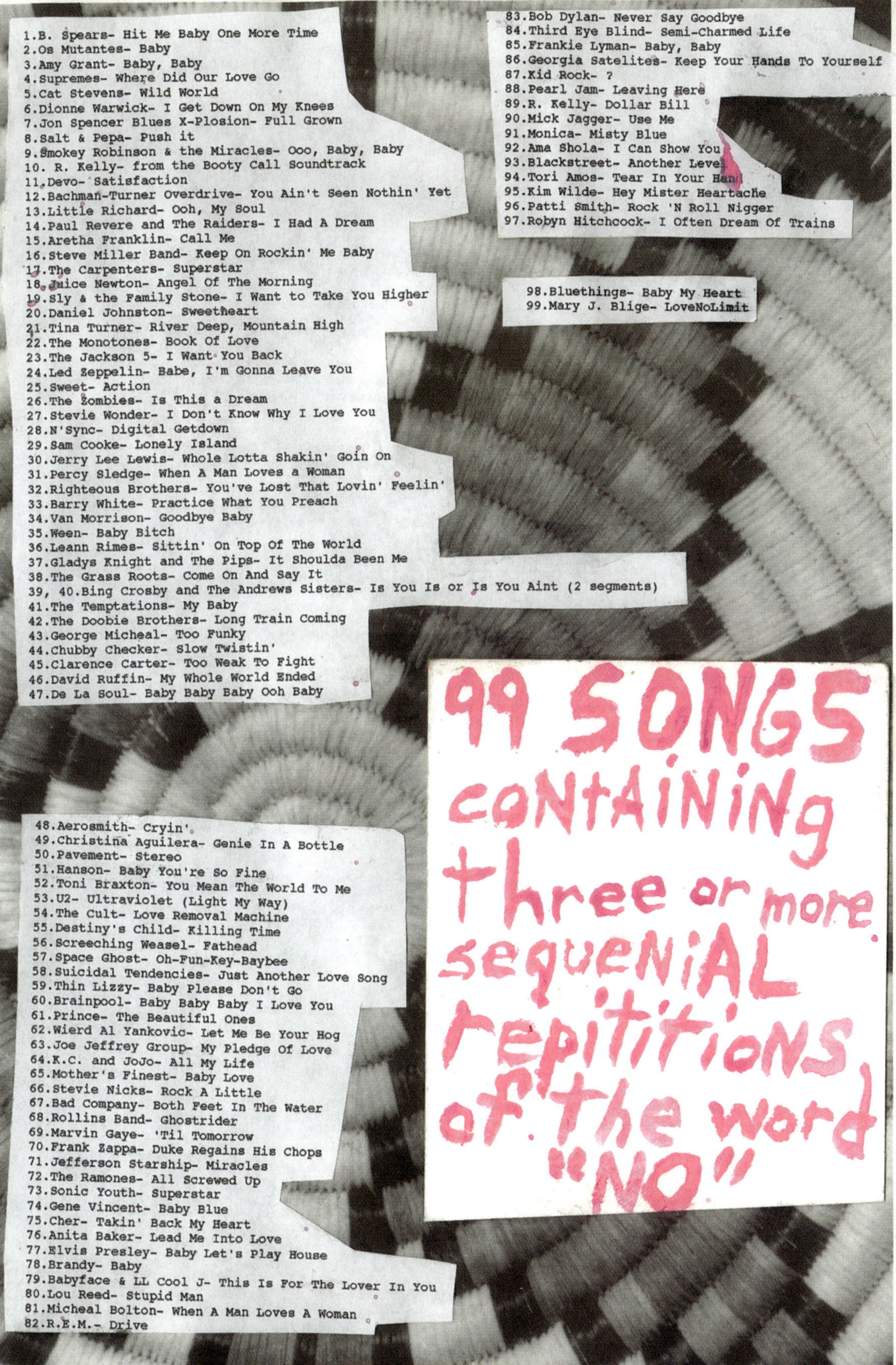

1.B. Spears- Hit Me Baby One More Time
2.Os Mutantes- Baby
3.Amy Grant- Baby, Baby
4.Supremes- Where Did Our Love Go
5.Cat Stevens- Wild World
6.Dionne Warwick- I Get Down On My Knees
7.Jon Spencer Blues X-Plosion- Full Grown
8.Salt & Pepa- Push it
9.Smokey Robinson & the Miracles- Ooo, Baby, Baby
10. R. Kelly- from the Booty Call Soundtrack
11.Devo- Satisfaction
12.Bachman-Turner Overdrive- You Ain't Seen Nothin' Yet
13.Little Richard- Ooh, My Soul
14.Paul Revere and The Raiders- I Had A Dream
15.Aretha Franklin- Call Me
16.Steve Miller Band- Keep On Rockin' Me Baby
17.The Carpenters- Superstar
18.Juice Newton- Angel Of The Morning
19.Sly & the Family Stone- I Want to Take You Higher
20.Daniel Johnston- Sweetheart
21.Tina Turner- River Deep, Mountain High
22.The Monotones- Book Of Love
23.The Jackson 5- I Want You Back
24.Led Zeppelin- Babe, I'm Gonna Leave You
25.Sweet- Action
26.The Zombies- Is This a Dream
27.Stevie Wonder- I Don't Know Why I Love You
28.N'Sync- Digital Getdown
29.Sam Cooke- Lonely Island
30.Jerry Lee Lewis- Whole Lotta Shakin' Goin On
31.Percy Sledge- When A Man Loves a Woman
32.Righteous Brothers- You've Lost That Lovin' Feelin'
33.Barry White- Practice What You Preach
34.Van Morrison- Goodbye Baby
35.Ween- Baby Bitch
36.Leann Rimes- Sittin' On Top Of The World
37.Gladys Knight and The Pips- It Shoulda Been Me
38.The Grass Roots- Come On And Say It
39, 40.Bing Crosby and The Andrews Sisters- Is You Is or Is You Aint (2 segments)
41.The Temptations- My Baby
42.The Doobie Brothers- Long Train Coming
43.George Micheal- Too Funky
44.Chubby Checker- Slow Twistin'
45.Clarence Carter- Too Weak To Fight
46.David Ruffin- My Whole World Ended
47.De La Soul- Baby Baby Baby Ooh Baby

83.Bob Dylan- Never Say Goodbye
84.Third Eye Blind- Semi-Charmed Life
85.Frankie Lyman- Baby, Baby
86.Georgia Satelites- Keep Your Hands To Yourself
87.Kid Rock- ?
88.Pearl Jam- Leaving Here
89.R. Kelly- Dollar Bill
90.Mick Jagger- Use Me
91.Monica- Misty Blue
92.Ama Shola- I Can Show You
93.Blackstreet- Another Level
94.Tori Amos- Tear In Your Hand
95.Kim Wilde- Hey Mister Heartache
96.Patti Smith- Rock 'N Roll Nigger
97.Robyn Hitchcock- I Often Dream Of Trains

98.Bluethings- Baby My Heart
99.Mary J. Blige- LoveNoLimit

48.Aerosmith- Cryin'
49.Christina Aguilera- Genie In A Bottle
50.Pavement- Stereo
51.Hanson- Baby You're So Fine
52.Toni Braxton- You Mean The World To Me
53.U2- Ultraviolet (Light My Way)
54.The Cult- Love Removal Machine
55.Destiny's Child- Killing Time
56.Screeching Weasel- Fathead
57.Space Ghost- Oh-Fun-Key-Baybee
58.Suicidal Tendencies- Just Another Love Song
59.Thin Lizzy- Baby Please Don't Go
60.Brainpool- Baby Baby Baby I Love You
61.Prince- The Beautiful Ones
62.Wierd Al Yankovic- Let Me Be Your Hog
63.Joe Jeffrey Group- My Pledge Of Love
64.K.C. and JoJo- All My Life
65.Mother's Finest- Baby Love
66.Stevie Nicks- Rock A Little
67.Bad Company- Both Feet In The Water
68.Rollins Band- Ghostrider
69.Marvin Gaye- 'Til Tomorrow
70.Frank Zappa- Duke Regains His Chops
71.Jefferson Starship- Miracles
72.The Ramones- All Screwed Up
73.Sonic Youth- Superstar
74.Gene Vincent- Baby Blue
75.Cher- Takin' Back My Heart
76.Anita Baker- Lead Me Into Love
77.Elvis Presley- Baby Let's Play House
78.Brandy- Baby
79.Babyface & LL Cool J- This Is For The Lover In You
80.Lou Reed- Stupid Man
81.Micheal Bolton- When A Man Loves A Woman
82.R.E.M.- Drive

99 SONGS CONTAINING three or more sequenial repititions of the word "NO"

List of songs containing three or more sequential repetitions of the word "No"

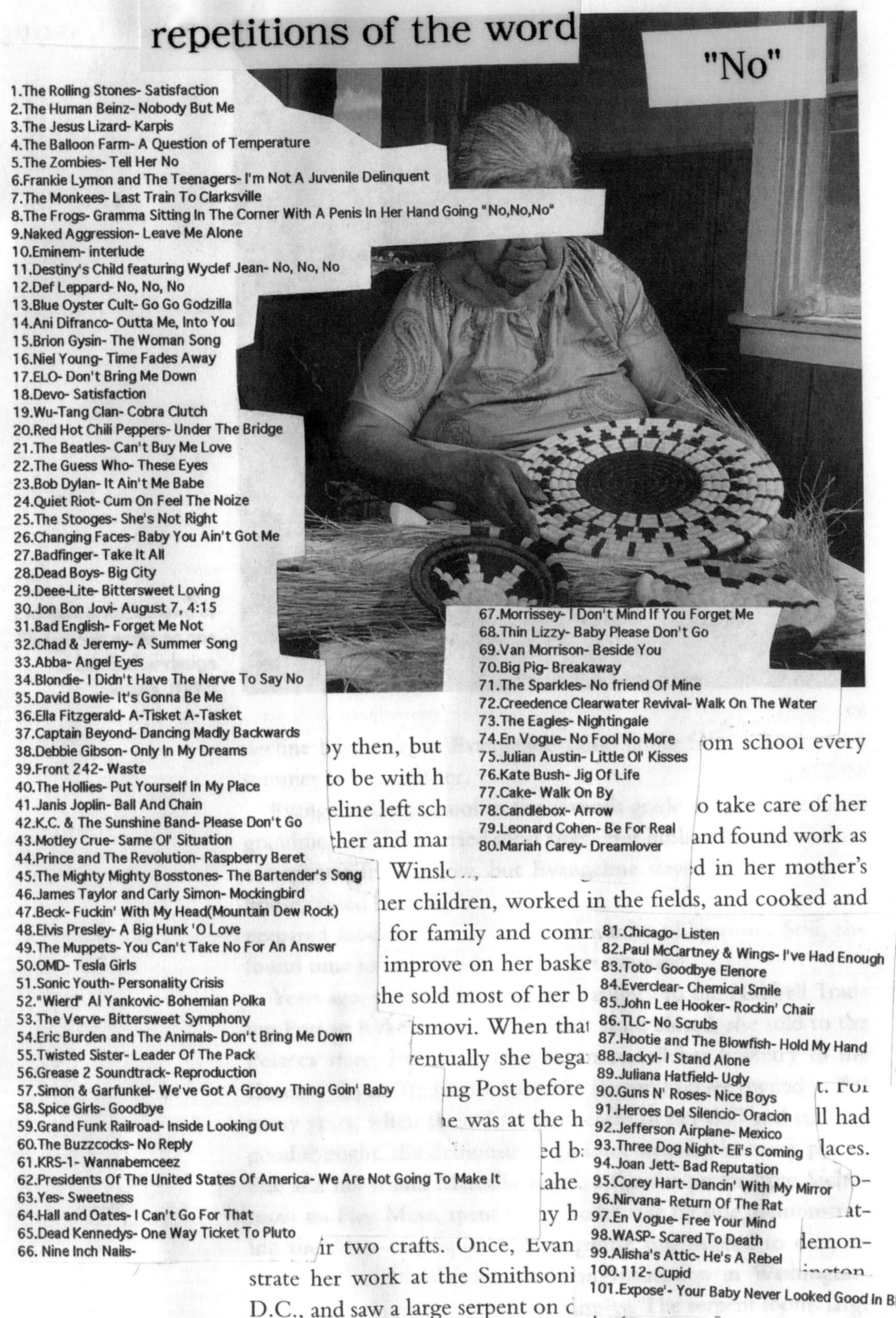

by then, but ... om school every ... to be with h ... eline left sch ... o take care of her ... her and mar ... and found work as ... Winsl... ...d in her mother's ... her children, worked in the fields, and cooked and ... for family and comr ... improve on her baske ... she sold most of her b ... tsmovi. When that ... entually she bega ... ng Post before ... t. For ... e was at the h ... ll had ... ed b: ... laces. ...ahe ... o- ...ny h ...at- ...ir two crafts. Once, Evan ...lemon- strate her work at the Smithsoni ...ington. D.C., and saw a large serpent on c

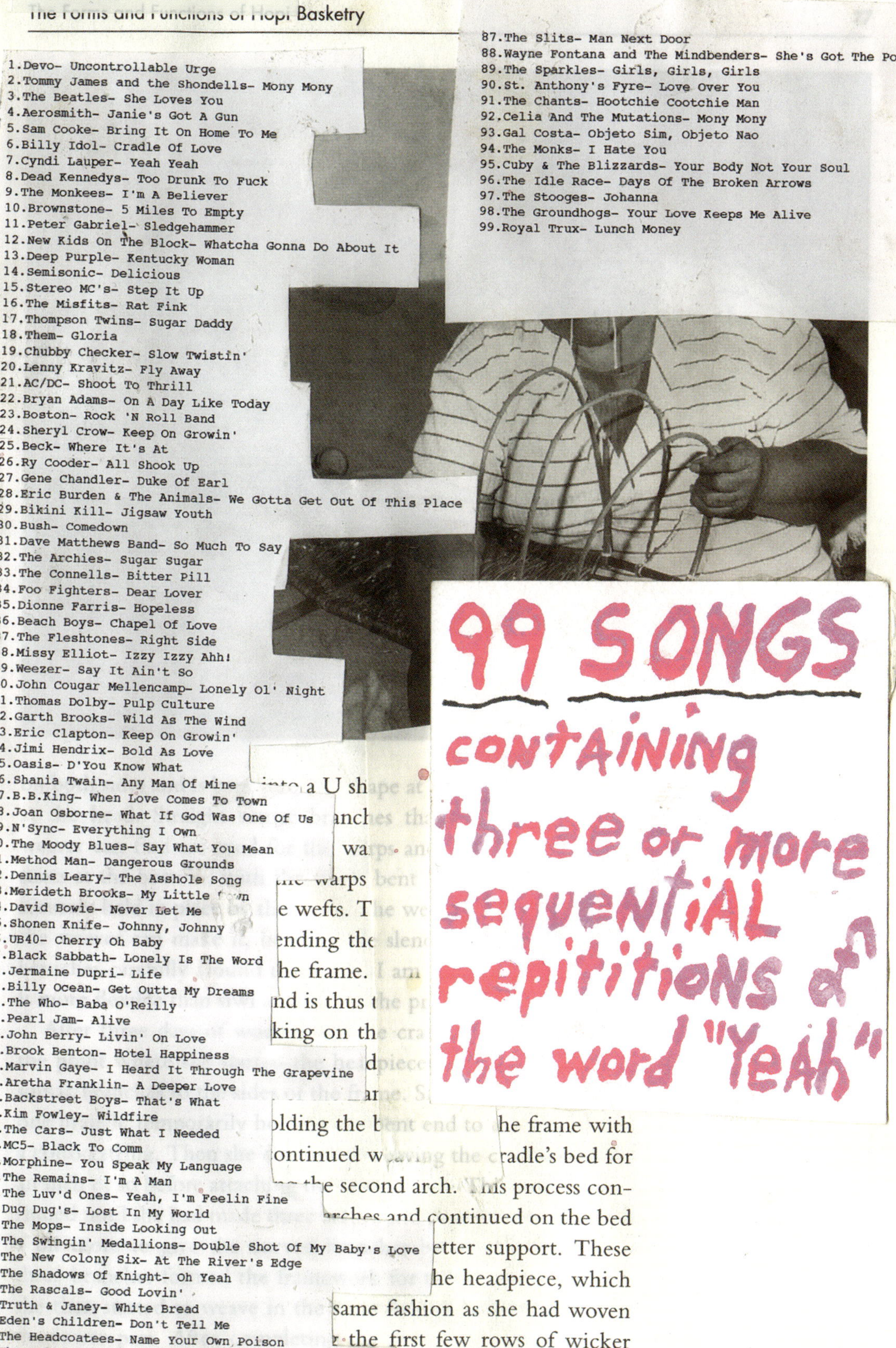

1. Devo- Uncontrollable Urge
2. Tommy James and the Shondells- Mony Mony
3. The Beatles- She Loves You
4. Aerosmith- Janie's Got A Gun
5. Sam Cooke- Bring It On Home To Me
6. Billy Idol- Cradle Of Love
7. Cyndi Lauper- Yeah Yeah
8. Dead Kennedys- Too Drunk To Fuck
9. The Monkees- I'm A Believer
10. Brownstone- 5 Miles To Empty
11. Peter Gabriel- Sledgehammer
12. New Kids On The Block- Whatcha Gonna Do About It
13. Deep Purple- Kentucky Woman
14. Semisonic- Delicious
15. Stereo MC's- Step It Up
16. The Misfits- Rat Fink
17. Thompson Twins- Sugar Daddy
18. Them- Gloria
19. Chubby Checker- Slow Twistin'
20. Lenny Kravitz- Fly Away
21. AC/DC- Shoot To Thrill
22. Bryan Adams- On A Day Like Today
23. Boston- Rock 'N Roll Band
24. Sheryl Crow- Keep On Growin'
25. Beck- Where It's At
26. Ry Cooder- All Shook Up
27. Gene Chandler- Duke Of Earl
28. Eric Burden & The Animals- We Gotta Get Out Of This Place
29. Bikini Kill- Jigsaw Youth
30. Bush- Comedown
31. Dave Matthews Band- So Much To Say
32. The Archies- Sugar Sugar
33. The Connells- Bitter Pill
34. Foo Fighters- Dear Lover
35. Dionne Farris- Hopeless
36. Beach Boys- Chapel Of Love
37. The Fleshtones- Right Side
38. Missy Elliot- Izzy Izzy Ahh!
39. Weezer- Say It Ain't So
40. John Cougar Mellencamp- Lonely Ol' Night
41. Thomas Dolby- Pulp Culture
42. Garth Brooks- Wild As The Wind
43. Eric Clapton- Keep On Growin'
44. Jimi Hendrix- Bold As Love
45. Oasis- D'You Know What
46. Shania Twain- Any Man Of Mine
47. B.B.King- When Love Comes To Town
48. Joan Osborne- What If God Was One Of Us
49. N'Sync- Everything I Own
50. The Moody Blues- Say What You Mean
51. Method Man- Dangerous Grounds
52. Dennis Leary- The Asshole Song
53. Merideth Brooks- My Little Town
54. David Bowie- Never Let Me
55. Shonen Knife- Johnny, Johnny
56. UB40- Cherry Oh Baby
57. Black Sabbath- Lonely Is The Word
58. Jermaine Dupri- Life
59. Billy Ocean- Get Outta My Dreams
60. The Who- Baba O'Reilly
61. Pearl Jam- Alive
62. John Berry- Livin' On Love
63. Brook Benton- Hotel Happiness
64. Marvin Gaye- I Heard It Through The Grapevine
65. Aretha Franklin- A Deeper Love
66. Backstreet Boys- That's What
67. Kim Fowley- Wildfire
68. The Cars- Just What I Needed
69. MC5- Black To Comm
70. Morphine- You Speak My Language
71. The Remains- I'm A Man
72. The Luv'd Ones- Yeah, I'm Feelin Fine
73. Dug Dug's- Lost In My World
74. The Mops- Inside Looking Out
75. The Swingin' Medallions- Double Shot Of My Baby's Love
76. The New Colony Six- At The River's Edge
77. The Shadows Of Knight- Oh Yeah
78. The Rascals- Good Lovin'
79. Truth & Janey- White Bread
80. Eden's Children- Don't Tell Me
81. The Headcoatees- Name Your Own Poison
82. The Helpful Soul- Peace For Fools
83. The Ronettes- Why Don't They Let Us Fall In Love
84. Blowfly- Maricon
85. Kim Fowley- Were Wolf Dynamite
86. Nite Hawks- Chicken Grabber
87. The Slits- Man Next Door
88. Wayne Fontana and The Mindbenders- She's Got The Power
89. The Sparkles- Girls, Girls, Girls
90. St. Anthony's Fyre- Love Over You
91. The Chants- Hootchie Cootchie Man
92. Celia And The Mutations- Mony Mony
93. Gal Costa- Objeto Sim, Objeto Nao
94. The Monks- I Hate You
95. Cuby & The Blizzards- Your Body Not Your Soul
96. The Idle Race- Days Of The Broken Arrows
97. The Stooges- Johanna
98. The Groundhogs- Your Love Keeps Me Alive
99. Royal Trux- Lunch Money

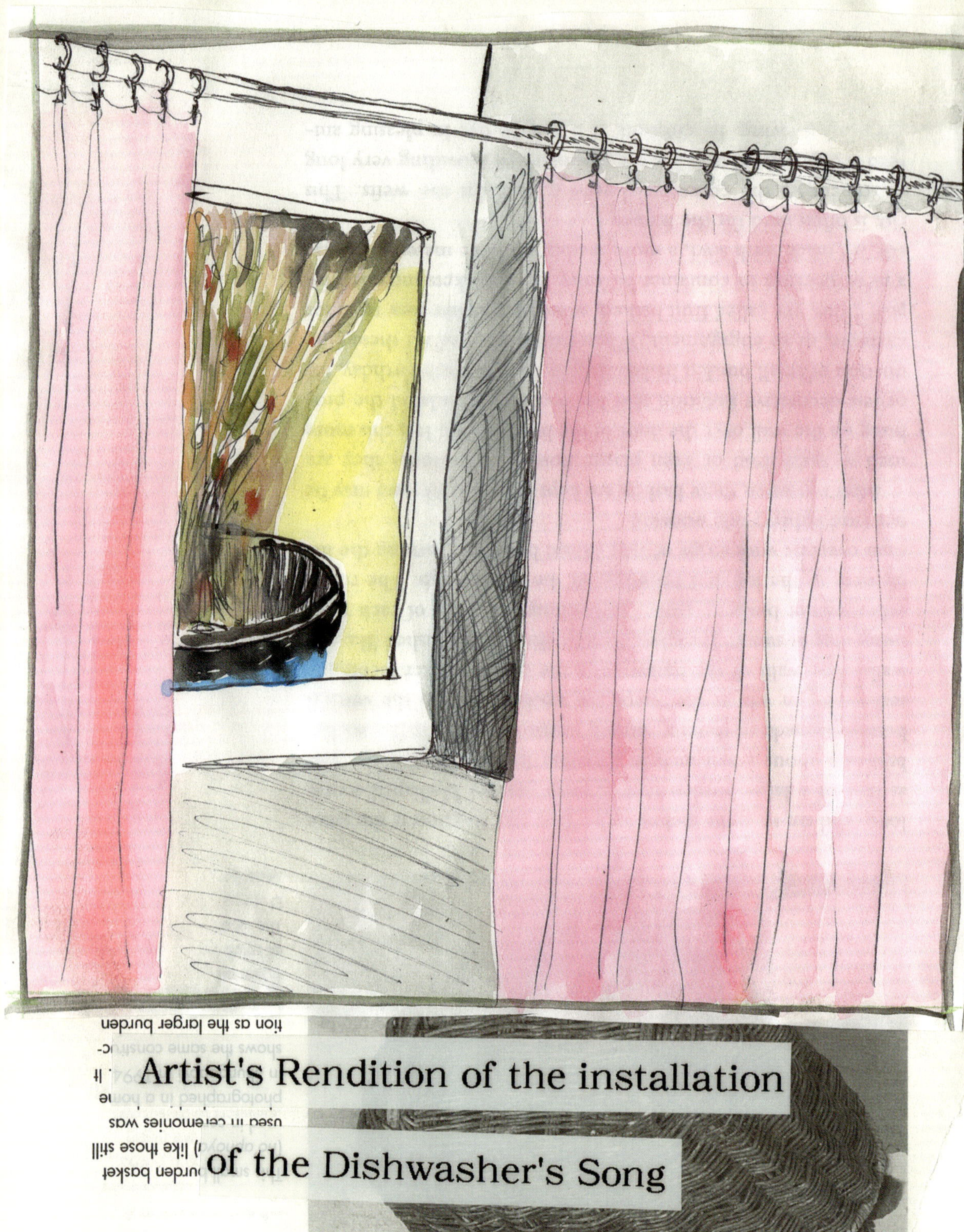

Artist's Rendition of the installation
of the Dishwasher's Song

The Dishwasher's Song is the next summer. an interactive video and multi-channel baskets sound used at installation created during my 9 month were made, period of employment this method as dishwasher at the Maharishi the growth Mahesh Yogi's branches. Fall Spiritual Center of the Americas. to be a This among the San Juan institution is a sort of camp for aging hippies and their basketry too. The new-agers where they are indoctrinated into decline among the Maharishi's astrological belief systems that it may be forgotten and instructed in his method of Transcendental weavers Meditation. These Leonora Quanimptewa followers are hongnovi referred to, repeatedly as the Maharishi's Thousand Headed Purusha. The sixties resort is located high from weaving. in the Appalachian scrub sumac, Mountain region of it is to North the branches of this Carolina decline in the manufacture of with views can be explained of beautiful vistas on anymore. Harvests all sides. For mentioned earlier, my own subject, however, mesas anymore because I chose an aspect of the Burden "Heavenly Mountain" a name so little used that goes seen less often. That a smaller is the gallons of and often used leftover food poured out into the trash at the end of each meal. Using my

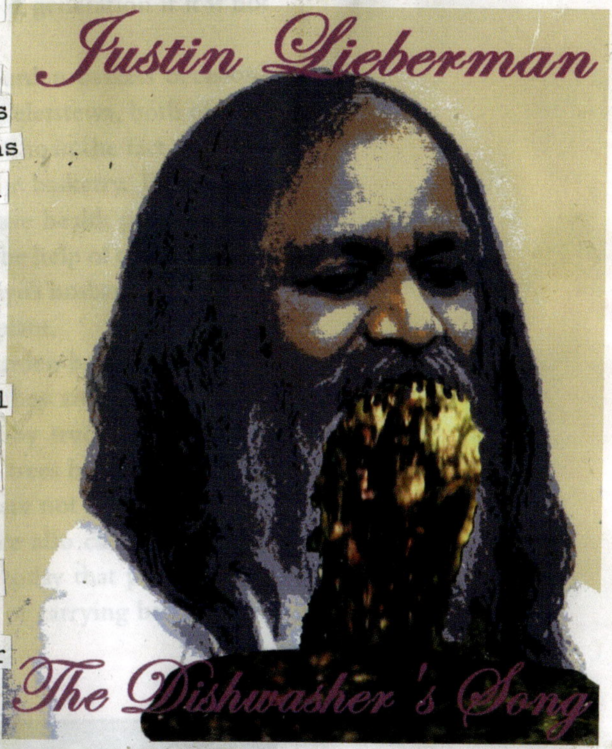

Justin Lieberman

The Dishwasher's Song

video camera, I would record each of these pourings at the end of the night and then bring home the footage to add to what I slowly burden basket came to perceive as a kind of "garbage poem". There are around 250 was made clips ranging in length from 3 to 15 seconds composing the final in 1931 by a piece which clocks in at around 20 minutes. At the same time Hopi man or woman named Sequoptewa. I was putting together this video, I was also creating basket is 27.5 inches long, the sound pieces that accompany and augment it. There are four 16.5 inches high, and 9 ide. It is made separate sound components of The Dishwasher's Song. The first with scrub sumac warps is merely the sound of the garbage itself. The other three are collages and made from excerpts of popular song. I sought out songs in which the words branches are oak. (1994; Museum of "Yeah", "No", or "Baby" were repeated a minimum of four times collection no. OC 2759) in a row. When I had 99 of these excerpts from 99 different songs by 99 different artists of each word I strung them together to create the final piece in which each of the three collages are played simultaneously in the same space as the video. The piece functions in several ways. Upon entering the space, we are confronted with cacophony. Our immediate reaction might be

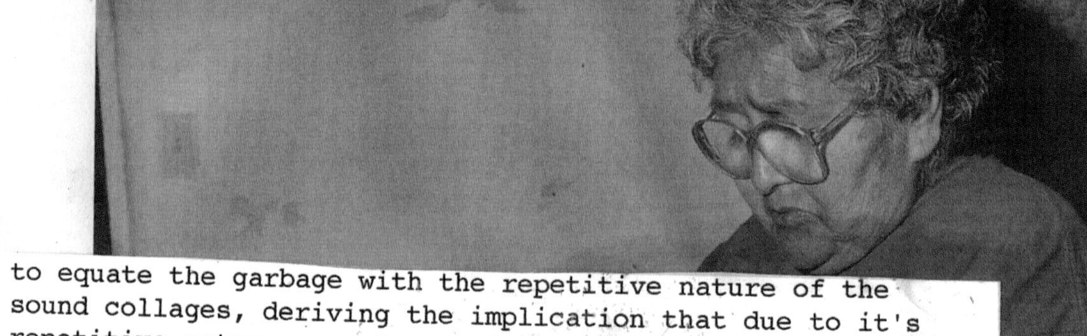

to equate the garbage with the repetitive nature of the sound collages, deriving the implication that due to it's repetitive nature, popular music is being declared garbage. Upon further reflection, this conclusion proves false. The repetition is an aspect of the work that is imposed by the work itself, thus relinquishing the original artists of any

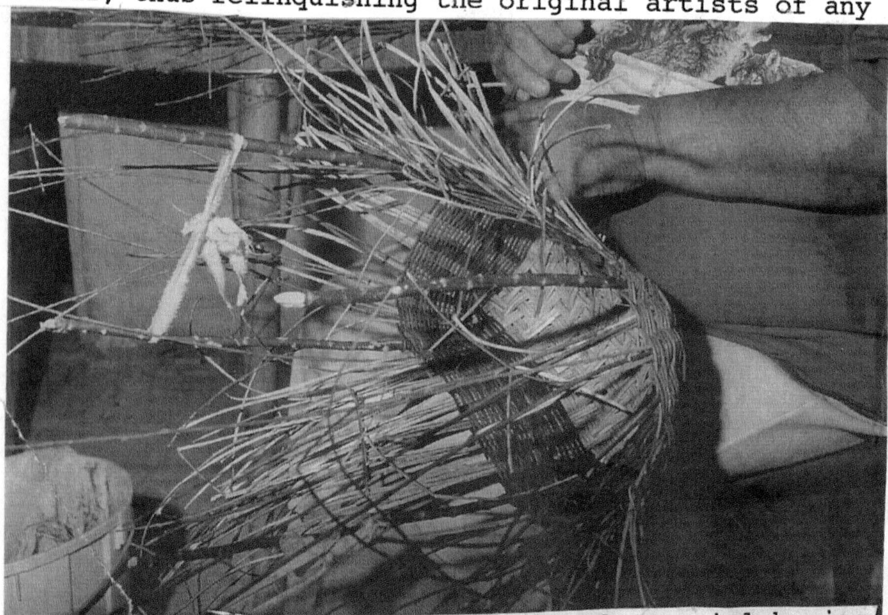

responsibility. At this point the variety of material begins to make itself apparent as the viewer explores the space, taking in the sound collages individually. What at first seemed repetitive now begins to unfold in time as the product of enormous labor. The sound collages do not actually repeat themselves for a full 12 minutes on any of the three tracks and the video continues for almost 20. With this second, closer inspection we begin to recognize individual excerpts of songs from our own listening. Time spent watching the video also induces a shift in our perception as its ever-changing contents

morph and swirl, recalling the language of abstraction. Surprise! The work is not a didactic lesson in popular culture after all. We are being presented with a sensory aesthetic experience in which meaning is a free-floating subjective that is left dangling like an unclipped hang-nail.

Justin Lieberman   2001

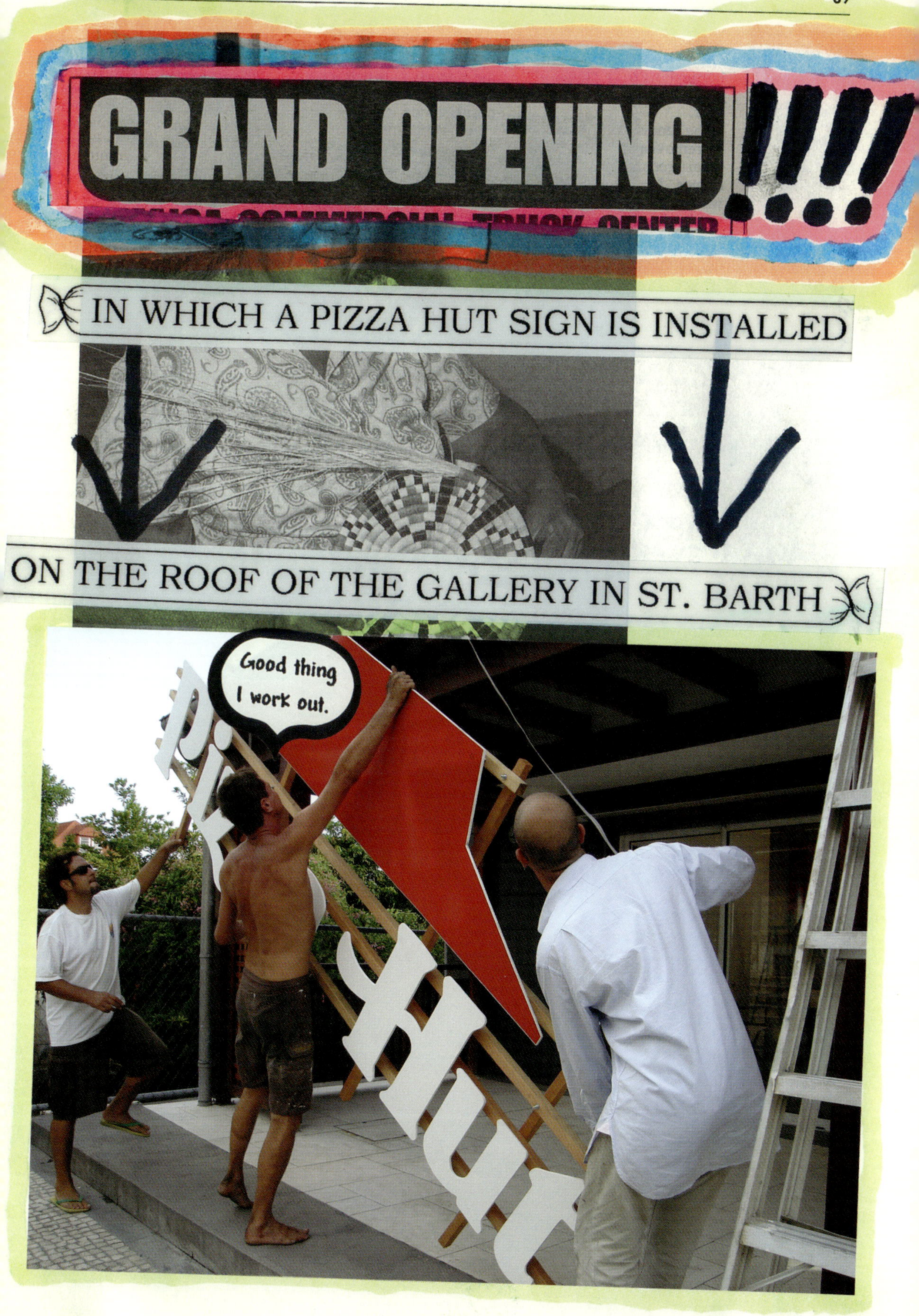

GRAND OPENING !!!!

IN WHICH A PIZZA HUT SIGN IS INSTALLED

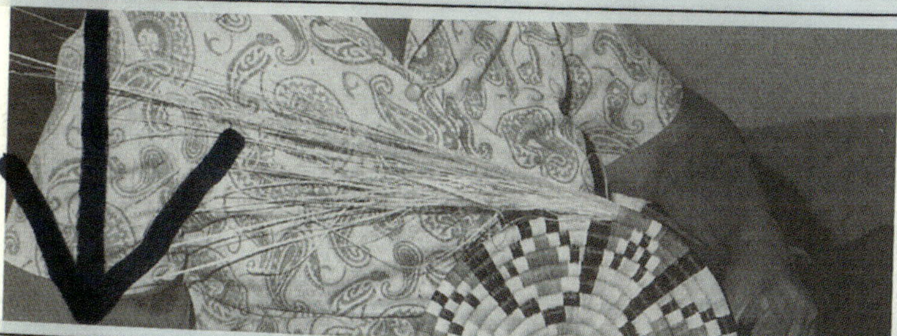

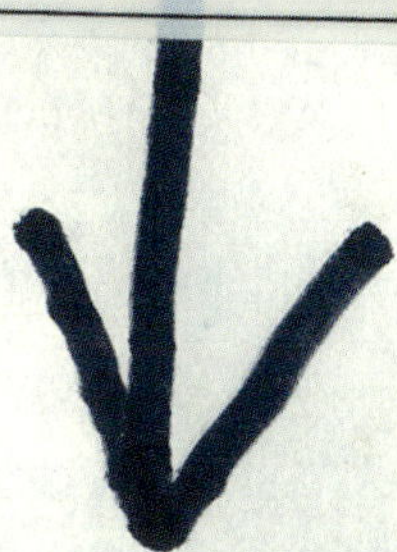

ON THE ROOF OF THE GALLERY IN ST. BARTH

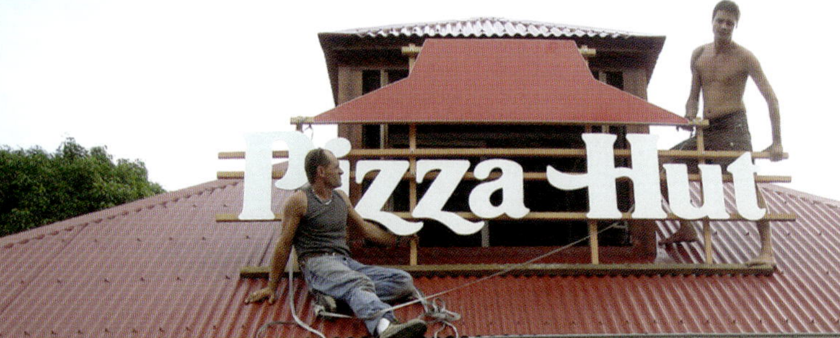

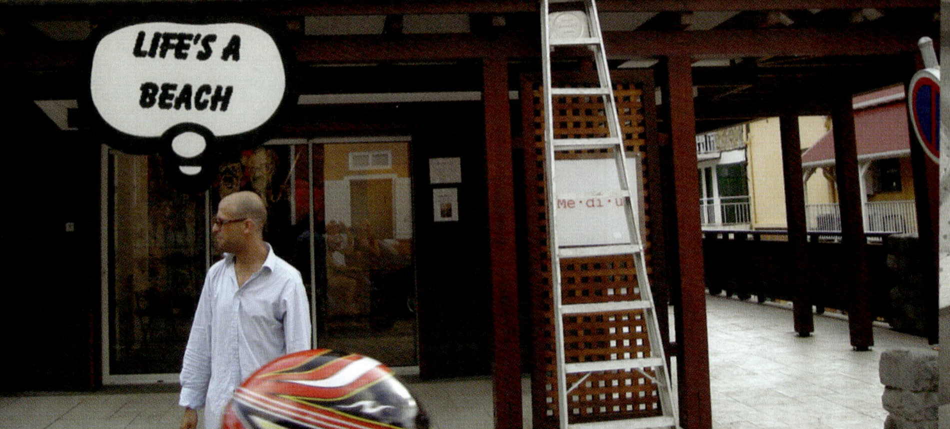

Left-Handed Katsina. In
the background is a coiled
plaque with a turtle

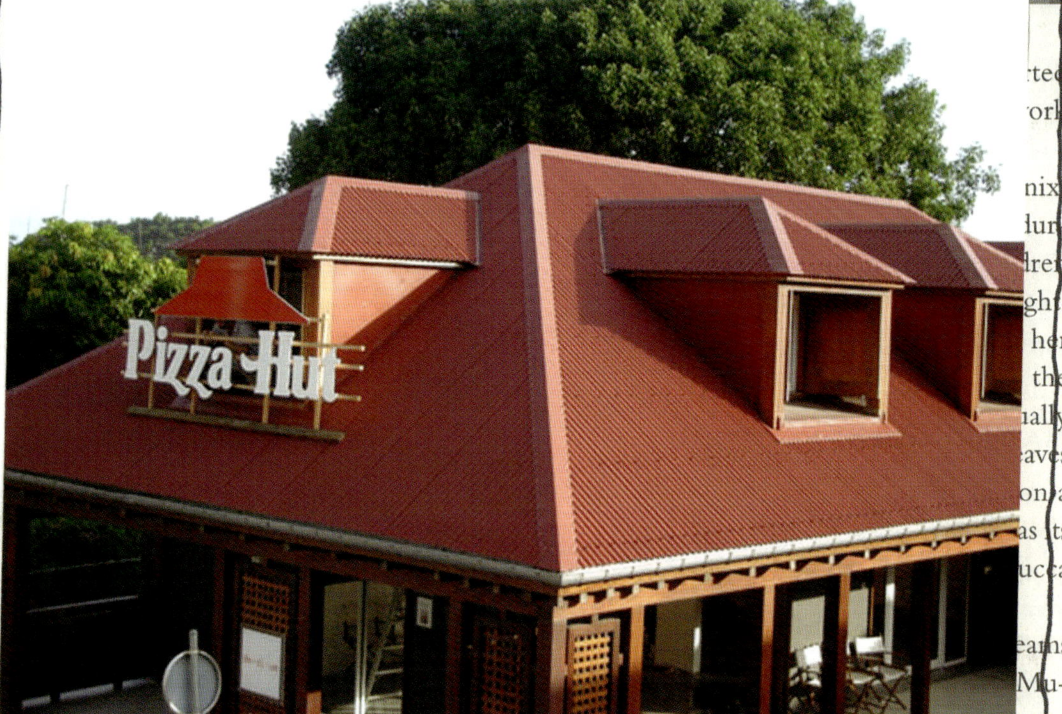

Coiled-l

Medium Gallery is pleased to present the exhibition
'Grand Opening!!!!!!!'. The following is an extract of an
extraordinary conversation between St. Barth veteran Jimmy
Buffet and contemporary New York based artist Justin
Lieberman.

loomed large there at the Smithsonian—so lar~ ~~~ ~~ only saw
its tail. She would like very much to be ~ ~~ to se~ ~~ of that
se~

to the Hop~ ~~~~~ ~~~h~
Fla~ ~~ ~~ ~~ before she star~~d enter~~ ~~ ~he
tio~ ~~ ~~ regularly enters work in both ~
19~ ~ ~p basket with the intention of ~
it i~ ~ ~ ~ Santa Fe. It was her first ent~
cov~ ~ ~ ~mptly won Best of Show and ~
ver~ ~ ~ ~g of the first day to a Ford e~
Ni~ ~ ~ ~ ~t repeated her achievement by ~
ora~ ~ ~ ~ for another large basket, clai~
Best of Division award and a First Prize in basketry. Over the

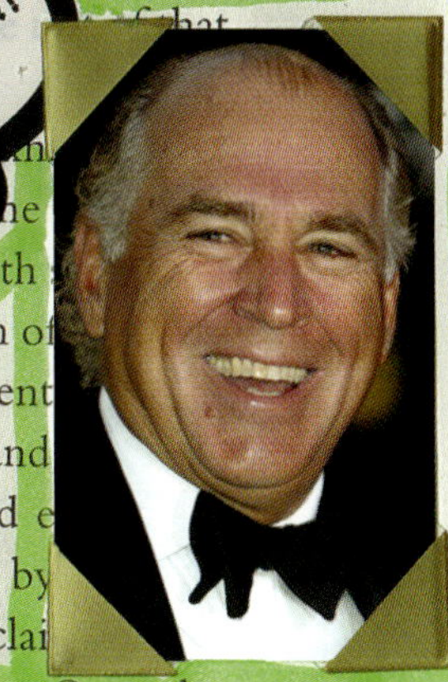

Jimmy Buffet: A Pizza Hut seems particularly out of
place in St. Barths. What did you have in mind?

merous Third Prizes and Honorable Mention ribbons. She usu-

Justin Lieberman: It first occurred to me when I saw a
picture of the gallery which is topped with a red peaked
roof that I thought was very strange for an art gallery. It
immediately reminded me of a Pizza Hut. It was only later
that I realized most of the buildings on the island have
these roofs. So it became a kind of transformation of the
island's architectural landscape. By naming one you kind of
name them all.

meant for the non-Hopi market, and Evangeline also ~~~
usually large plaques for this market. When I photographed her,

Buffet: Did you have problems with local zoning
boards?

enter it in the 199~ ~~~~ ~~ ~~~~~~~~~ ~~~~~~~~~ Th~
she made this particular design, which she created, was in 1969

Lieberman: Not yet. When you don't ask permission, nobody
can say "no". Of course there are strict regulations
concerning chain stores and their signs on the island.
Cartier and Louis Vuitton are allowed, K-Mart and
McDonald's are not. So there is a democratic component as
well. Why should the rich be the only ones to benefit from
the corporate commercialization of the island?

craft Cooperative Guild (commonly known as the Hopi Guild)
for ten years. She left when Fred Kabotie, its founder, retired

Buffet: Obviously the luxury brands want a piece of
the action but for K-Mart, McDonalds or comparables
it really is an issue of the economy of scale. There
simply are not enough people on the island, enough
children and schools for McDonald's to meet their
expectations, same I guess with K-Mart but you have
the equivalent, local supermarket (one is under the
facing the harbor & vis a vis the wine store) and you
have JoJo for burgers. I mean there are a lot of
regular folks with kids that live on the island and
shop at the local supermarkets.

Lieberman: Hmmmm. You may be right. Really I was just trying to set up a situation where I would be able to say: "Why should the rich be the only ones to benefit from the corporate commercialization of the island?" It kind of refers back to the anti-corporate sentiments of "culture jamming" (a term and practice I can't stand, except for Cattelan, Marc Bijl, and a few others who have done projects here and there that could be likened to it). Like when someone takes a corporate logo and turns it into something that criticizes the corporation (the magazine Adbusters is full of this kind of stuff). Most of it is hopelessly idealistic and righteous, as well as didactic in an extremely formulaic way. With the Pizza Hut sign I was trying to create a situation where the meaning of the intervention was less determined, more absurd, and yet still reflected back onto the economic and aesthetic situation of the site. I suppose it could also be read in a more apocalypic way, as though corporate globalization has penetrated even here.

Buffet: The poor benefit from the tone of work opportunities on the island. There is plenty of work. The island has an economy with no unemployment. Corporate globalization is dependent on the island on the economy of scale. Based on the high end traffic its easier to sell 100 gold watches by Cartier then a hundred Big Macs.

Lieberman: Well you have cut right to the heart of it. I feel that while Karl Marx was astute and often brilliant in his critique of capitalism, his solutions neglected to take into account that people work in order to satisfy libidinal drives rather than for a communal good. So I hope that the sign will reflect this uncertainty as to solutions and maintain a certain ambiguity of purpose rather than just seeming like a big Fuck You to everybody.

Buffet: And the hand-painted "ART SHOW" signs placed around the island?

Lieberman: Those are a kind of reversal of context. The gallery has a very professional, New York kind of feel, white walls and polished cement floors, as opposed to the other galleries on the island which take a much more rural approach. Many of them have similar hand-painted signs. Basically I wanted to turn the gallery into a Pizza Hut and then create the impression of a "local" art exhibition going on inside.

Buffet: St. Barths is great, huh?

Lieberman: You know it Jimmy, It's good to be us.

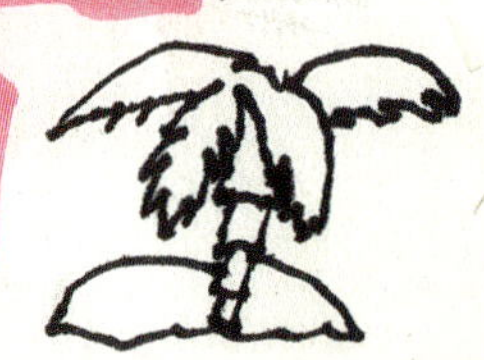

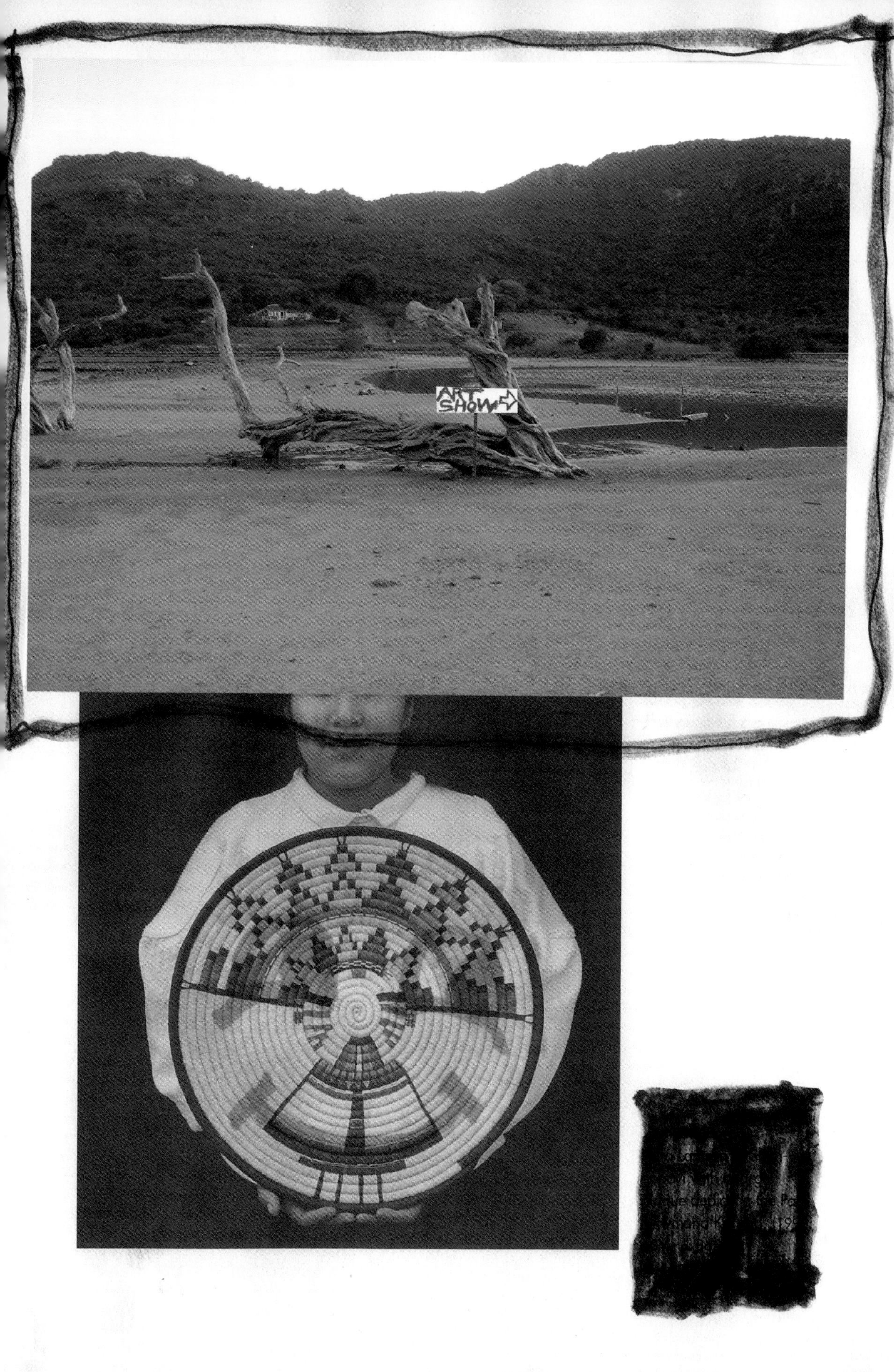

ART
SHOW

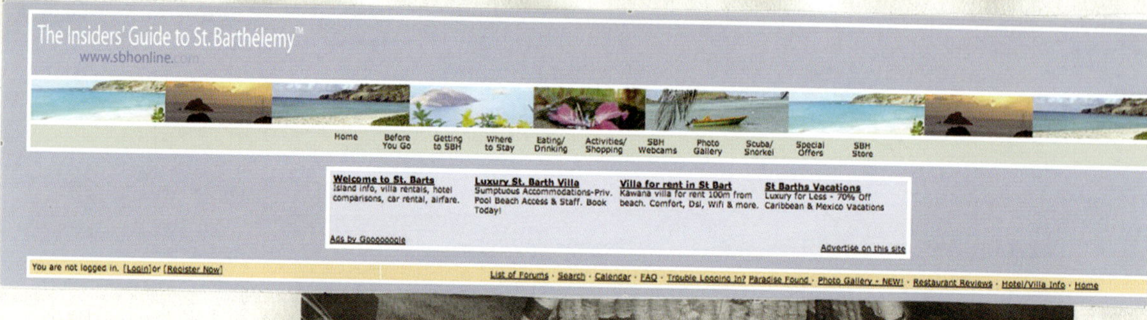

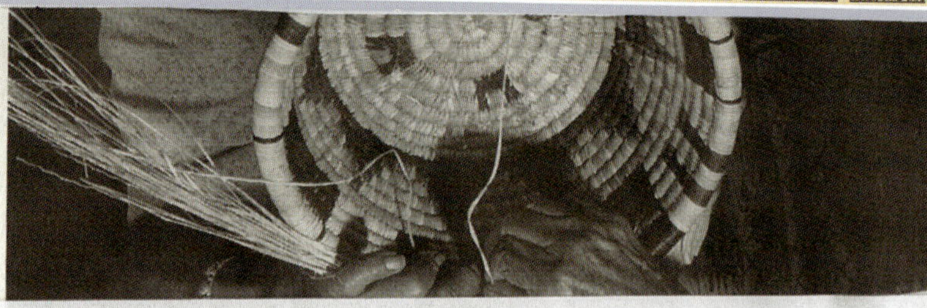

http://www.sbhonline.com/ubbthreads/printthread.php?Cat=0&Board=sam&main=70112&type=thread   08/15/2006 01:27 PM

greg0425 () 07/05/06 06:53 AM	**pizza hut????** I've just returned from a week on the island. For background I've been a visitor for nearly 15 years and a villa owner for the past two. My wife and I typically visit 4-5 times per year. Having witnessed a much of the change that has occurred over the past decade, I generally have supported the "evolution" of the island into a more complete and full service vacation destination. However, having said all that I did see something yesterday that really surprised me. There is a giant Pizza Hut sign going up on a new structure that is on the left side of the upper road that takes you out of Gustavia toward the light house. Its right before the back side of the ASB grocery. I'm all for competition and while I don't think that the presence of such an outlet is the downfall of the island experiene as we know it, it seems like a strange busness decision. Needless to say there is no shortage of great Pizza and other take away food. There are also a number of retail spaces turning over this year and if any thing there may now be too much retail of the same type in Gustavia. Interesting decisions.
julia () 07/05/06 11:17 AM	**Re: pizza hut????** Say it isn't so!--maybe it was a mirage. While I'm all for entrepreneurship, it's hard to think of a Pizza Hut on St. Barth. Perhaps JimD or someone else from the island can enlighten us.
wickhamlane () 07/05/06 11:23 AM	**Re: pizza hut????** Coals to New Castle!I don't get it.Pizza Hut pizza is pretty abysmal compared to any pizza in SB.Even here in Pittsburgh we can find excellent artisanal pizza which some consider (dare I say it) even better than Andy's or L'Entracte.We've been visiting for over 15 years as well and "fuuny little SB" has undergone some unwelcome changes but this is really a surprise.
Island Visitor () 07/05/06 11:23 AM	**Re: pizza hut????** Two things: 1. Kara - FOR GOD'S SAKE MOVE THIS THREAD BEFORE MIKER SEES IT ;) 2. That is almost certainly meant for the locals and not for us. As a chain, Pizza Hut can probably do some things more cheaply than a local restaurant. And, as much as we like to enjoy French culture when in France, French people actually enjoy Playing The Cowboy once in a while and dabbling in our culture. Of course, this place could also do a bustling Cruise Ship Business on days that ships are in port. Given the abysmal record of survival of the Pizza Huts where I live, here's an idea: If WE dont go to it, and the French people dont go to it...
NYCFred () 07/05/06 11:34 AM	**Re: pizza hut????** Hmmm can the 'Golden Arches' be far behind?
Cheri () 07/05/06 11:40 AM	**Re: pizza hut????** I second "say it isn't so", Julie!!! But there are pizza huts in France. http://www.pizzahut.fr/ Even so, this is very unfortunate news. ;-(Like it has already been mentioned, Pizza Hut cannot begin to compare to Andy's, Le Entracte, La Saladarie, etc. However, even though none of us like it, it's their island and, different strokes, and all that....

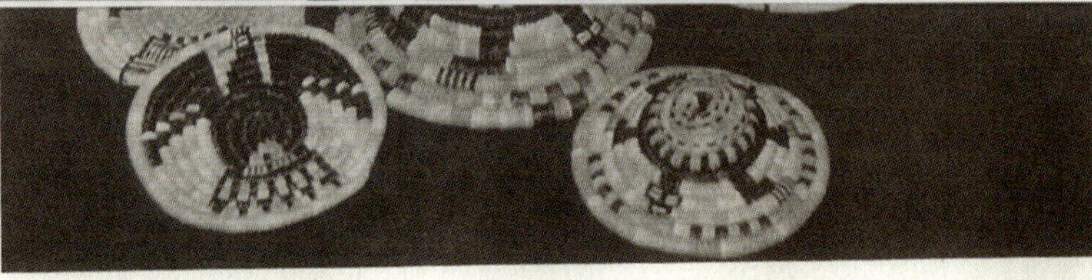

Martha Leban of Shungopovi. (1992; ASM no. 86506)

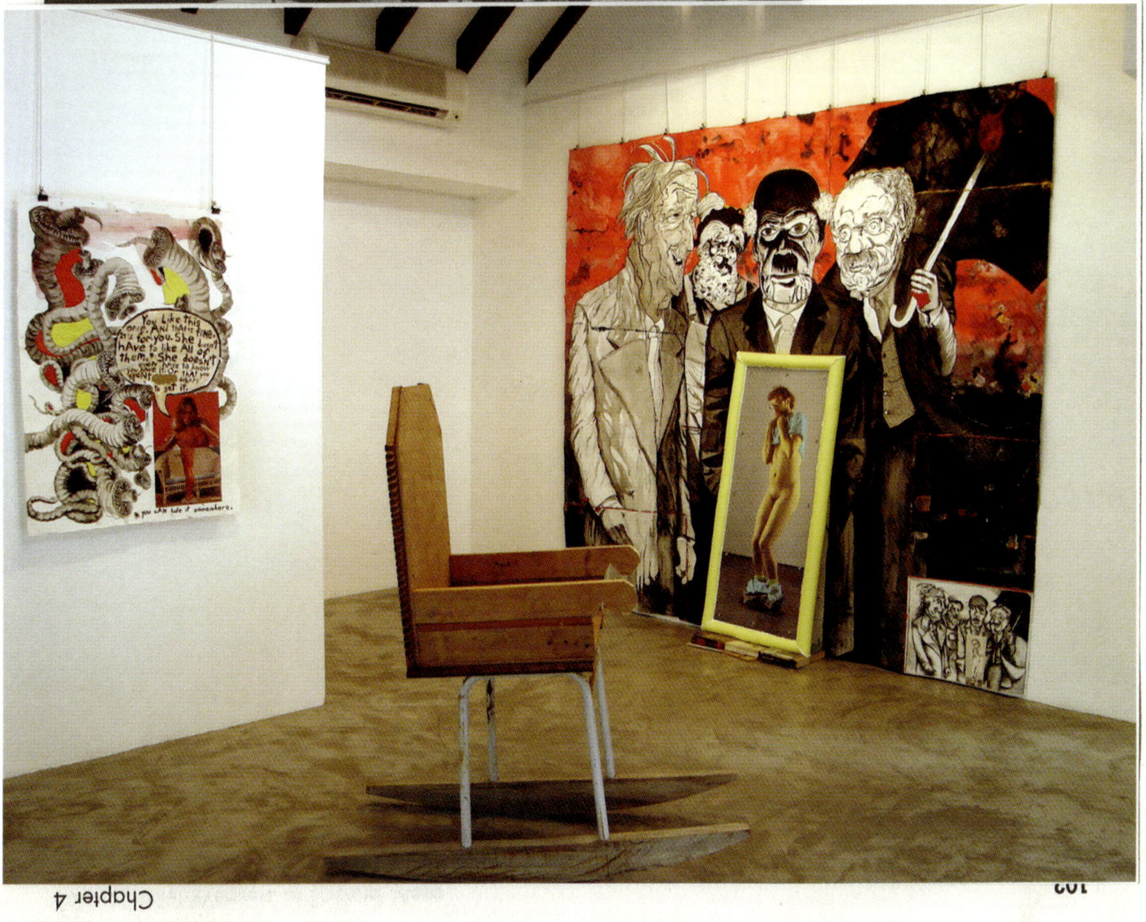

her warm in winter. In 1991 Martha made a medium-sized deep coiled basket with four Katsina heads. It was so well made and so beautiful that she won the Governor's Award for it. The governor invited her to the award dinner in Phoenix, which made her happy and proud.

IN THE GALLERY

REMEDIOS was born into the Bearstrap/Spider Clan on June 3, 1938, in Shungopovi. She learned her art from her mother and grandmother. She does not make baskets ... etry ... that ... very large baskets very often—only one about every ten years—but

AND ARTWORKS ARE INSTALLED

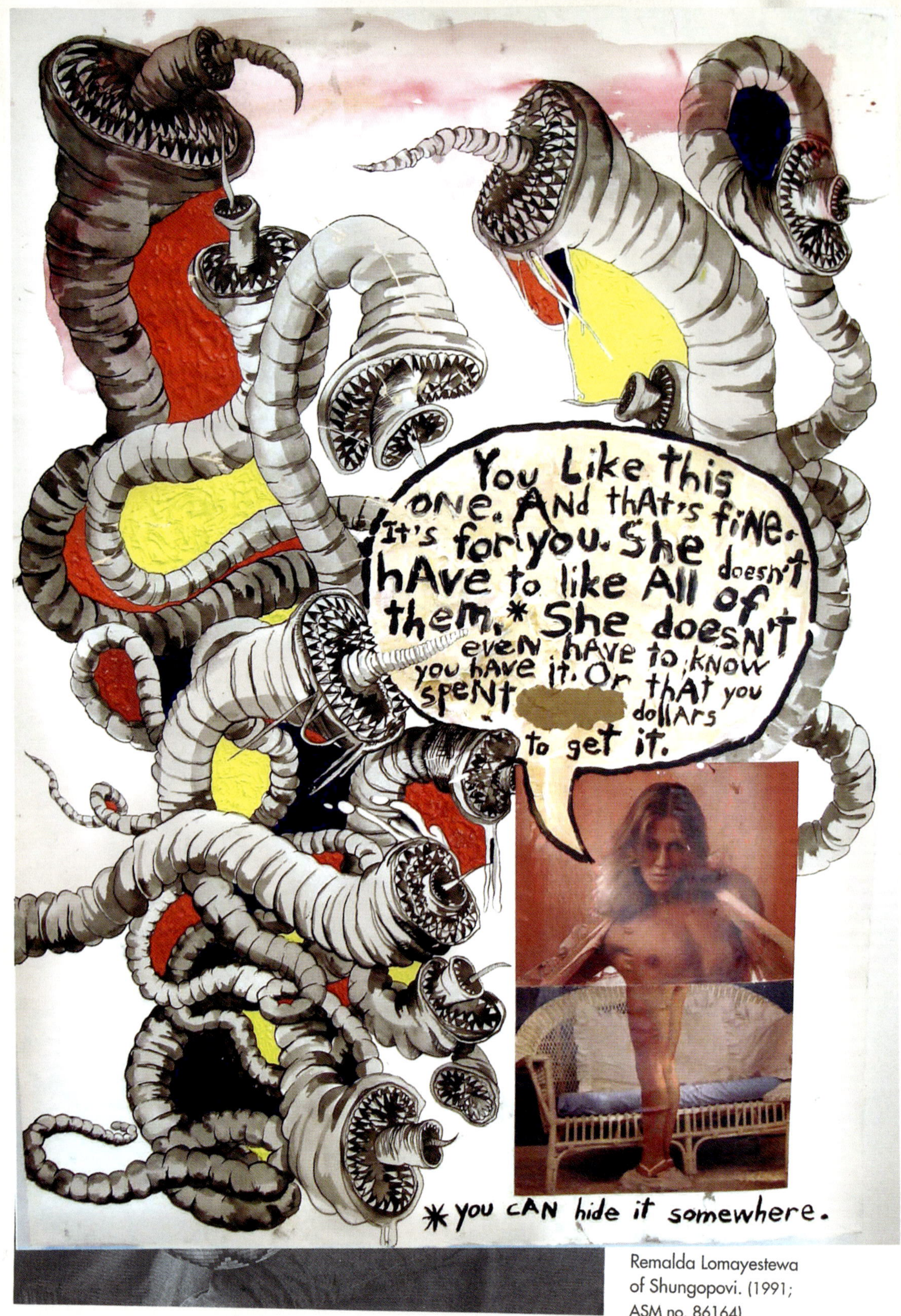

Remalda Lomayestewa of Shungopovi. (1991; ASM no. 86164)

Call of Cthulu
2006

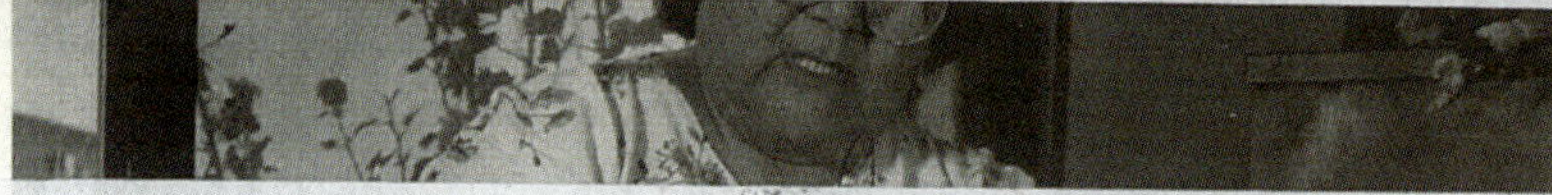

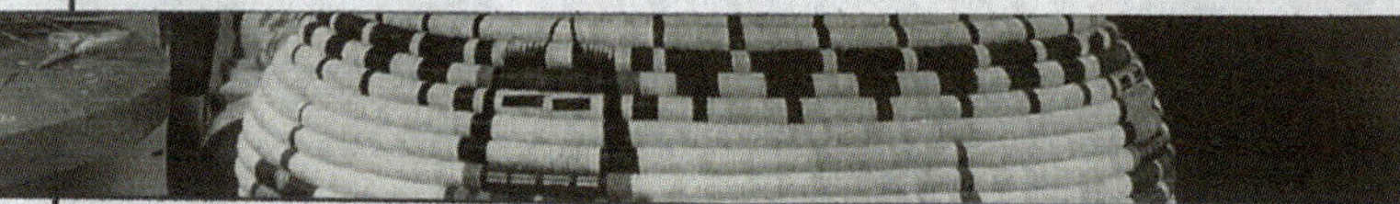

ing on a large basket with
four full-figure Longhair

baskets. She also weaves beautiful plaques and plaited sifter baskets out of yucca. She often makes more plaques than large

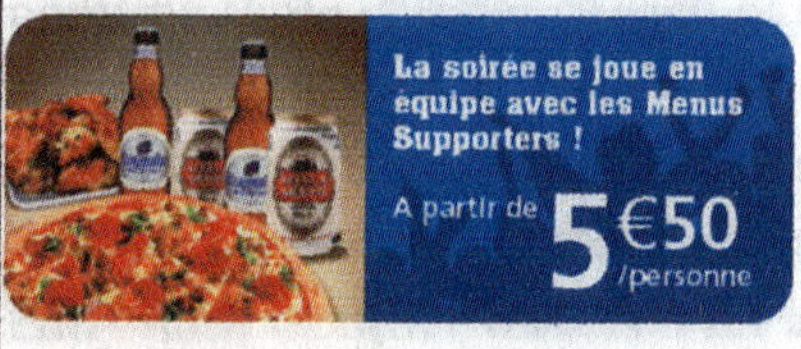

at the O'odham Tash in Casa Grande, Arizona, in 1989, and a
First Prize in Denver in December 1990. She has won other
prizes at the Intertribal Indian Ceremonial in Gallup and the In-

LOL..oh Bill I'm still gonna hang around here and make you crazy and illicit your very predictable responses...come on!!!...what would life be without that?? ?....you can sleep well mon ami....you aint gettin rid of me that easy..Im havin too much fun with ya

the same corporation which owns Pizza Hut..also owns Taco Bell, Baskins Robbins and KFC...woo hoooo!!!!...think of the possibilities here

Joyce Ann Saufkie, still goes on her own collecting trips to find the yucca and galleta grass she needs for weaving and also the

Island Visitor () 07/06/06 07:38 AM	📖 Re: Un Jour En Ville
	You pays your money, you takes your chances. If some of the import workers feel a bit pinched in the pocket but still want to go out for pizza with Da Boys, or if a local french family watching Dallas reruns decided to Play Cowboy and go to an "american" restaurant, what does it yearn me? Of course, if this new resto becomes a cultural sink into which the cruise ships can disgorge their Bluehairs thereby taking the stress off Our Local Favs, where have I lost in that deal? I have several choices here: 1. Do go to the PH. Hmmmm, maybe not. 2. Don't go to the PH but do go to St Barth. Ja sure, you betcha 3. Don't go to St Barth.

JERRI LOMAKEMA

Jerri Lomakema belongs to the Bear Clan. She was born in Shungopovi on December 15, 1960. When growing up, she watched

My understanding is that no PHs are currently planned for Bequia, Necker Island or Redonda. Then again, there are no boulagneries on Redonda either.

Island Visitor () 07/06/06 07:52 AM	📖 Re: Un Jour En Ville
	One other thought. We read about the "bored youth" with nothing to do. Perhaps this kind of hangout, a place where their parents would not DREAM of going, might be kind of cool. Goodness knows we hung around the PH in my little town Back In The Day. The Youth have to rebel a little. It is in the job description. If this serves as The Naughty Place for vigorous youth to go and be away from Prying Eyes, L'Etat will probably survive. My gut feeling if the place lasts two years (I give it 50 - 50) is that the patrons will be migrant workers, cruiseshippers, St Martin Daytrippers and teenagers. Of course, if any of you guys choose to go, you are free to do so.

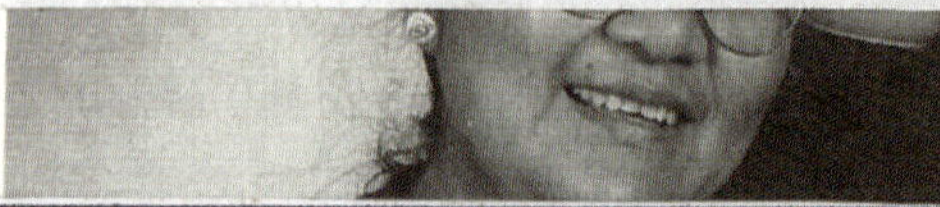

Mike R () 07/06/06 08:21 AM	📖 Re: Un Jour En Ville
	IV...I still say you HAVE to be a brother or cousin to the guy who in Iraq was screaming that "we are beating back the American soldiers" while at the same time we were taking down the statue of Saddam and securing Baghdag...LOL whatever happens... happens .....you must admit that, at the very least, a once thought unthinkable concept has been breached.....its awfully hard to put the genie back into the bottle.....it will be interesting to see what happens next... two New England resort towns swore they would never let fast food into their towns...those towns were Freeport Maine (home of the flagship LL bean store) and right here in P Town....both towns got challenged in court and lost...Freeport now has a Mickey D's (the compromise was no golden arches, they had to fit into a building which was in code with the "historical codes" for buildings....and P Town now has a Subway which ironically is right next to an institution here for fast food, which has been here forever and is very good and wildly successful (MOJO's), and is just kicking SubWays ass..also the locals here mostly refuse to patronize the Subway and I hear, that other then July and August, its struggling quite a bit, and regreting coming here....and the wheel keeps going round and round

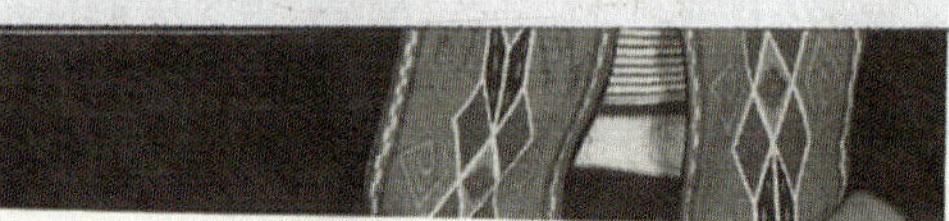

Jerri Lomakema of
Shungopovi. (1994)

andynap () 07/06/06 08:26 AM	📖 Re: Un Jour En Ville
	If this place is on the upper road I doubt that daytrippers and cruisers will be going there. It's the SIGN that is objectionable not the place.

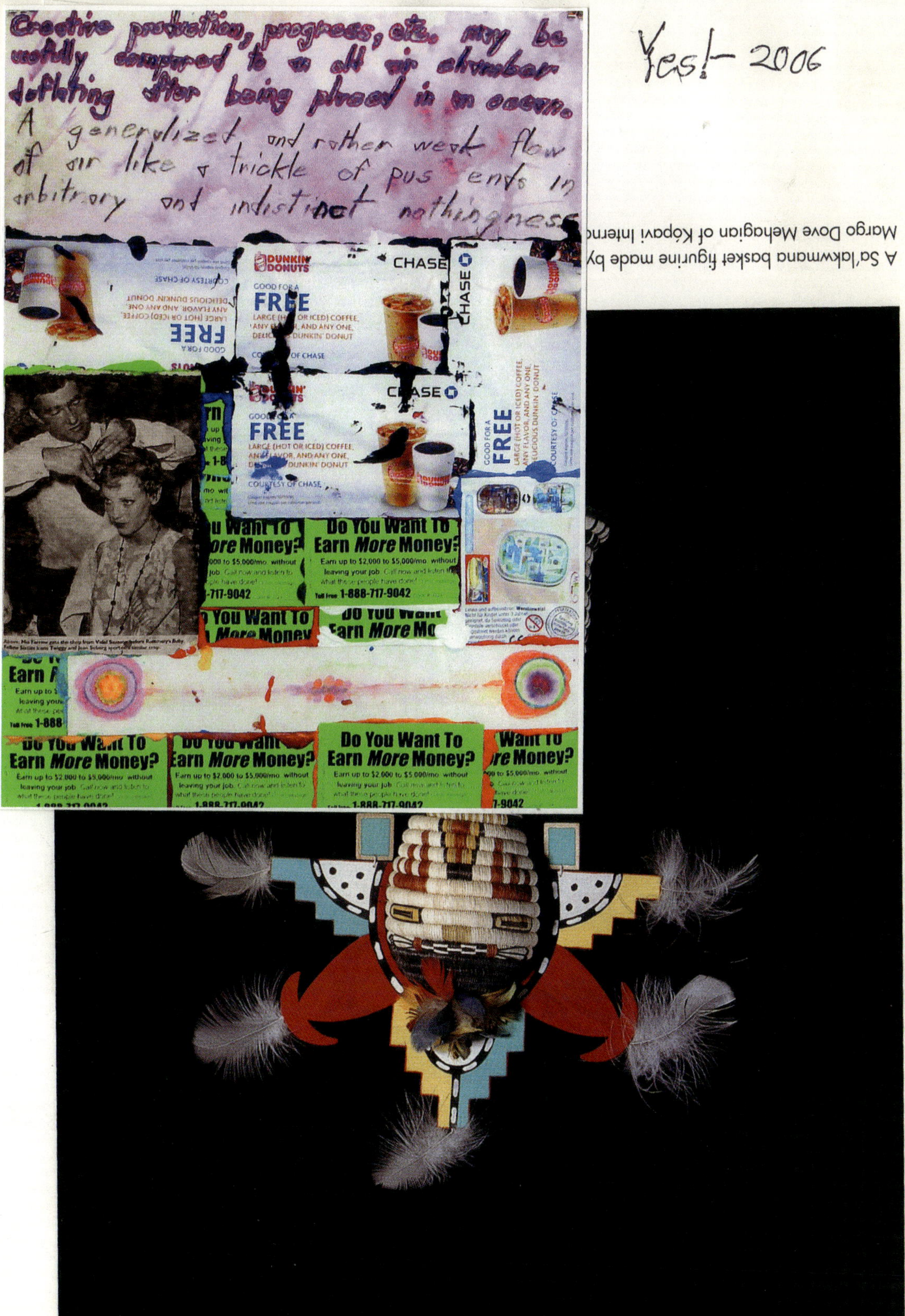

Creative protestation, progress, etc. may be usefully compared to an old air chamber deflating after being placed in an ocean.
A generalized and rather weak flow of air like a trickle of pus ends in arbitrary and indistinct nothingness
Yes!- 2006
A Sa'lakwmana basket figurine made by Margo Dove Mehagian of Kopavi Intern

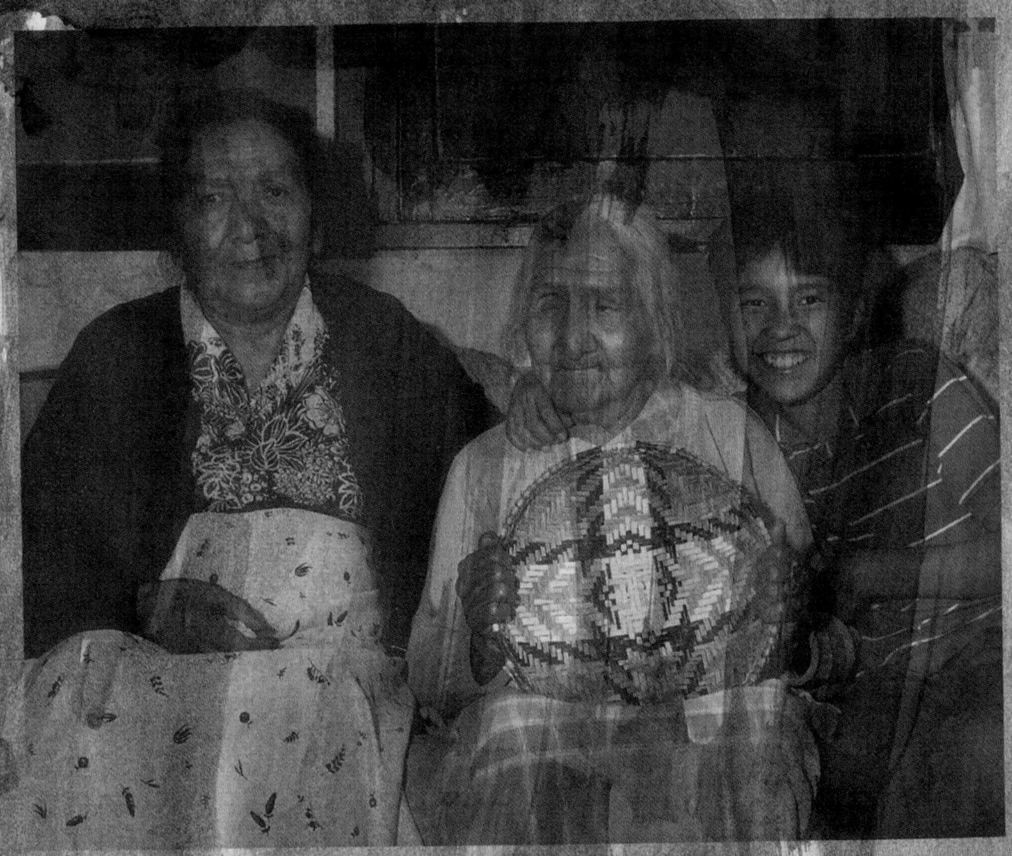

Josie Tyma of Shungopovi with her daughter Gladys Kagenweama and her ten-year-old great-grandson Benny Naseyowma. (1992; ASM no. 87103)

life she traveled to Chicago to demonstrate her art and to bring Hopi coiled basket weaving to that large city.

RETTA LOU ADAMS

Retta Lou Adams belongs to the Bearstrap/Spider Clan. She was born on June 6, 1940, in Shungopovi. When she was fifteen years old, her mother, Gladys Kas

Painting is an excellent hobby if you are the kind of person who likes to spend a lot of time by yourself. Which is everyone, really. Each of us lives alone, is born alone, and dies alone. Even when you fuck, you're alone. Alone with your flesh, alone with your life, which is a tunnel impossible to share. And the older you get, the lonelier you are, replaying memories of a self-destructing life. A life is like a tunnel, and to each his own little tunnel. At the end of the tunnel there is not even light. Even memory goes before the end. A little life, a little savings, a little retirement, and then a little grave.

THANK HEAVEN FOR LITTLE GIRLS

Thank Heaven For Little Girls is a print of a collage made on Photoshop
of elements appropriated from three sources: Jock Sturges's
photography, headshot photography from pre-teen beauty pageants, and
watercolors by Henry Darger. It is first and foremost a piece about the
intersection of these elements. Pre-teen beauty pageants are a cultural
phenomenon that thrives on visuals dismissed by elite culture as kitch.
Heavy make-up, frilly dresses, bright colors, and artifice pervade the

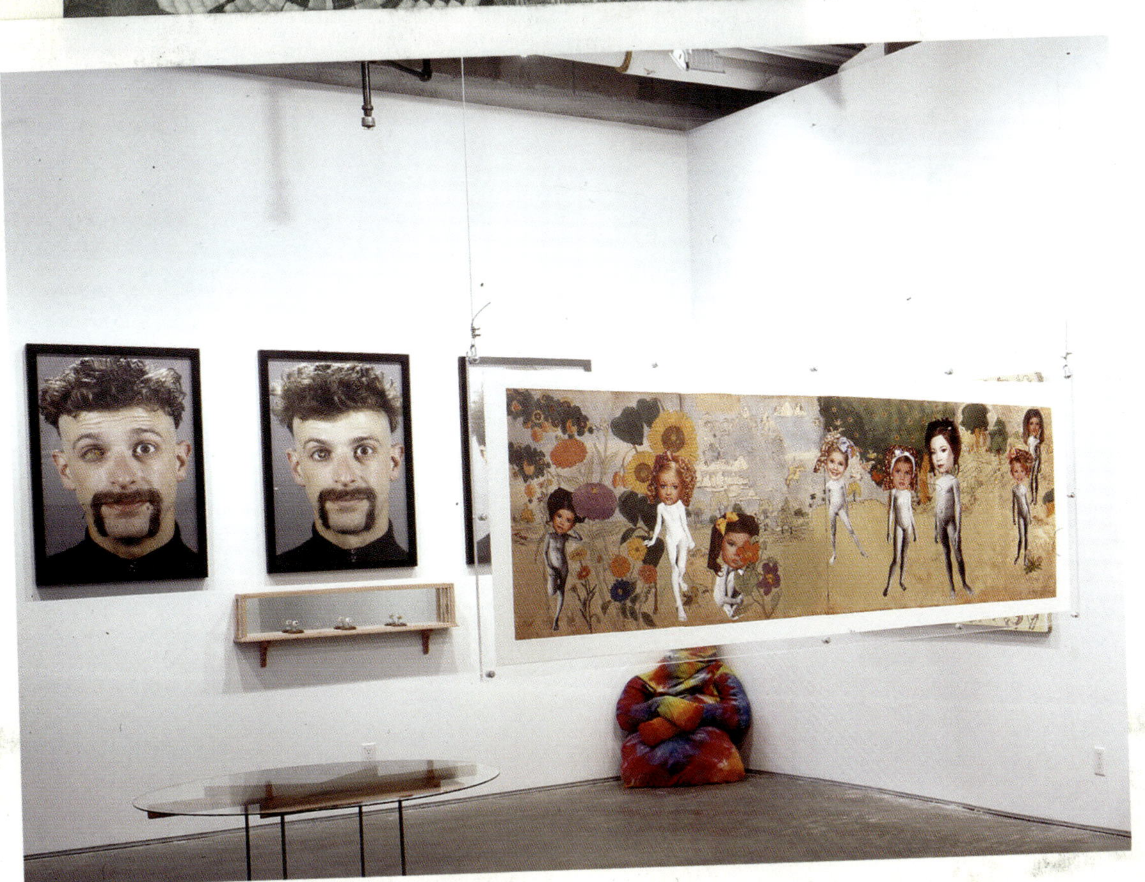

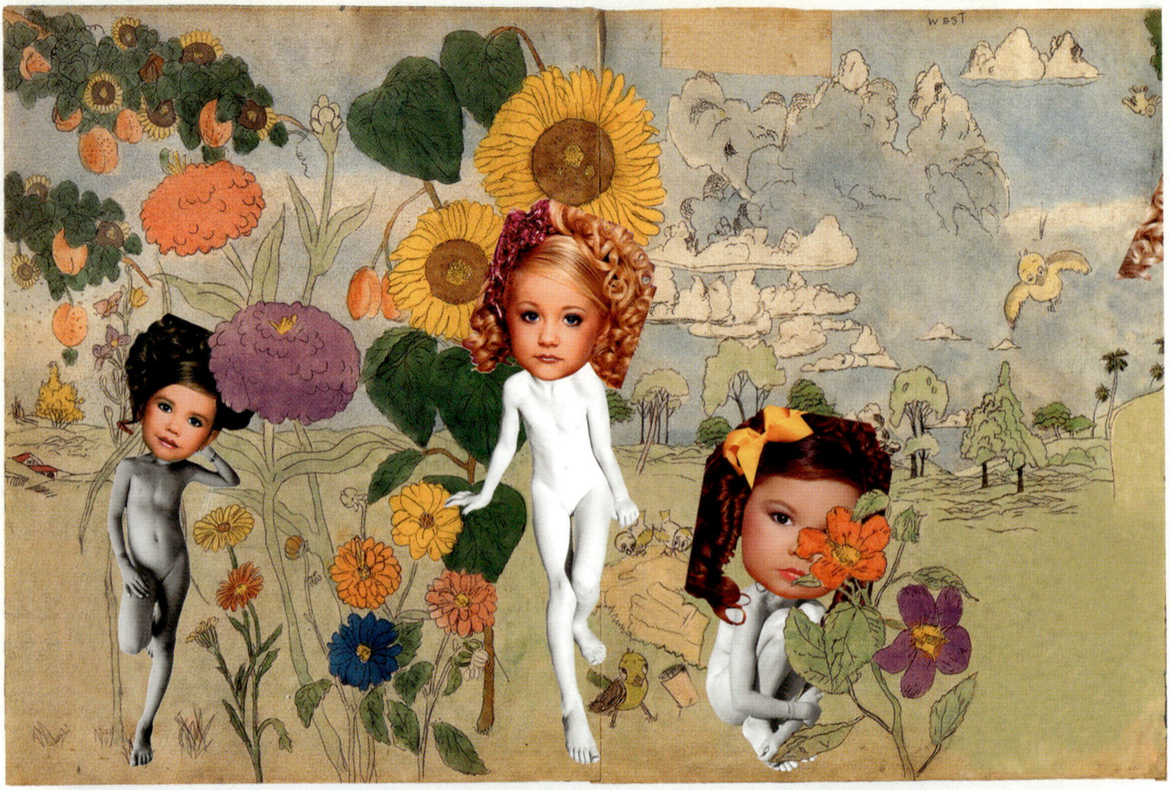

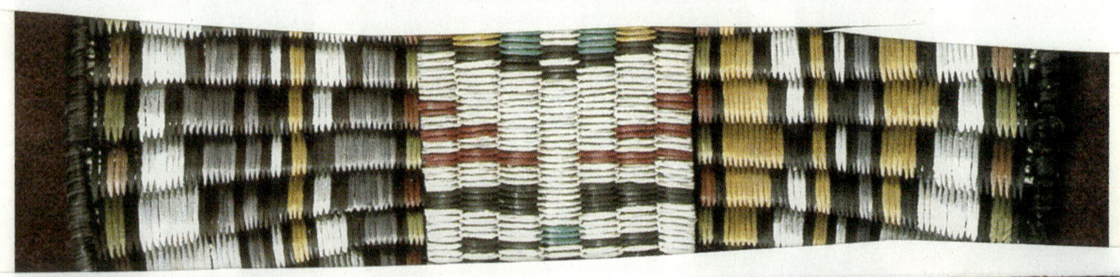

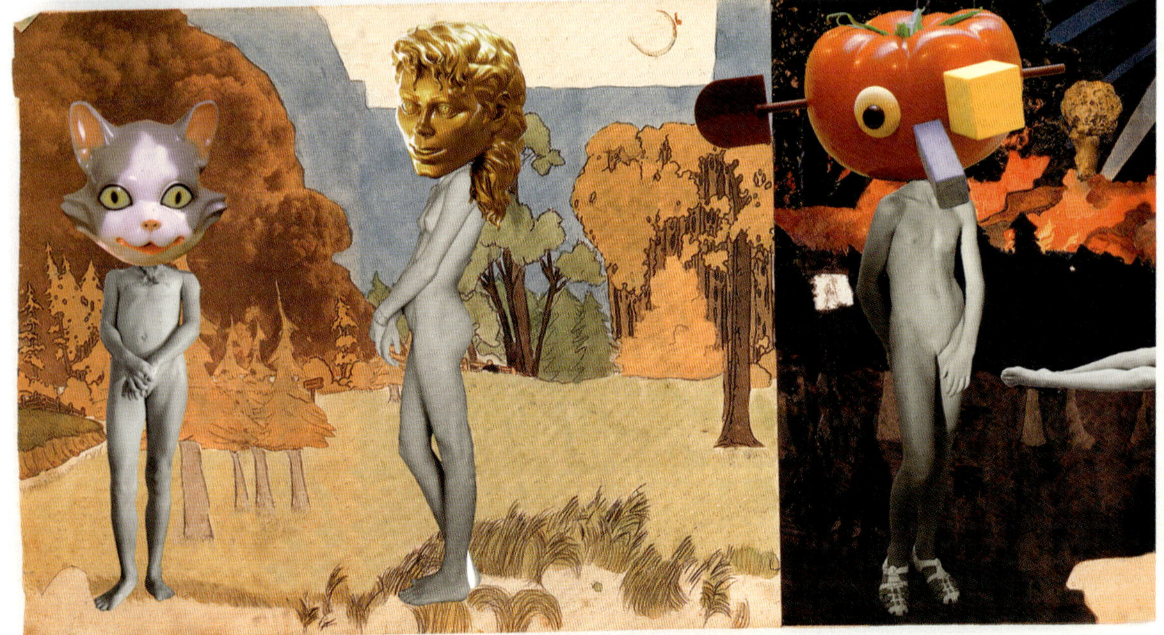

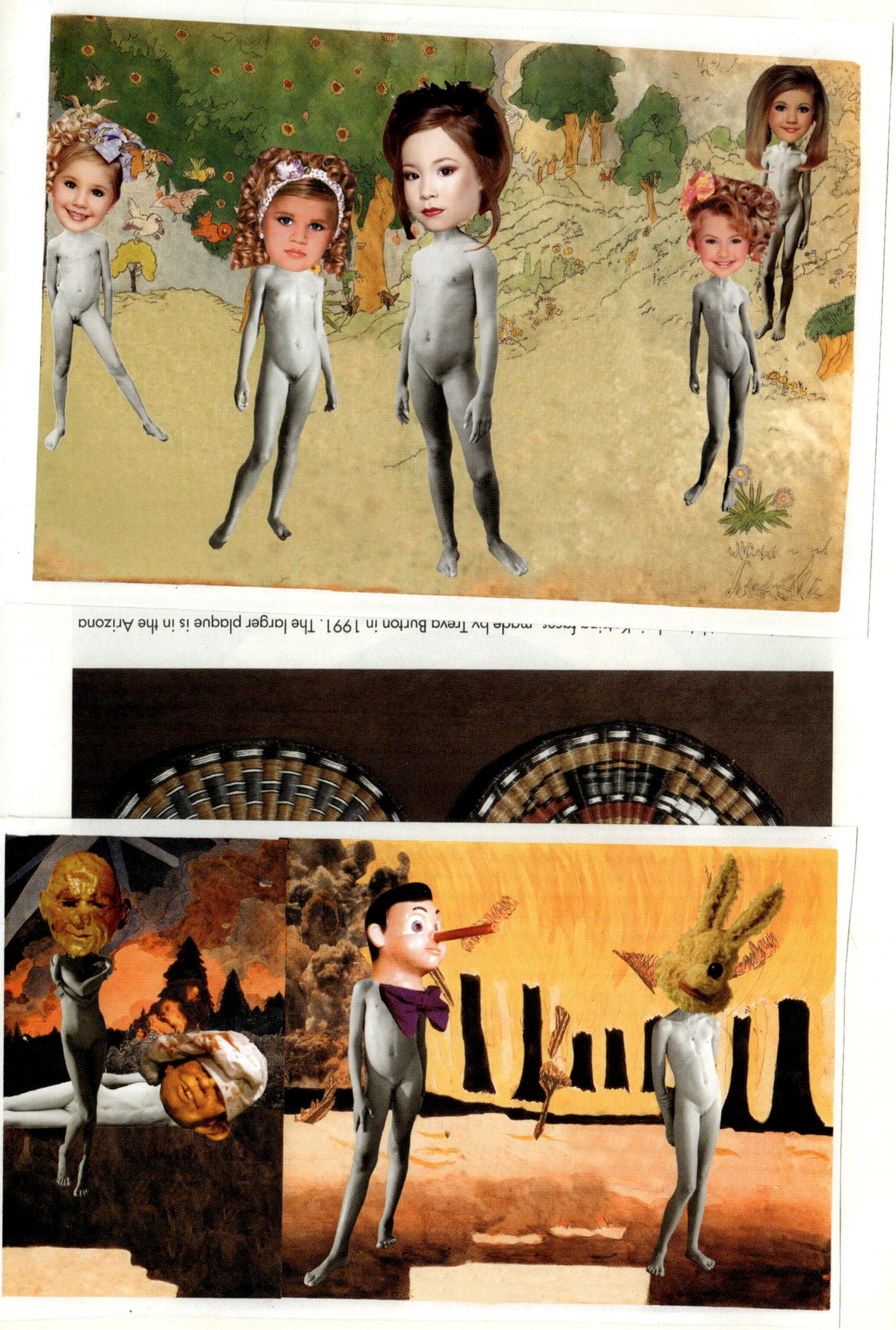

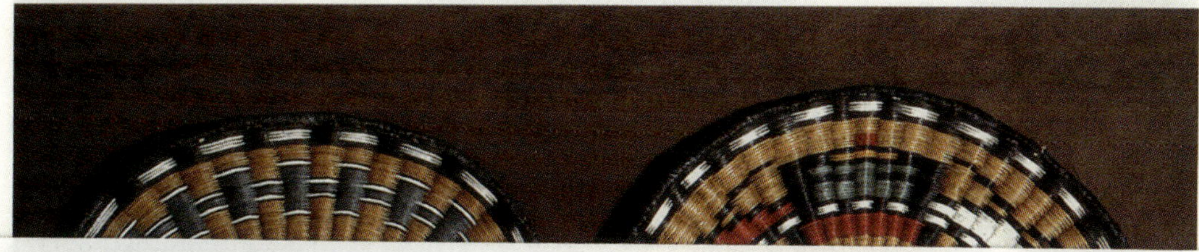

White faces made by Treva Burton in 1991. The larger plaque is in the Arizona

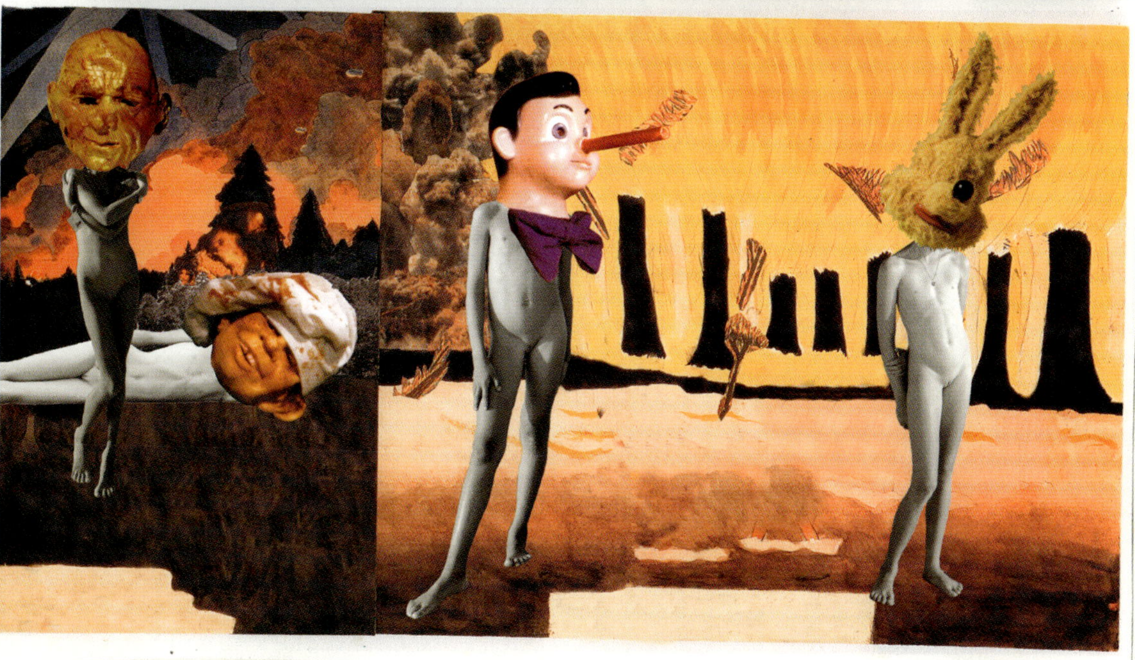

images. Sturges's long row of their pictures are her sofa. It was the exact
opposite. They are often taken and one of her daughters in natural settings and
his use of B&W photography trays for this daughter's wedding serves to highlight
the formal aspects of one daughter who has to make her the medium children In a
perfect inversion of the very proud of their situation surrounding the pagean
photos, they can make are frequently basketry item. Her labeled by the
mass media as artsy kiddy porn. , but in addition she can make plaited sifter baskets, The
Frankensteinian figures that , small square trays, and result from their combination
function the way they do precisely the materials herself, usually because of this
formal conflict. It struck me she finds the yucca leaves upon completion of the
figures that there sifters. She was a possibility because she uses every leaf that
they might be read as Along the road pathological; created out of desire. I
recognition of this interpretation I employed willow twigs for the wicker weave of the
background from a Henry Darger painting trays. Instead she uses the commercial reed from
which I removed his own painted craft store, which gives her figures in Photoshop.
The use of an artist's sifter baskets in small and work that was interpreted
almost exclusively in terms of dyed yucca leaves. Furthermore, the pathological
re-directs interpretation towards the more ceremonial kilts. She truly is a general
question: Do we attempt to figure out the psychology appreciated by collectors of the
artist, or do we ascribe tourists. the meaning to his stated intentions and
focus on the formal qualities often demonstrated of the work?

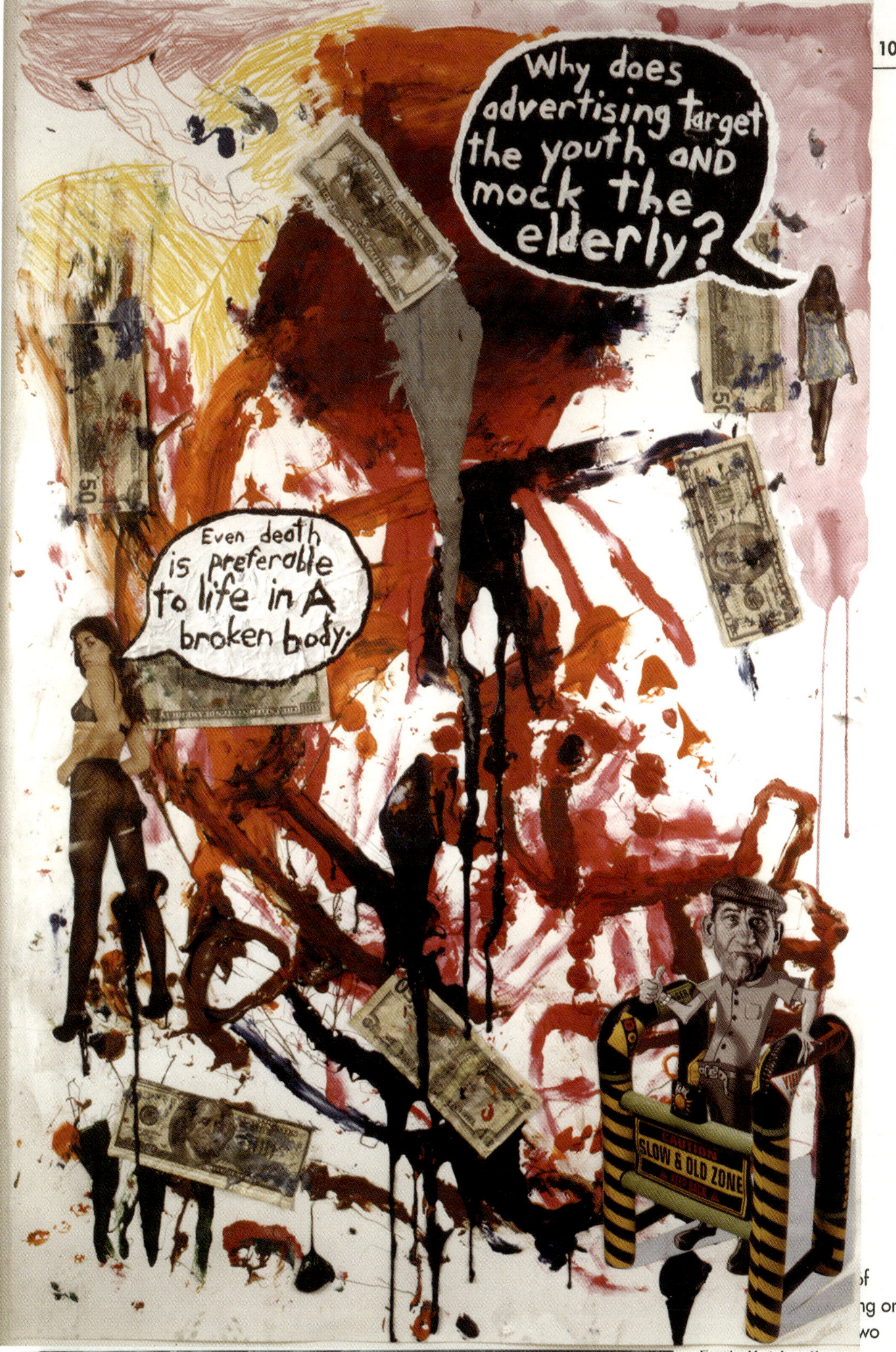

of
ng on
wo
Eagle Katsina figures.
(1994)

Picture for Children
2005

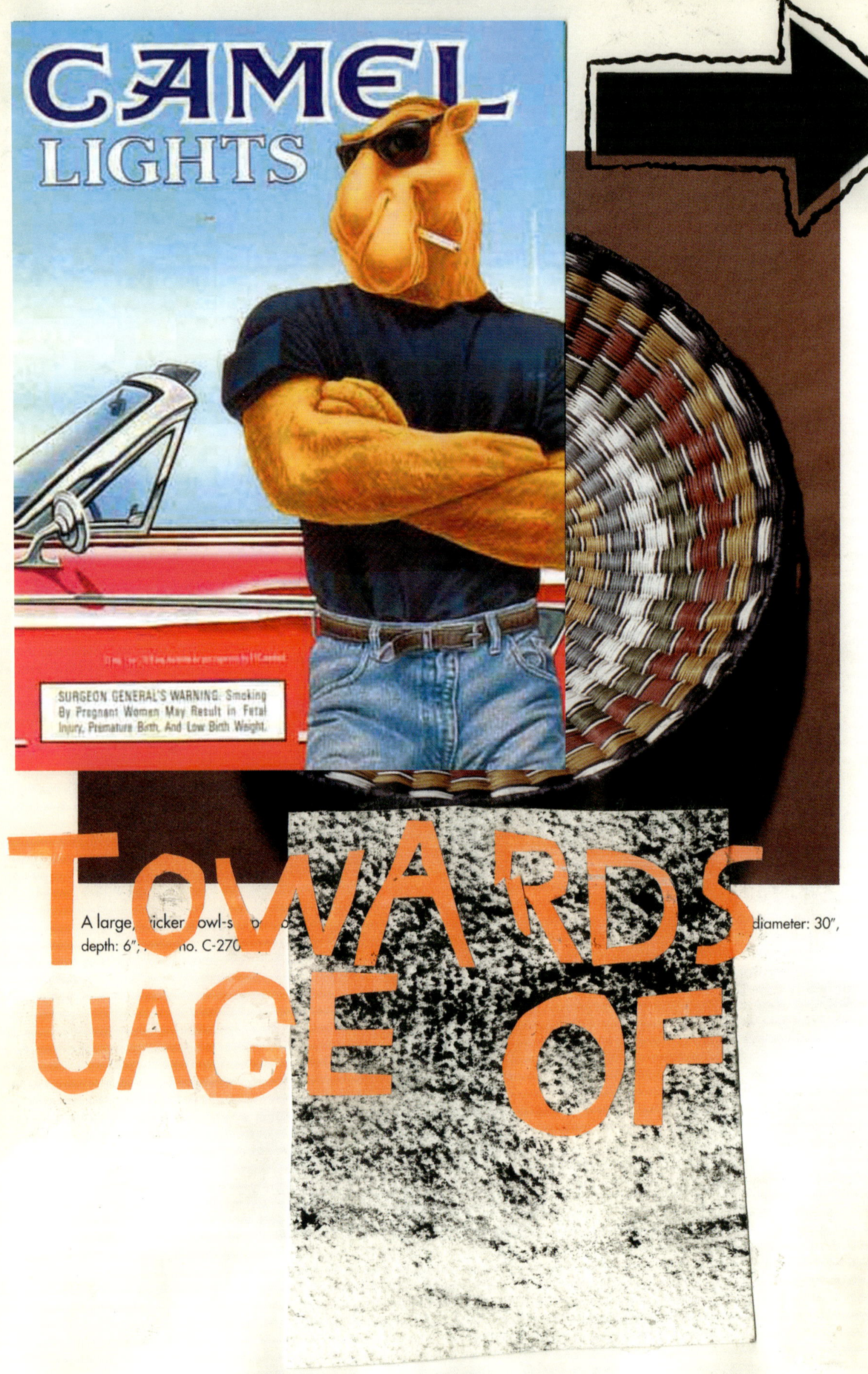
CAMEL
LIGHTS
SURGEON GENERAL'S WARNING: Smoking
By Pregnant Women May Result In Fetal
Injury, Premature Birth, And Low Birth Weight.
A large, wicker bowl-shaped   diameter: 30",
depth: 6",   no. C-270
TOWARDS
UAGE OF

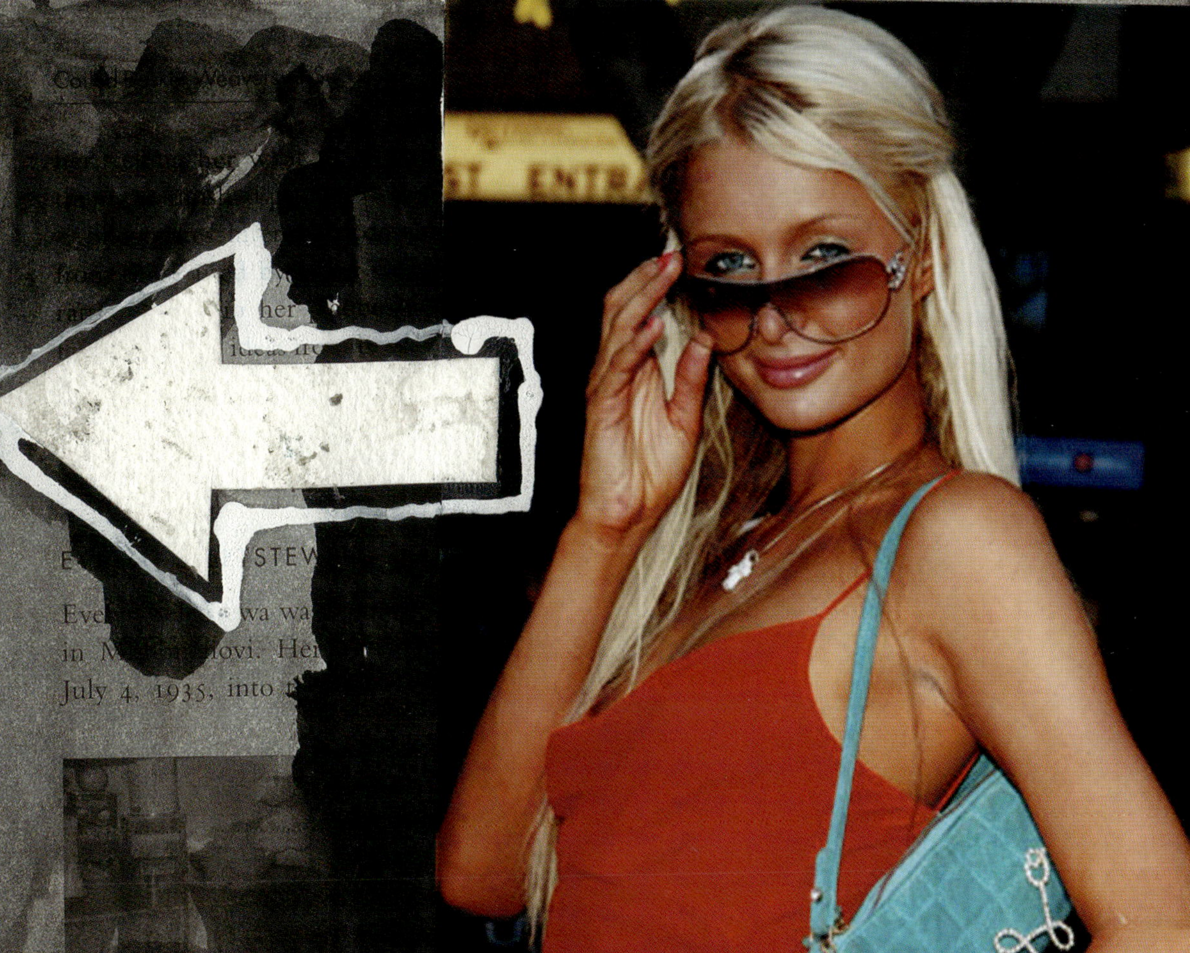

A MetaLang-
Collage

Collage, more than most other mediums, may be said to exist on the front lines of representation. That is to say that since subjects need only be chosen (and not rendered, as in painting), content can be arrived at rather quickly, both in execution and perception. Content in collage as I speak of it is formulated through the selection and juxtaposition of elements (subjects) and may be appreciated as such. This differs from painting because were the content to be arrived at in such a way in painting, the execution of the painting wound surely stand in the way of the clarity of *this type* of communication, since all forms of painting contain within their representations ideologies, historical significance, and personal expression which cannot be ignored and constitute the subject (rightfully) in terms of an understanding of the picture.

A painting is a unified image. A collage is a fragmented one.

   Nor does collage share the semiotic language of appropriation as it was evinced by artists in the 80's with their focus on identity, authorship and distinctions between high and low culture. Sherrie Levine's re-photographing of the work of Walker Evans points directly at the relationship of the author to the work, and Levine's own identity as a female artist. Now, when we view these photographs, having witnessed her act of appropriation, it is the question of authorship that springs immediately to mind. The use of appropriation in the work of Jeff Koons takes on a different character. In Koons's case, there is no question about the author of the images. They are considered authorless, as they belong to the realm of mass culture, and as Mike Kelley has pointed out, their meaning hinges on this distinction. Koons's aesthetic resuscitation of his banal subjects would be impossible if they did not already carry with them an explicit history of their elevated status as aesthetic objects and subsequent descent into kitsch through their mass production and proliferation. Collage as I speak of it functions in almost the opposite way.

A new metalanguage of collage must take into account both
the medium's inherent directness as well as recognizing its
potential to easily overshoot the mark and wind up with
only platitudes. Much of the politically oriented collage
of the 1980's suffered this affliction. Tibor Kahlman and
Winston Smith both allowed the aspects of the political in
their work to be eclipsed by the heavy-handed way in which
they dealt with highly charged subjects. It is not within
the artist's power to change the meaning of a sign.
Startling juxtapositions are just that: juxtapositions.

She says that when she started to put color designs into her
into the Lalkont and O'waqol societies.

Combinations of images that imply something about one
another but are never more than the sum of their parts.
This is the weakness of collage that underlies its apparent
bravado and ultimately forms the building blocks of its
language. If collage itself is the sign, then in order to
understand it's meaning it is this very weakness that must

she was twelve or fourteen at the time of the Oraibi split in that
she and her family still lived in Oraibi before 1906. She thinks
Vera remembers that she went to school in Kykotsmovi when

be utilized. It is not enough to work with material
appropriated from undervalued areas of culture. These
materials must be put to use with the understanding of one
to whom they are directed. For example:

deep wicker
Hotevilla
Vera

* Celine Dion makes a guest appearance on Friends.

   * Jar Jar Binks stars in an edutainment CD-ROM for use in
schools.

* An entire room is plastered with pictures from magazines
of the Backstreet Boys.

This is following the directions prescribed by these signs to the letter.
These are the "little projects" approved of by the culture industry. Like
Pringles, they target an extremely wide demographic, and their design is
based on the idea of being the least
offensive to the largest number of
potential consumers. Their genesis comes
from a place where culture no longer
serves as a medium for self-expression,
but as a medium for design and
consumption. The mixing and convergence of
various cultural conventions causes a kind of premature aging of the subjects of
the work, the conventions being utilized, and the work itself. As though with
an understanding of the internal logic of the work comes a recognition that the
idea being presented has become like Dorian Grey when the picture of him was
slashed, aging a hundred years in a second and crumbling to dust in the space
of an instant.

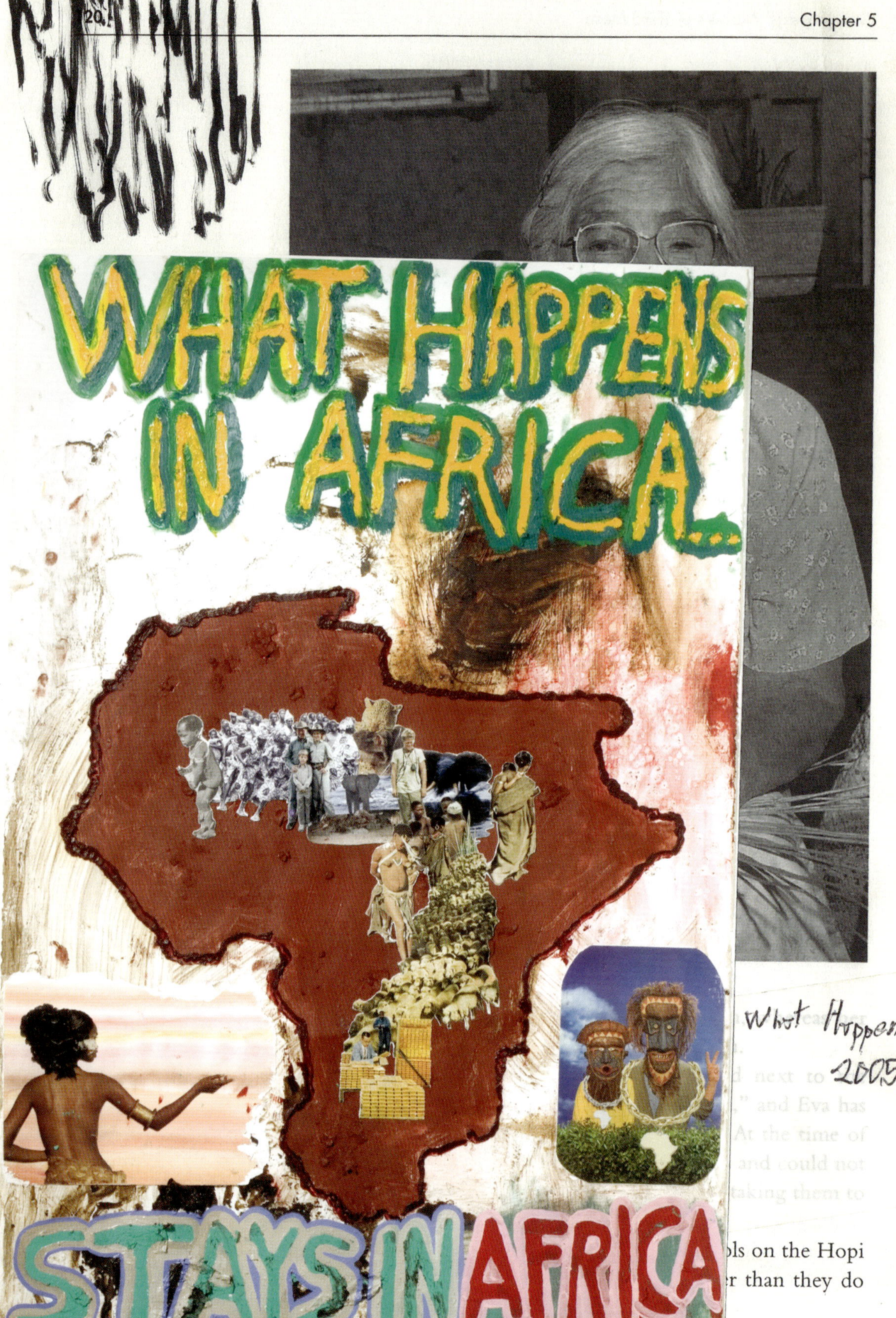

d next to
" and Eva has
At the time of
and could not
taking them to

ols on the Hopi
er than they do

The Bug Chasers is a painting in which I attempt to recuperate the morality of this bizarre sub-cultural activity. Bug chasers are attempting to contract the AIDS virus on purpose. Like suicide, it is an activity that can only be dealt with in the mainstream through pathologizing it's participants. The text in the painting is a mash-up/paraphrase of three separate quotations. Pat Robertson on the AIDS virus, then Dennis Cooper, writing from the standpoint of one of his more apathetic characters, and finally Susan Sontag from her beautiful book, Aids and its Metaphors.

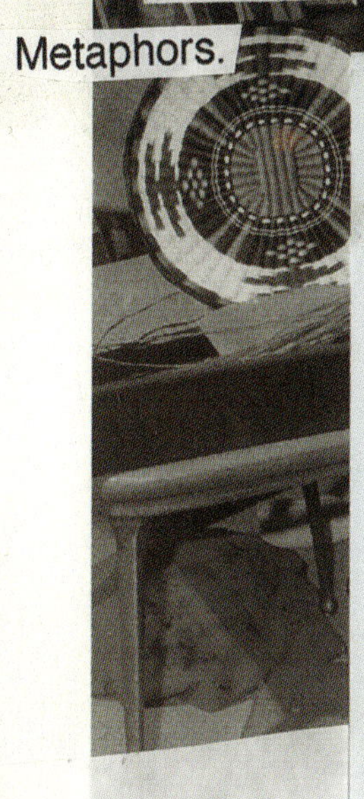

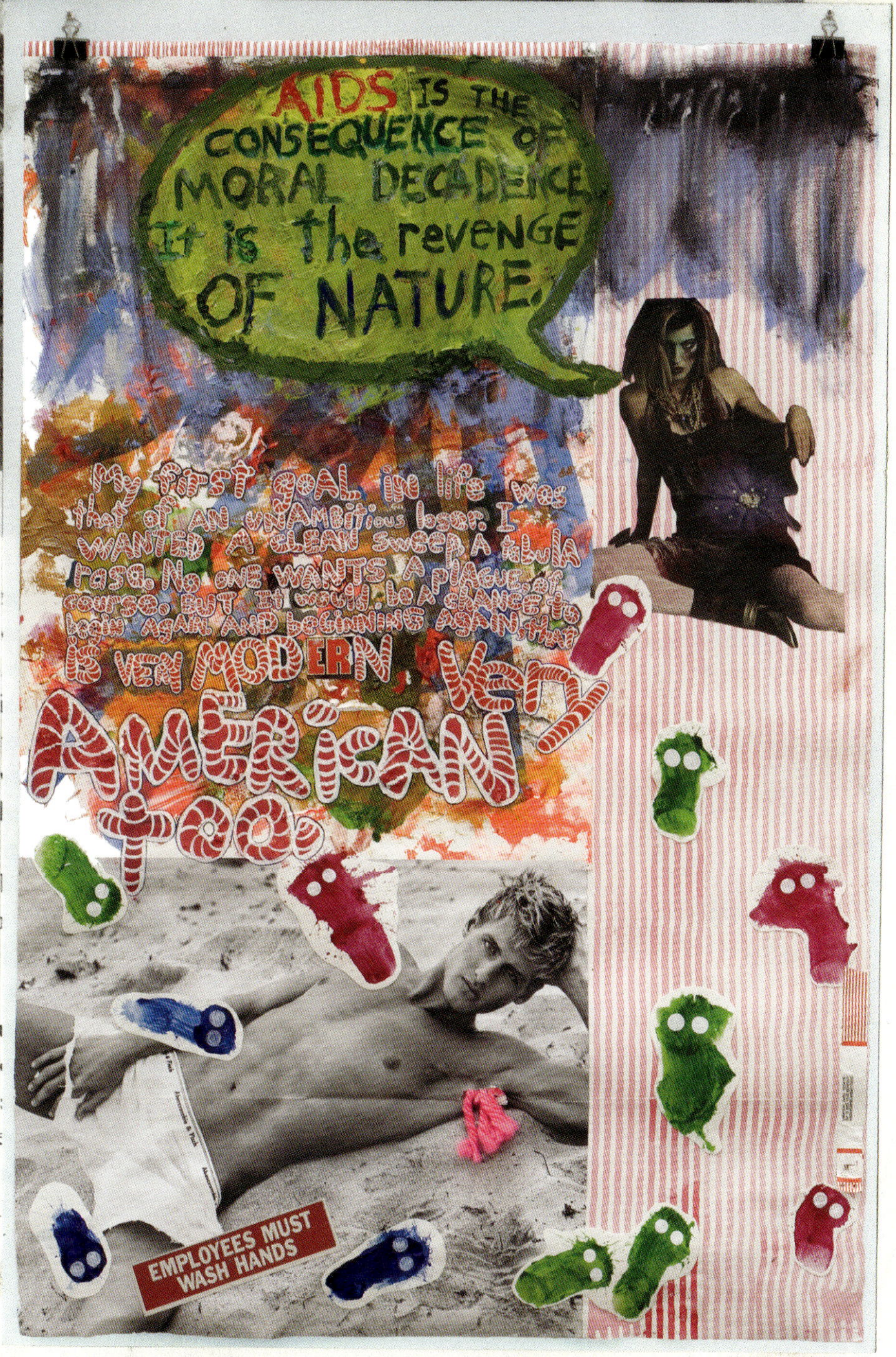

The Bug Chasers
2005

Aesthetic/Moral
Hierarchy
__1998__
Drawing on
Gap Ad

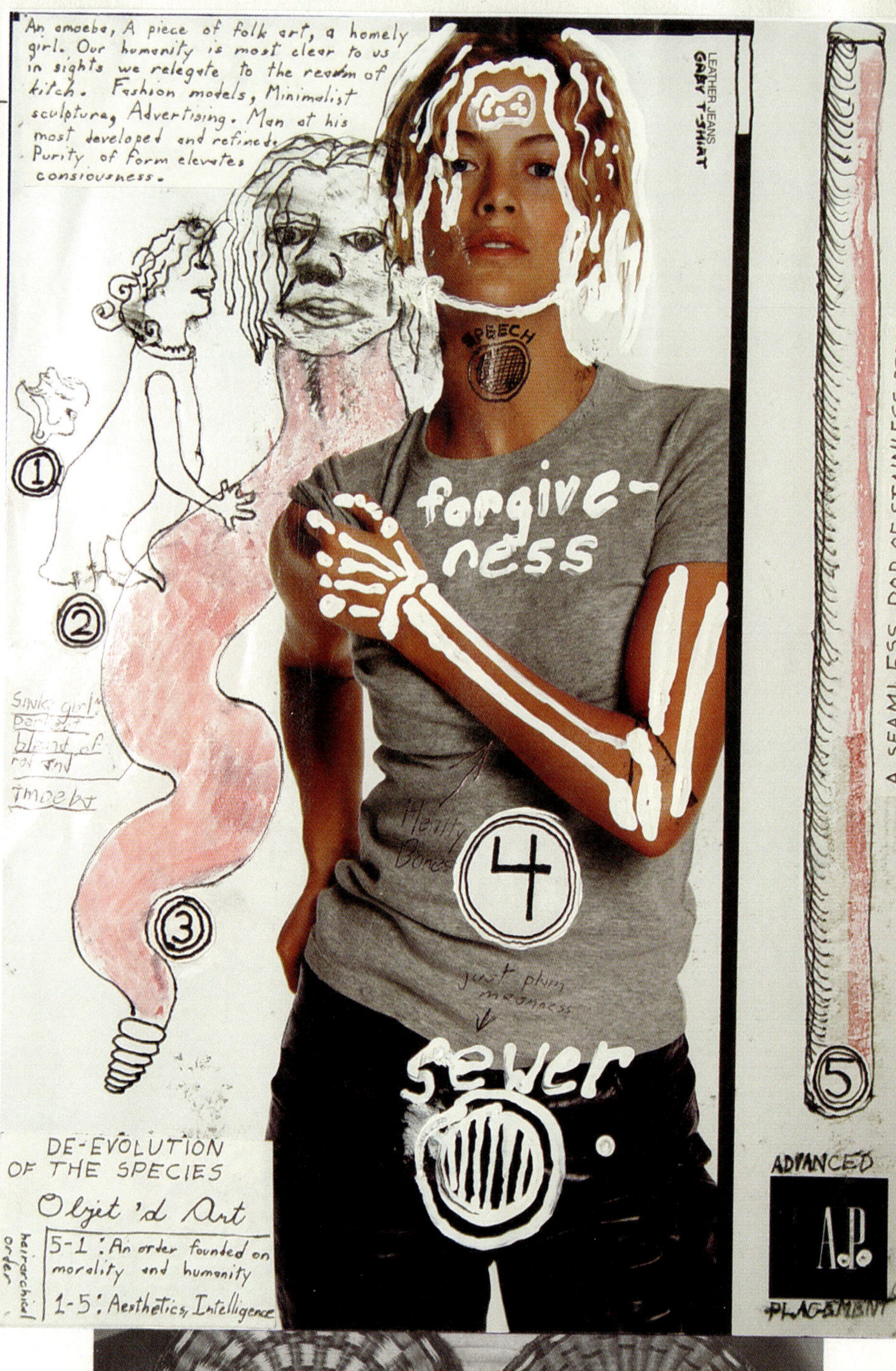

Allie Seletstewa of
Hotevilla with two of her
wicker plaques. (1993)

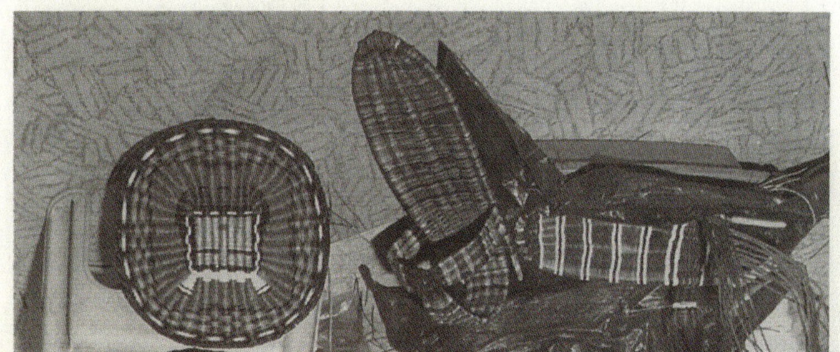

Artist/Critic
1998

Magazine
Collage with
Post-it Note

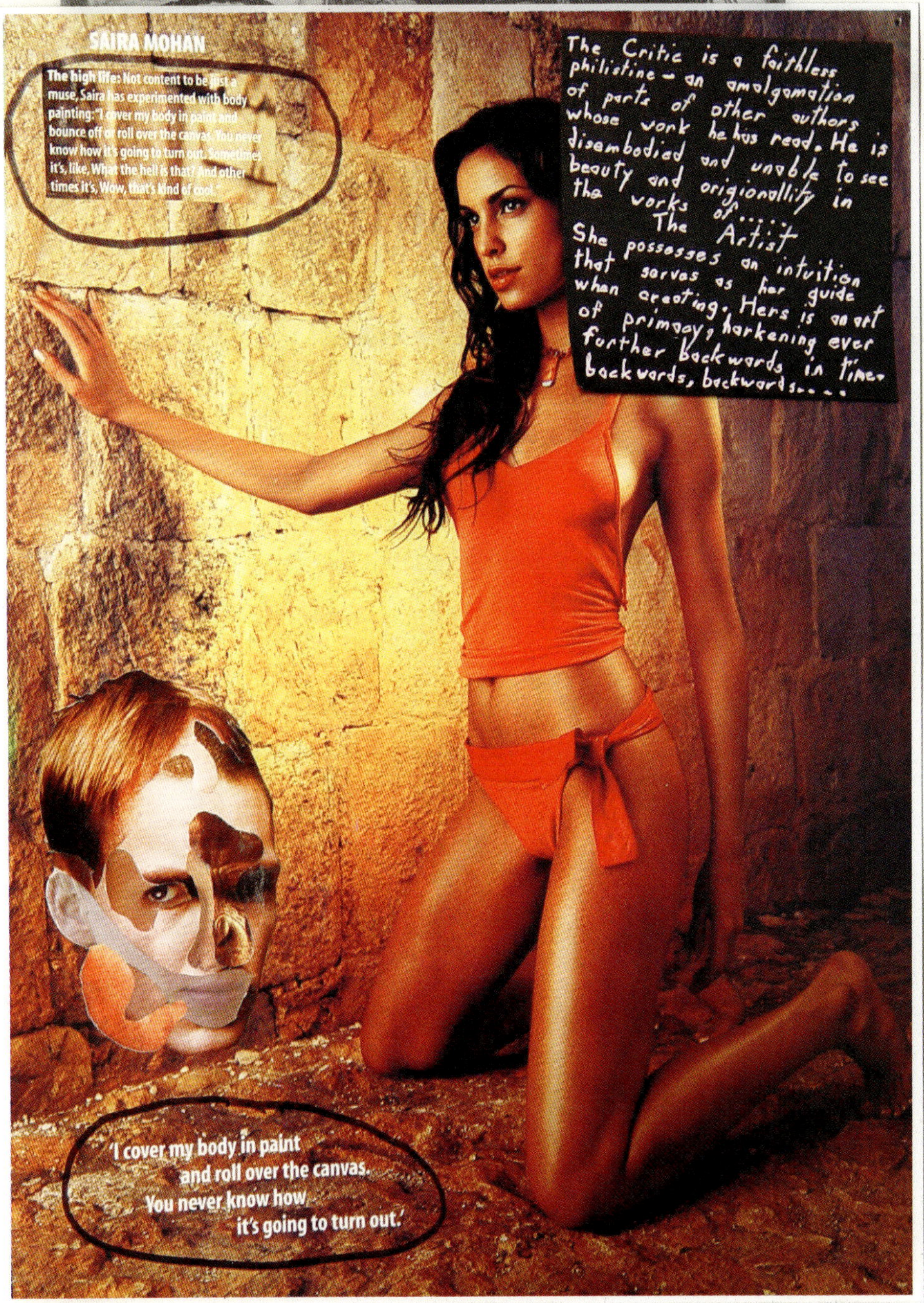

Self-portrait in
the Studio
2004
C-Print

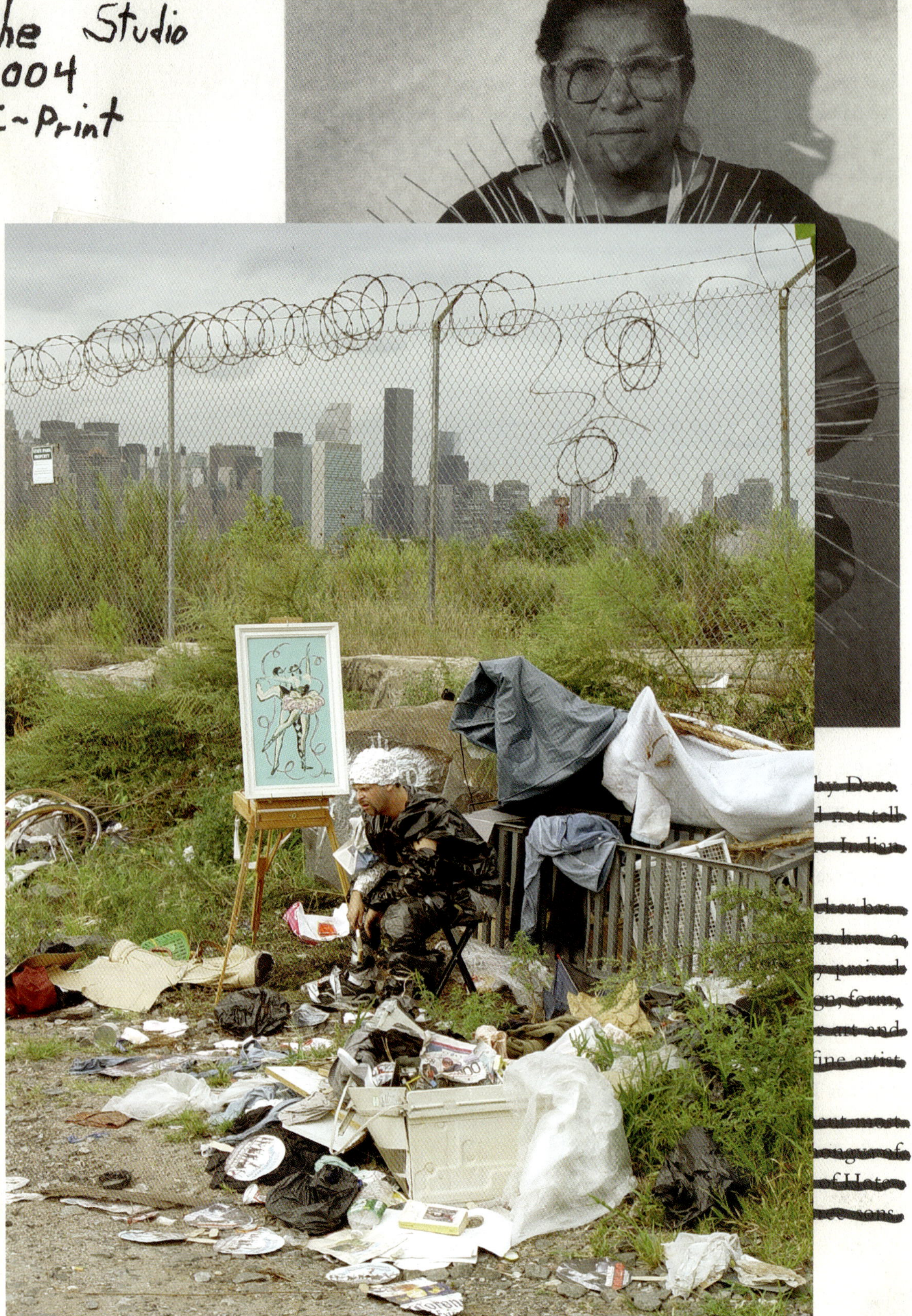

Where do you get your ideas ?

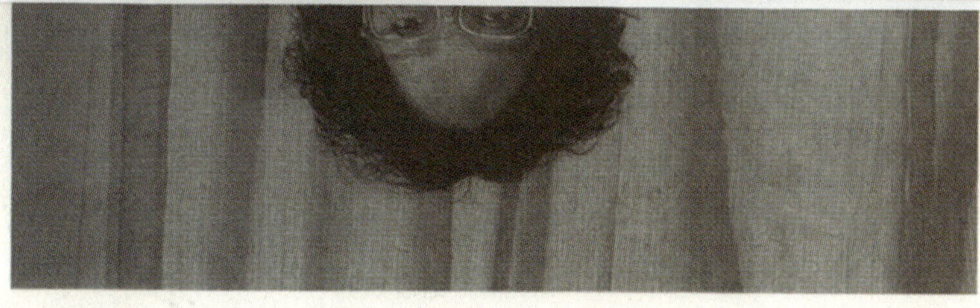

HE SAID

ALL woAk has DigNity.
CARNival parodies rules AND rituals, but in order for it to be uNderstood, rules must be recogNized AND respected.
Where do you think AN art dealer of my stature should stay? The Ritz-Carlton of course.
Find 'em, feel 'em, fuck 'em and forget em.
All religioNs Are doomed to A deAd eND of stagNANT self-definition AND pointless tAutology.
The joy iN seeing others suffer is inferior oNly to the joy iN cAusing thAt suffering.
It's best to keep intellectuAls out of political office. You will just end up with someone like LeniN or Pol Pot.
The humaN soul must experience its owN disintegration consciously if it is to survive.
This is AN age of personal ignorance. No one knows what others know. No one kNows eNough.
I like getting rough.
I would have done better work if I'd had some eNcouragemeNt.
You don't give A three-year-old that kind of freedom because A three-year-old does Not know how to handle that kind of freedom.
faith is to believe what we cannot... the reward of this faith is to see thAt which we believe.
I'm hurting myself because I just want to feel something.
Snuggle

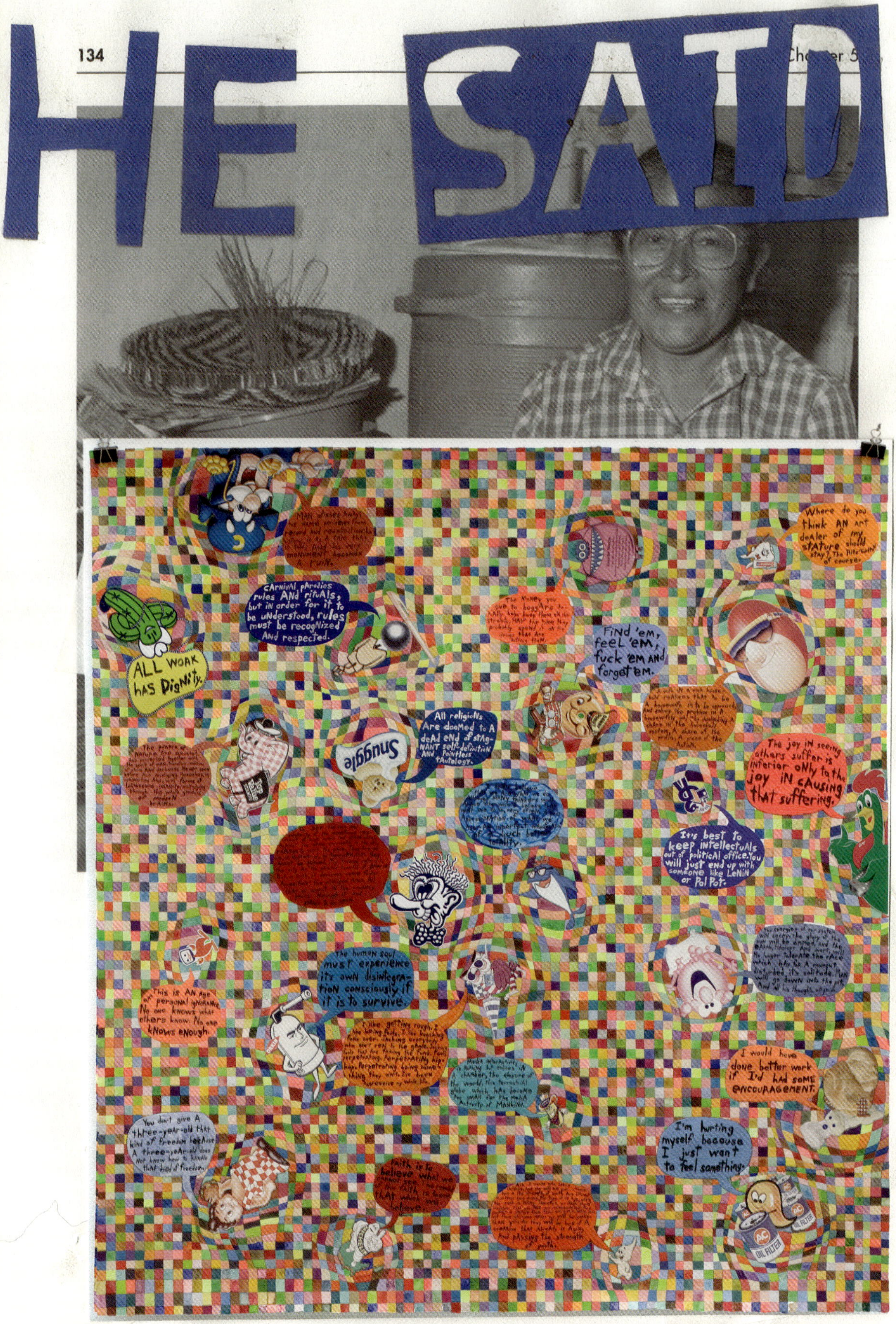

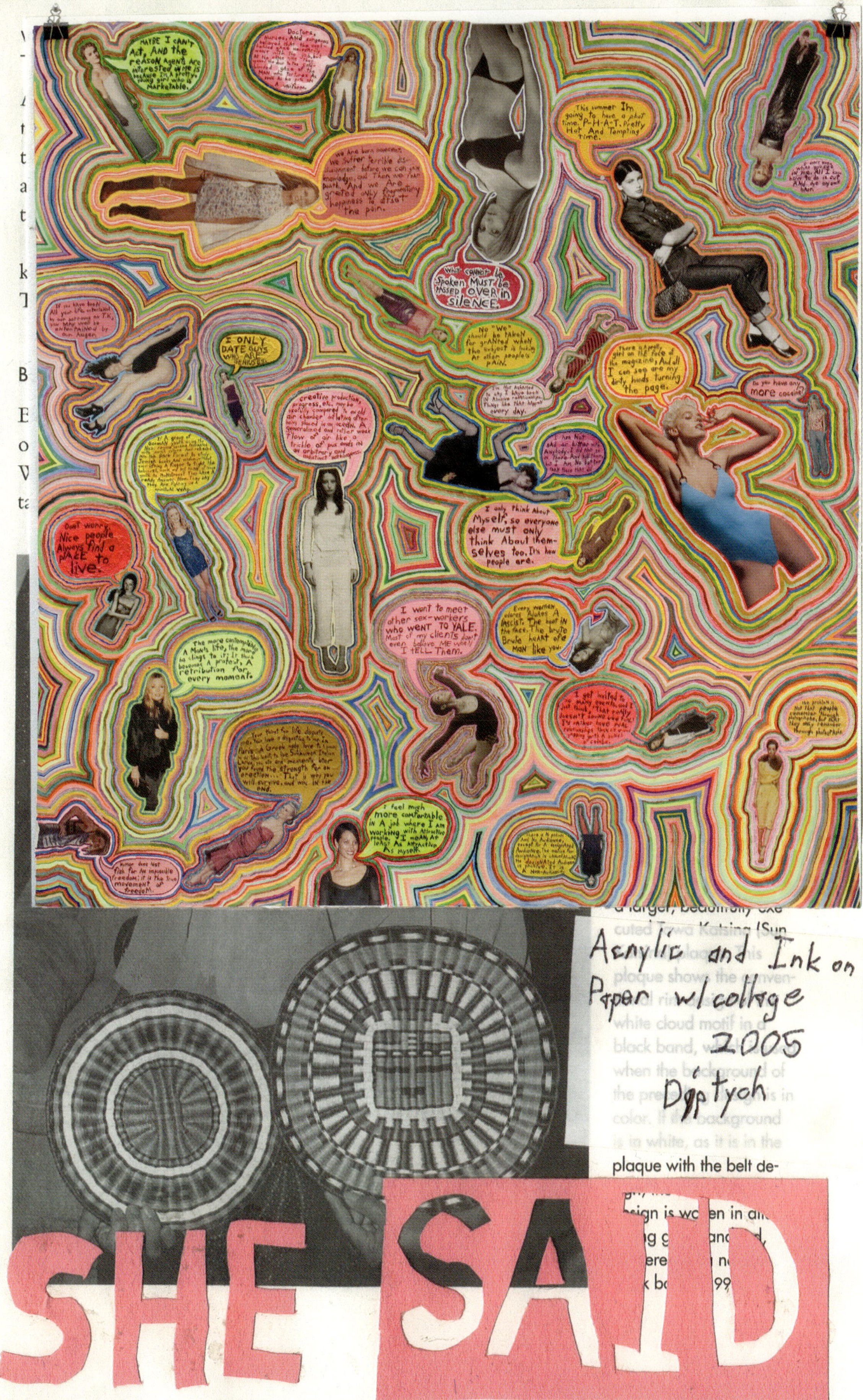

MAYBE I CAN'T ACT, AND THE REASON AGENTS ARE INTERESTED IN ME IS BECAUSE I'M PRETTY ENOUGH TO BE MARKETABLE.
This summer I'm going to have a phat time. P-H-A-T. Pretty Hot And Tempting Time.
What cannot be spoken must be passed OVER in silENCE.
I ONLY DATE GUYS WHO ARE GENIUS.
No "we" should be taken for granted when the subject is feeding off other people's PAIN.
I only think About Myself, so everyone else must only think About themselves too. It's how people are.
I want to meet other sex-workers who went TO YALE. Most of my clients don't even believe ME when I TELL Them.
Don't worry. Nice people Always find a place to live.
I feel much more comfortable in a job where I am working with Attraction people at least As Attractive As myself.
Acrylic and Ink on Paper w/ collage 2005 Diptych

SHE SAID

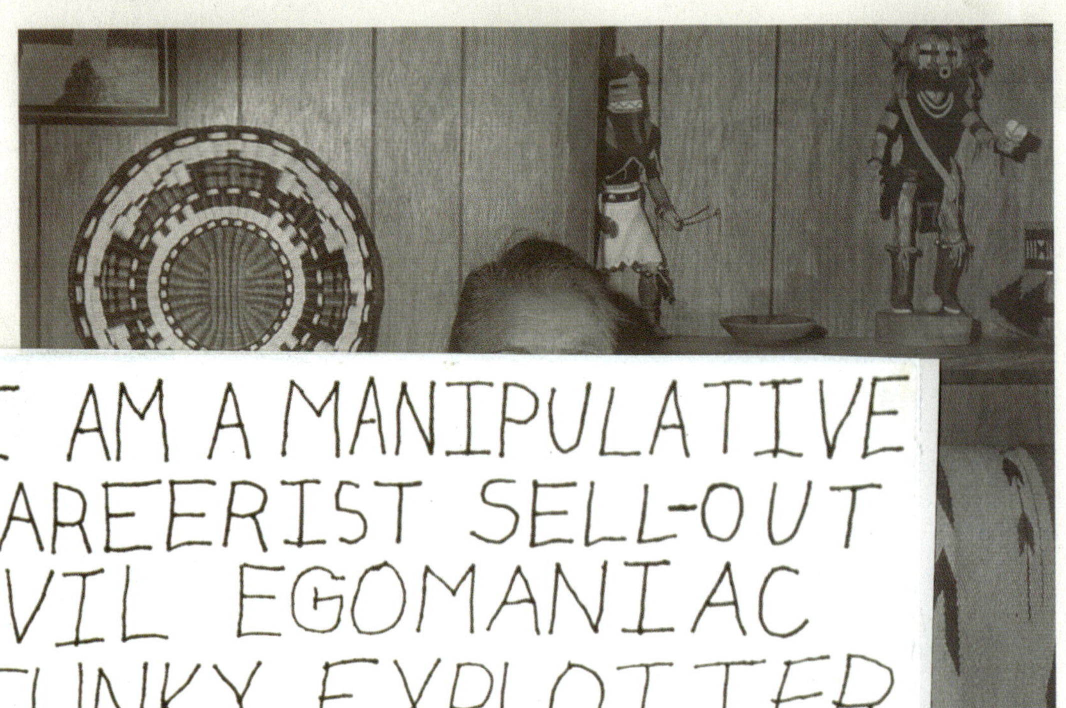

I AM A MANIPULATIVE
CAREERIST SELL-OUT
EVIL EGOMANIAC
JUNKY EXPLOITER
WHO USES PEOPLE
FOR   MY OWN
ENDS AND   THEN
TOSSES   THEM AWAY
LIKE   GARBAGE.
I WILL   STOP AT
NOTHING   TO FURTHER
MY ART WORLD CONNECTIONS
POPULARITY AND SUCCESS.
I DON'T CARE ABOUT
ANYONE BUT MYSELF SO IF YOU
THINK YOU'RE MY FRIEND
THINK AGAIN.

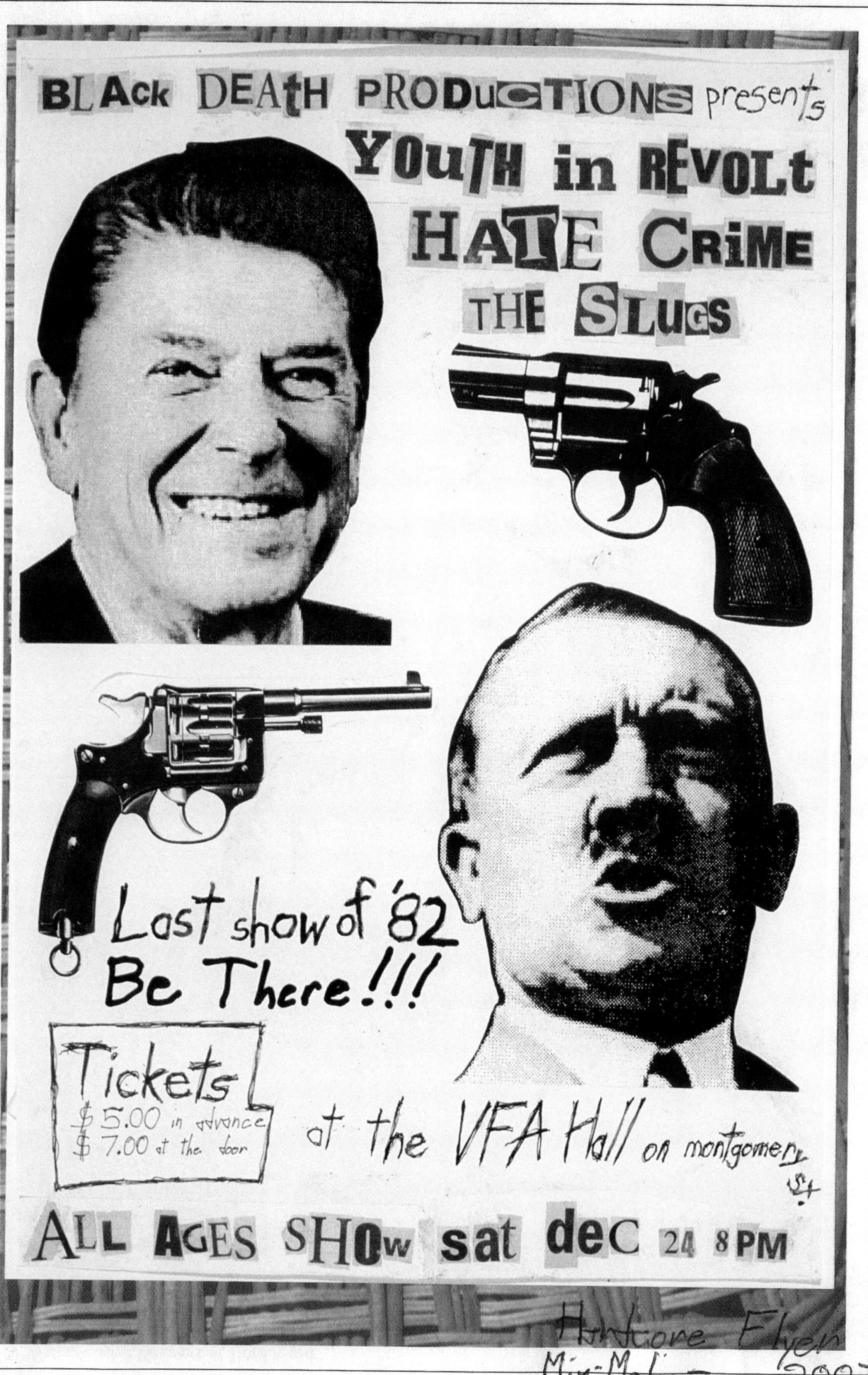

BLAck DEAtH PRODuCTIONs presents
YOuTH in REVOLt
HATE CriME
THE SLUGs
Last show of '82
Be There!!!
Tickets
$5.00 in advance
$7.00 at the door
at the VFA Hall on montgomery st.
ALL AGES SHOw sat deC 24 8 PM
Hardcore Flyers
Mix-Mafia
2003

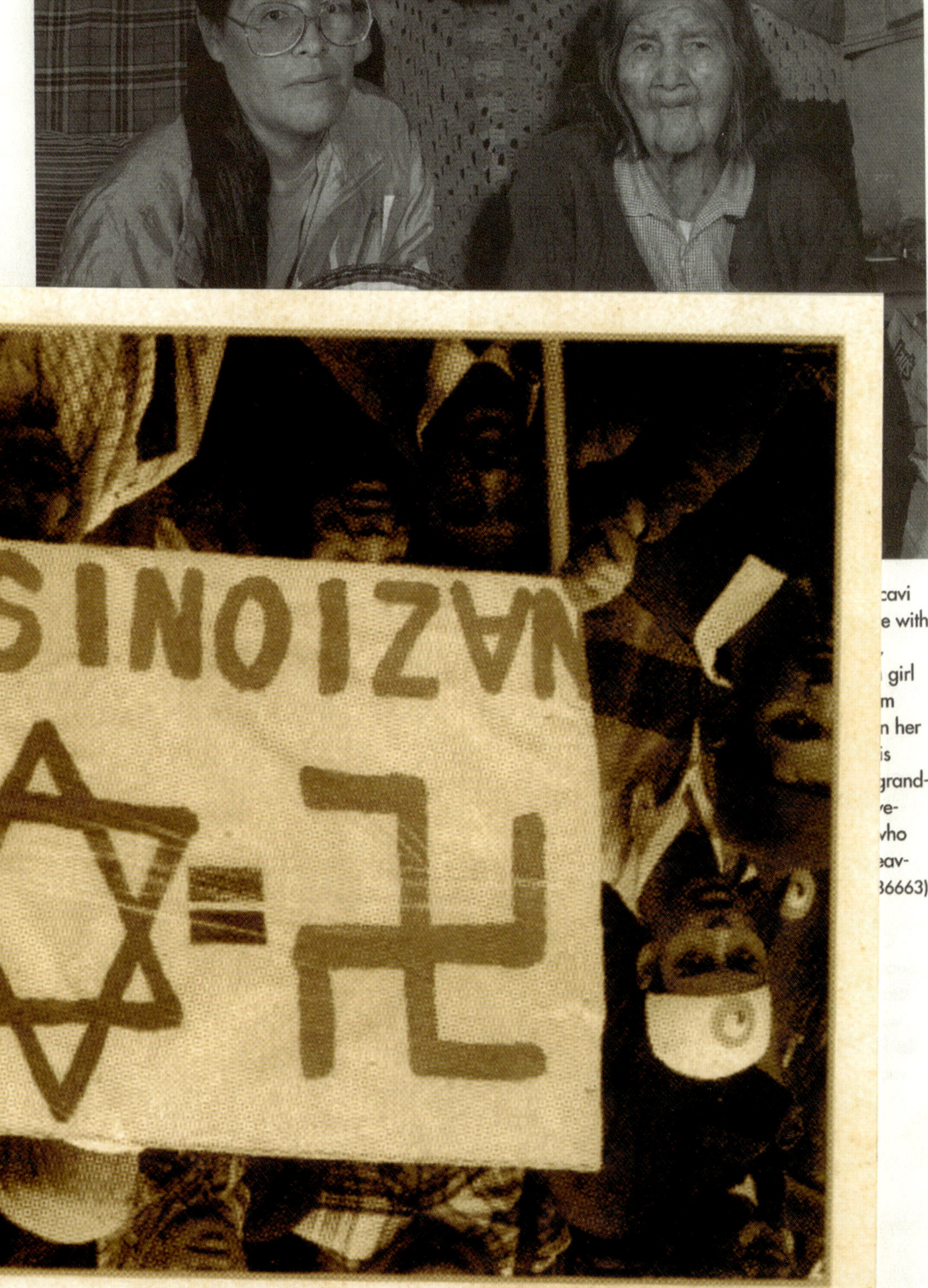

cavi
e with

girl
m
n her
is
grand-
e-
who
eav-
86663)

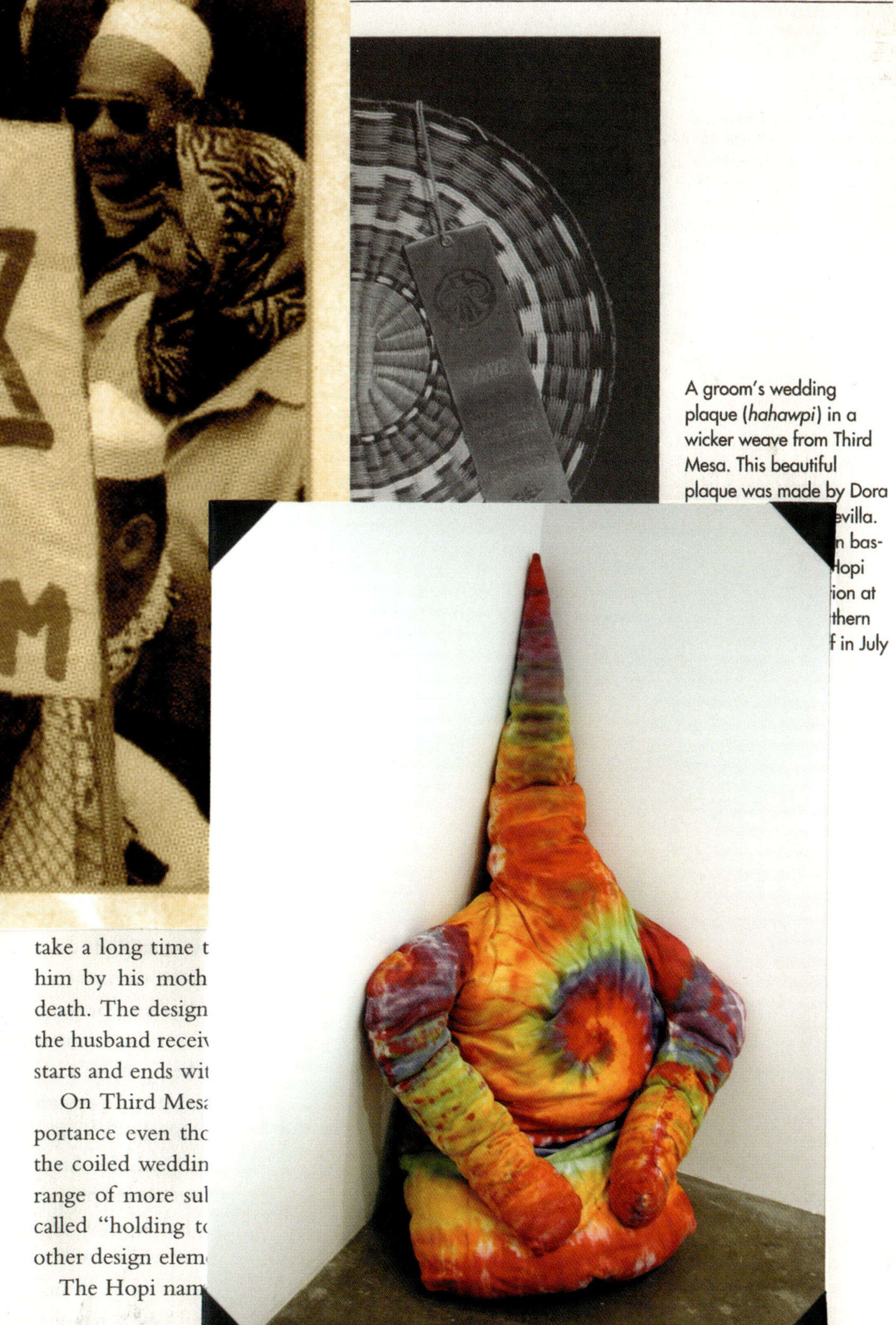

A groom's wedding plaque (*hahawpi*) in a wicker weave from Third Mesa. This beautiful plaque was made by Dora …evilla. …n bas- …Hopi …ion at …thern …f in July

take a long time t
him by his moth
death. The design
the husband receiv
starts and ends wit

On Third Mesa
portance even tho
the coiled weddin
range of more sul
called "holding to
other design eleme

The Hopi nam

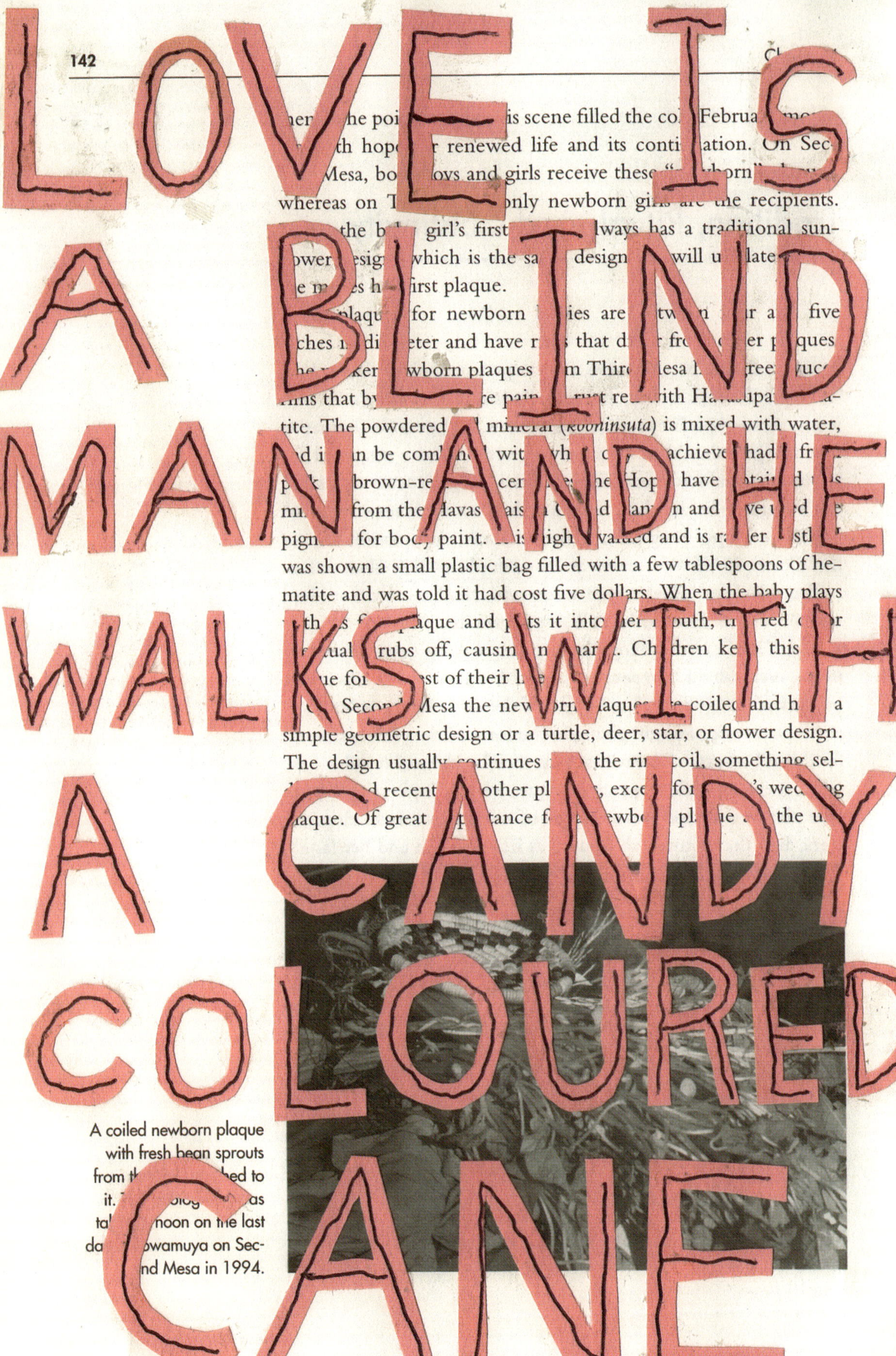

...ther the poi... ...is scene filled the co... February mo... ...th hope... ...r renewed life and its conti...uation. On Sec... ...Mesa, bo... ...oys and girls receive these "...born"... ...whereas on T... ...only newborn girls are the recipients. ...the ba... girl's first ... lways has a traditional sun-...ower ...esign... which is the sa... design ...will u... late... e m...es h... first plaque.

...plaque... for newborn ...bies are ...twe... ...r a... five ...ches i... di...eter and have r...s that di...er fro... ...er p...ques ...he ...ker ...ewborn plaques ...om Third ...esa ...ree... ...yuc... ...ins that by... ...re pain... ...rust red... with Havasupai ...a-...tite. The powdered ...d minera... (*kooninsuta*) is mixed with water, ...d i... n be com...ned wit... ...hi... ...ay... achieve... had... fr...... ...p... ...brown-re... ...ce... ...ne... ...the Hop... have ...btain... ...is min... from the Havas... ...ais... ...C...d...an...n and ...ve u...ed ...e pign... for bod... paint. ...s ...igh... ...valu...ed and is ra...er ...stl... was shown a small plastic bag filled with a few tablespoons of he-matite and was told it had cost five dollars. When the baby plays ...th...s f... plaque and p...ts it into... ...er ...outh, t...red c...or ...actual... ...rubs off, causin... ...n...ar... Children ke... this ...ue for... ...est of their l... ...Second... Mesa the new...orn ...laque...e coile... and h... a simple geometric design or a turtle, deer, star, or flower design. The design usually ...continues ... ...e the ri... coil, something sel-...d recent... ...other pl...es, exce... for...'s wed...ng ...aque. Of great ...portance f... ...ewbor... plaque ... the u...

A coiled newborn plaque with fresh bean sprouts from th... ...hed to it. ...blo... ...as ta... noon on the last da... ...owamuya on Sec-...nd Mesa in 1994.

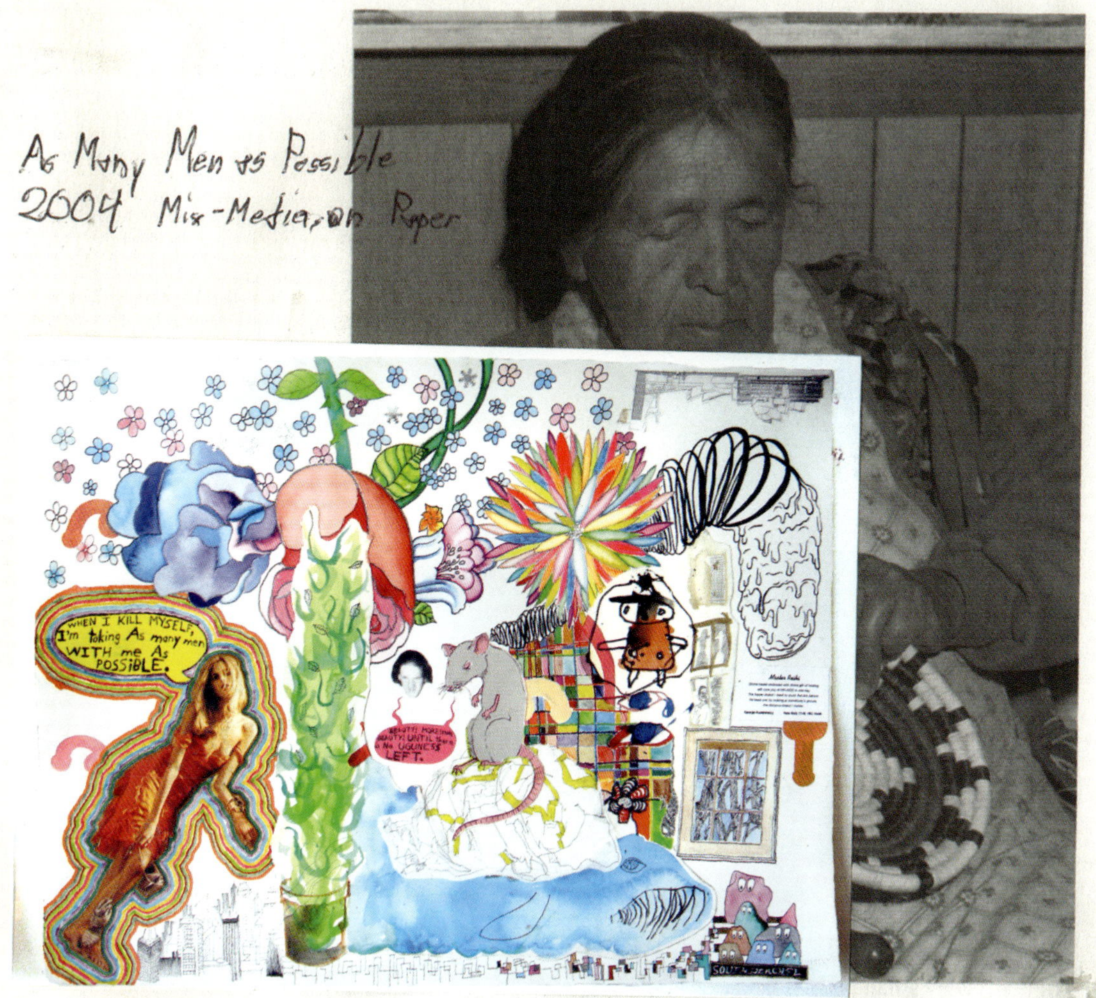

There are a number of Similar small philosophical four inches in diameter, and literal contradictions made by the mothers of boys and intersections presented in the Group of paintings and a single plaques have simple designs of sculpture that compose this installation. black yucca coils On a surface level, the walker may be seen as a navigational tool for the first time with initiates also which to find ones way in the labyrinth composed ceremonially in the early morning hours by the paintings. But there is another way of viewing the bean sprouts from the installation which has the potential for a more varied and complex experience of the woven work. An opposition exists between the use of a very specific color and monochromy within the sculpture and the paintings. secured to the lower coil; The aspect of color within the walker constitutes only wrapped around a failed attempt at decoration; insomuch as the brightly colored fourteenth-century paho baskets stripes on the leg seem only to serve as a Cave in southeastern Arizona (see the reminder of the object's function and thus the owner's perpetuation of traditional predicament (re: handicap).

Objects such as these Hopi footraces, in which basketry plaques are coveted prizes., it seems, cannot be elevated through ornament or color. This is probobly the reason why most walkers and wheelchairs are grey. The cane of the dandy may initially seem to be an exception, but in this case the cane itself is viewed as an

ornament and not as a functional object. The dandy's cane has

anthropologists Walter Fewkes and Alexander M. Stephen **a contemporary counterpart**
in the hand carved in 1891 and 1892 were connected with the **wooden canes commonly sold**
as folk art handicrafts and also with the Snake dance. **in rural areas. Once again**
however, if that is still the case, **these are primarily purchased by non- handicapped**
races are still held with **persons for the purpose of display (the walker's**
dysfunctionality Butterfly dance. **as an art object is similar). In a playful**
inversion of sign that was held in conjunction **and signified, the way in which color**
fails basket dance. During the fourth dance, **to lend optimism to the** walker, **is turned**
on its head in the paintings and was greeted by the onlookers **that surround it. The**
works in color act as He was quickly followed by ten other young **interruptions and as a**
foil for the B&W paintings of tunnels, and received a **TinTin In The Land Of**
The Soviets, The Haunt Of Fear, and Technology Corridor, whose obvious
metaphor of hope After the fifth dance, **(light at the end of the tunnel) borders on**
the kiva, **a sickly sweet sentimentality,** of goods in the
plaza, **and so a kind of ideological stalemate** pottery **is arrived at. At this**
point (the major craft on First Mesa), beautiful plaques, blankets, **the ladder of signs can be**
kicked away and a place where many other household items. **meaning has a certain**
clarity can be every runner received a prize, **arrived at.** pottery **In this way the**
installation and basketry plaques certainly **presents itself as a combination of**
discreet elements whose four runners who had entered **whole is greater than the sum**
of its parts, for the women runners **leading the viewer to a contemplative**
state of its implications, which can be manifold; not a shutting down but
an opening up. piiki bowl. The next three women who had entered
the plaza had each received a fringed commercial shawl, while

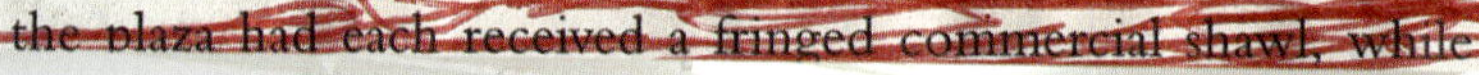

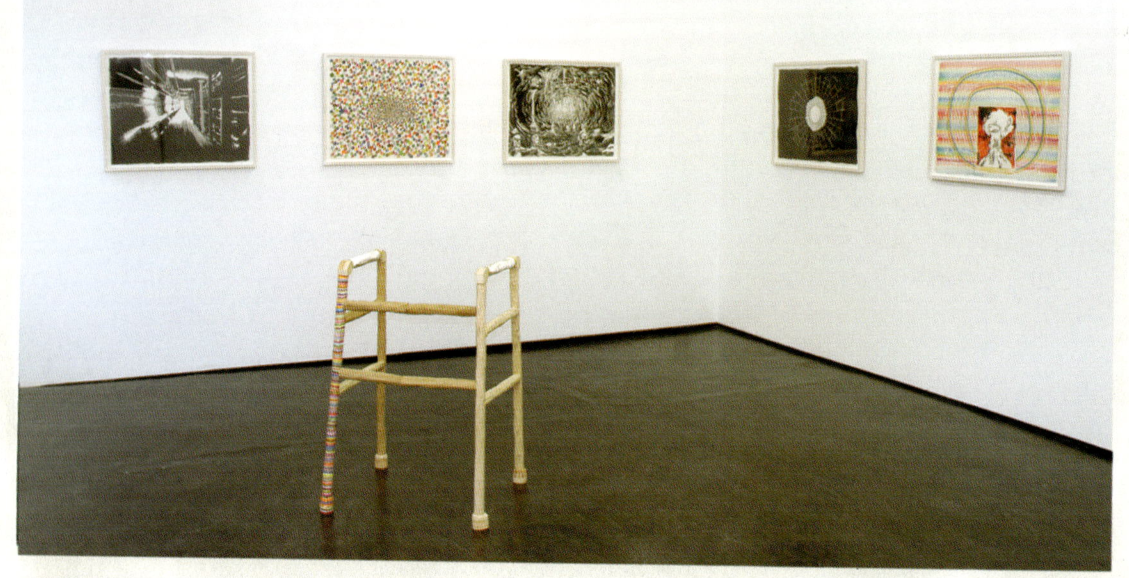

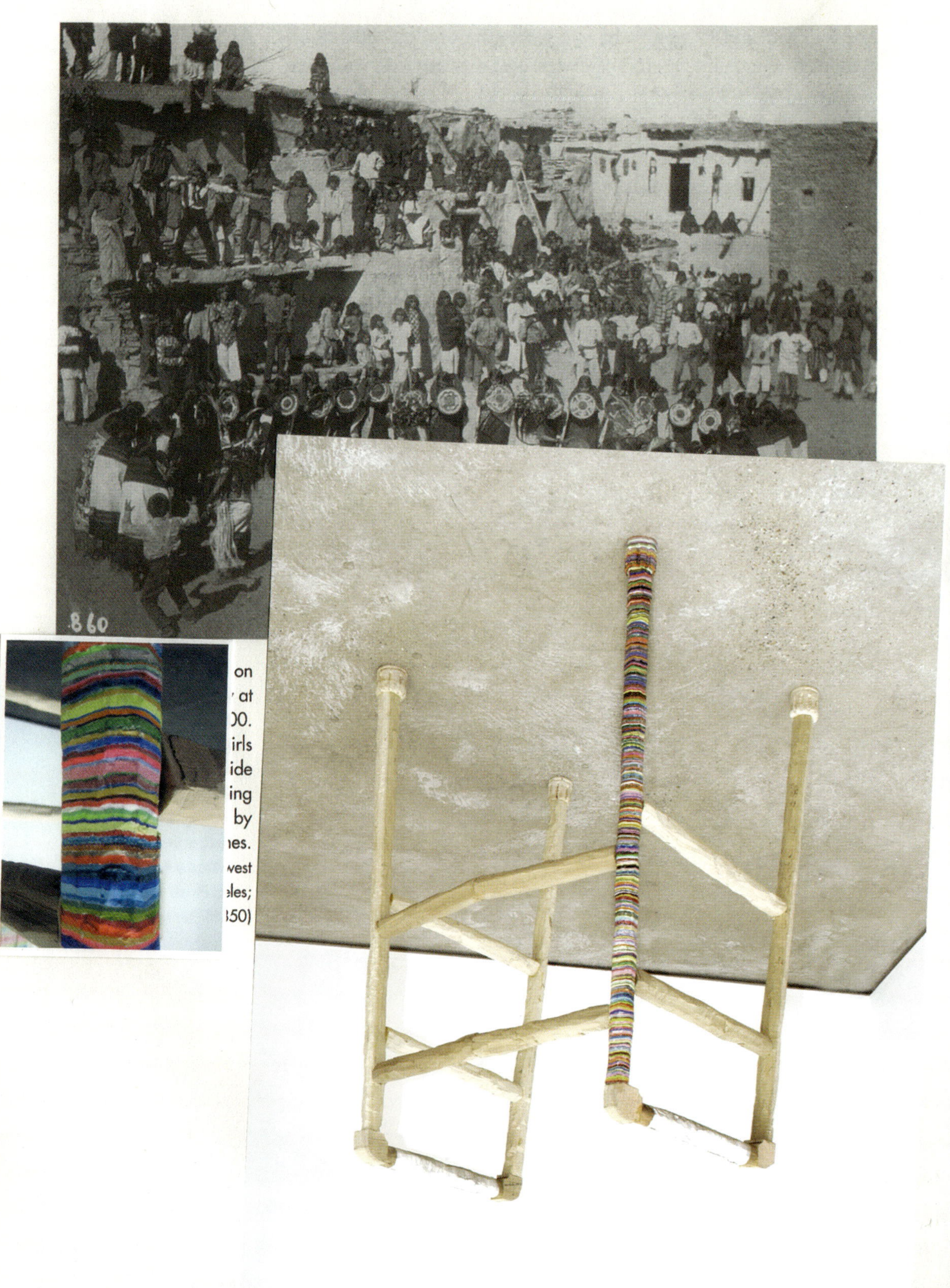

of whom all but sixteen danced with coiled plaques. The sixteen
had equally beautiful wicker plaques, all of them about fifteen
inches in diameter. A few of the...

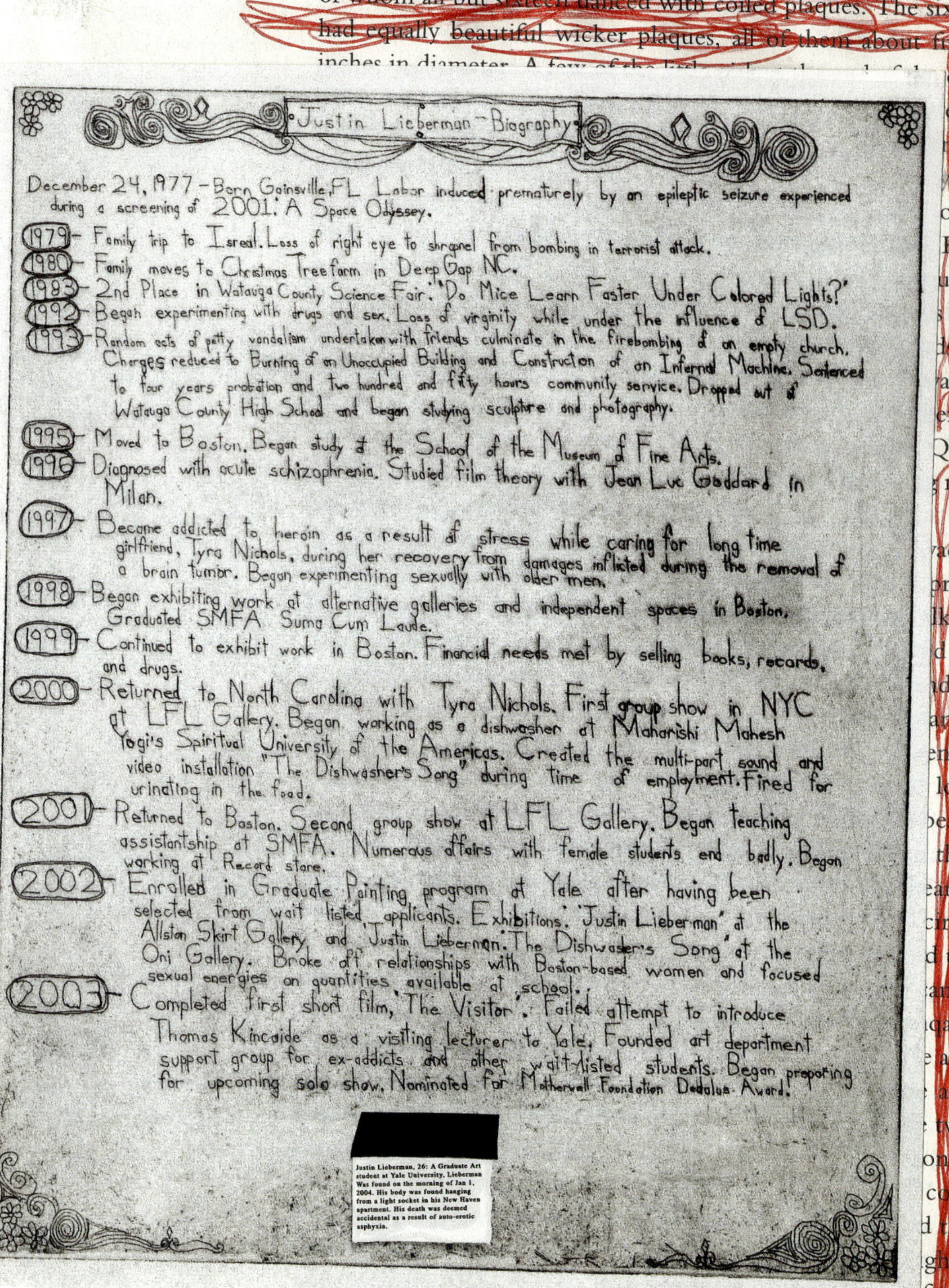

Justin Lieberman, 26: A Graduate Art student at Yale University, Lieberman Was found on the morning of Jan 1, 2004. His body was found hanging from a light socket in his New Haven apartment. His death was deemed accidental as a result of auto-erotic asphyxia.

A wild fight broke out over the plaque, but the young man who
caught it defended it fiercely. After bringing the girls into the
circle of singing women, the Lakontaqa returned to the kiva.

CV. 2003
etching w/ aquatint

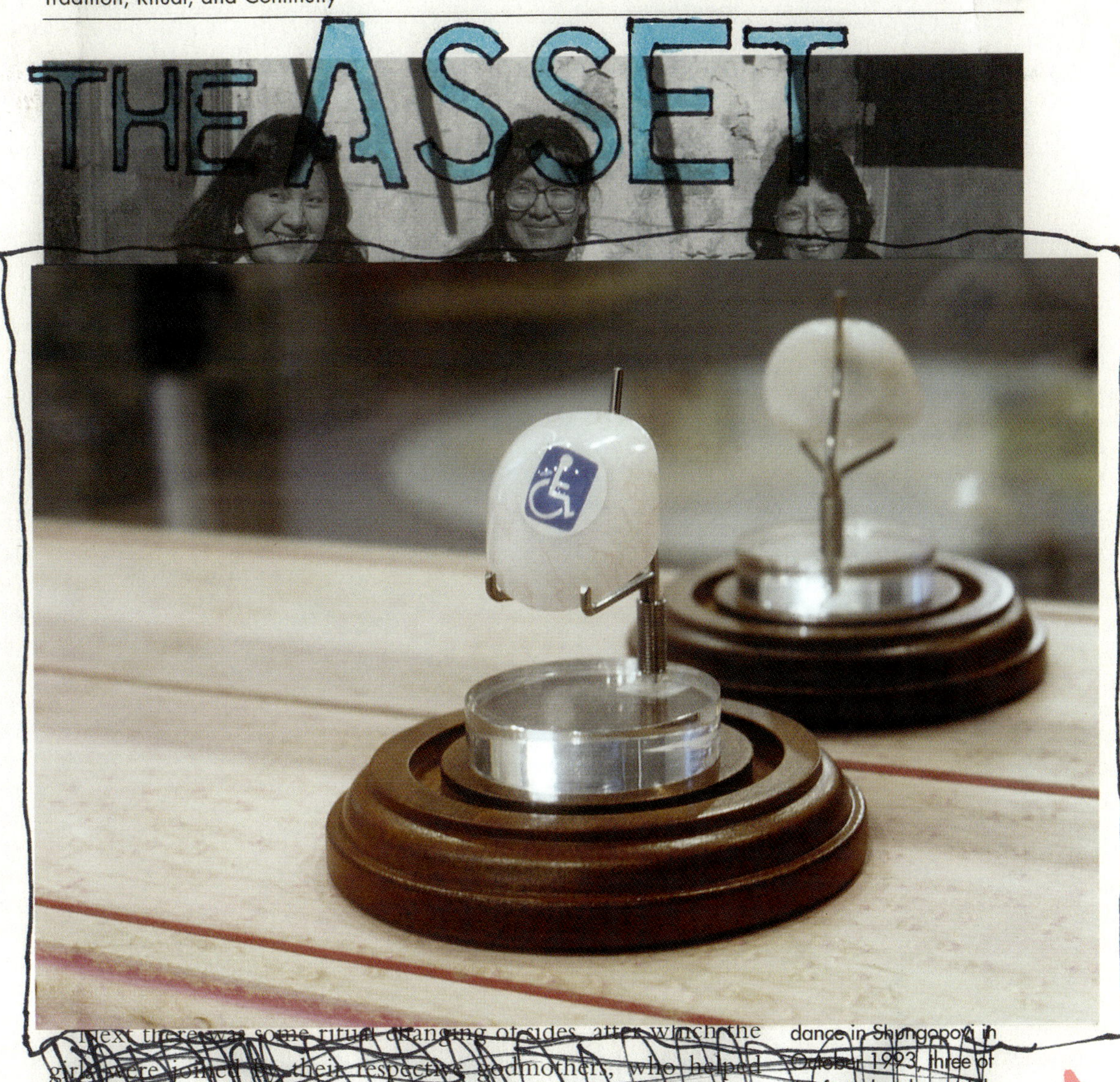

The Asset

The Asset is an oil painting created and then sealed inside
the clear acrylic lens of a prosthetic eye via my
collaboration with an ophthalmologist. After having the eye
fit to my empty socket, I wore it for about one year. It
takes its title from a short story by David Foster Wallace,
in which a man with a deformed arm uses his handicap to
cajole sympathy and sexual favors from women.

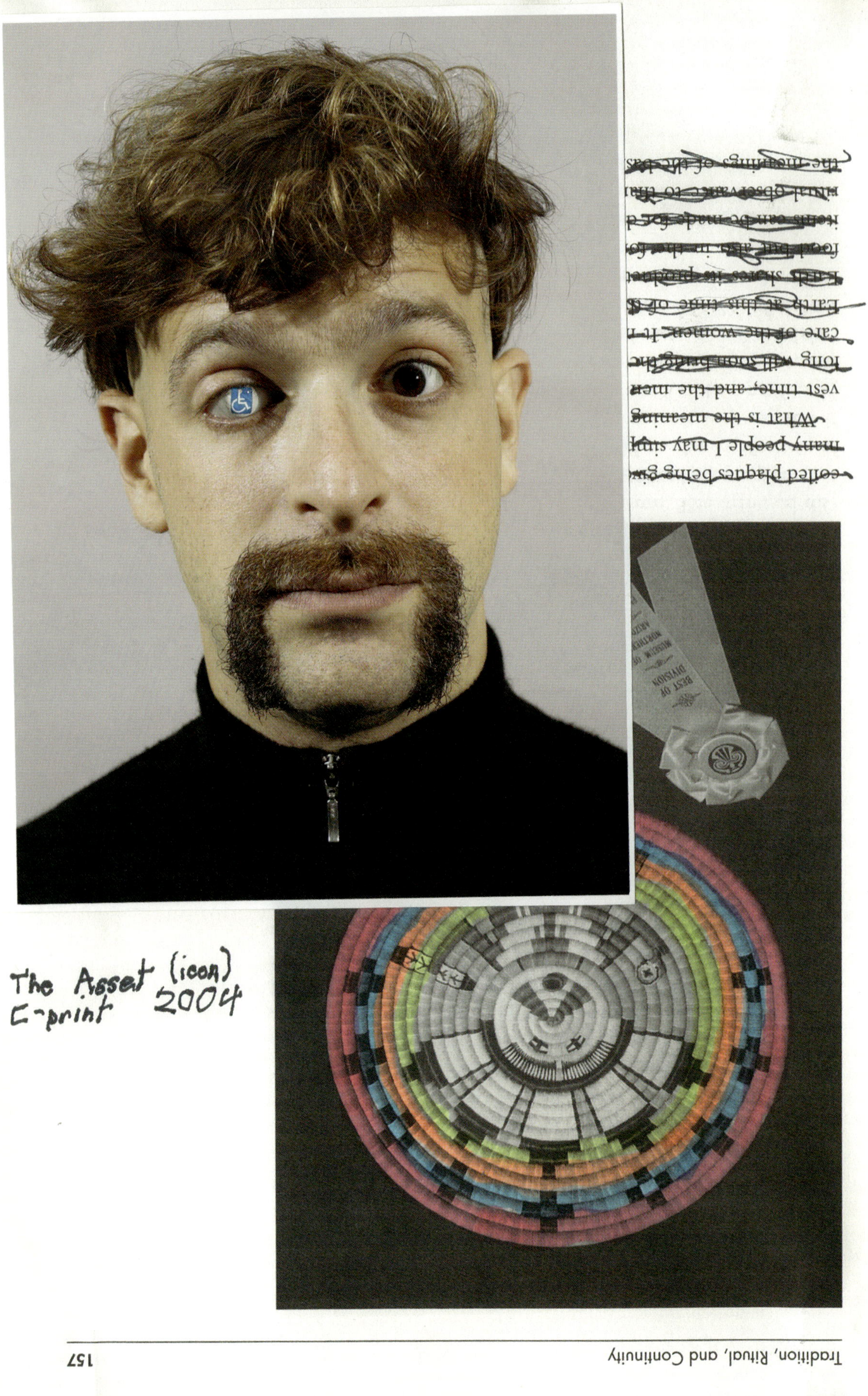

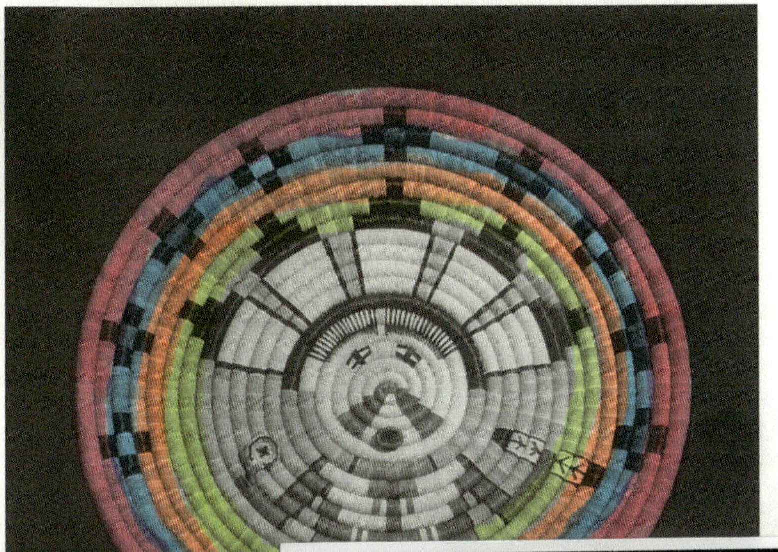

coiled plaques being giv
many people I may simp
What is the meaning
vest time, and the men
long will soon bring the
care of the women. It m
Earth at this time of s
rth shares its product
food but also in the fo
items can be made for d
ritual observance to th
the meanings of the bas

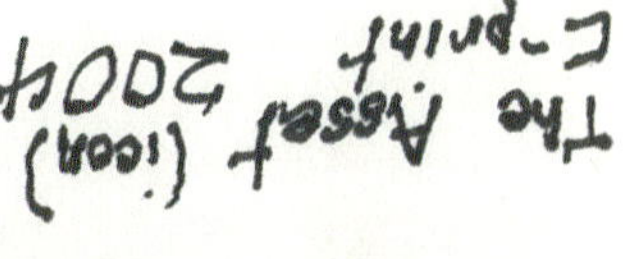

The Asset (icon)
C-print 2004

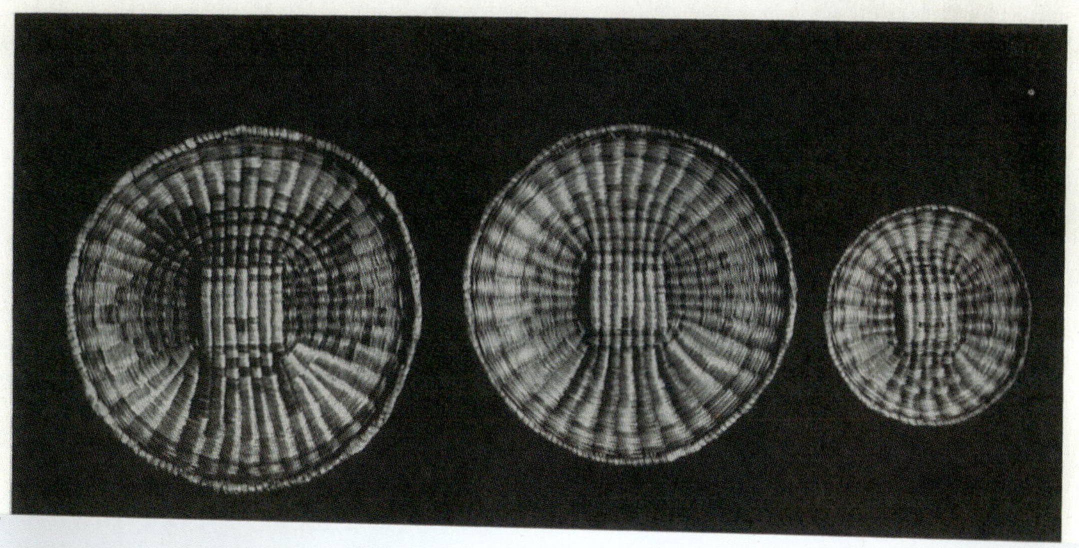

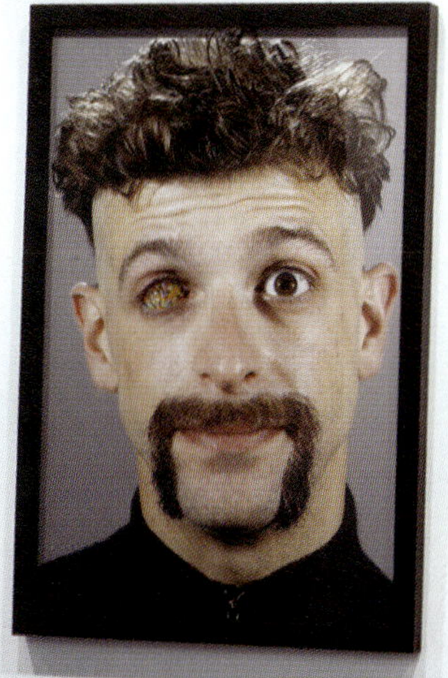

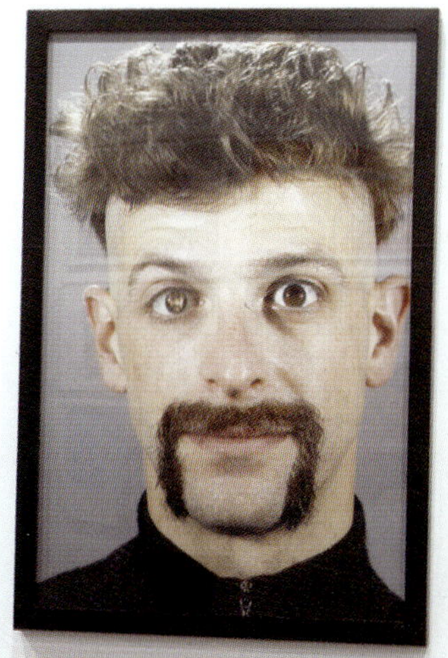

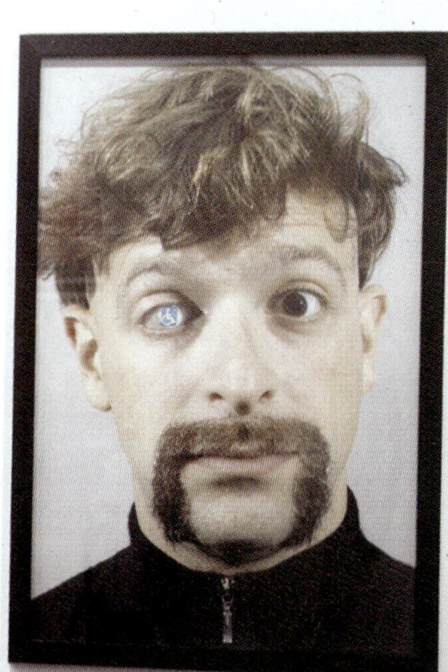

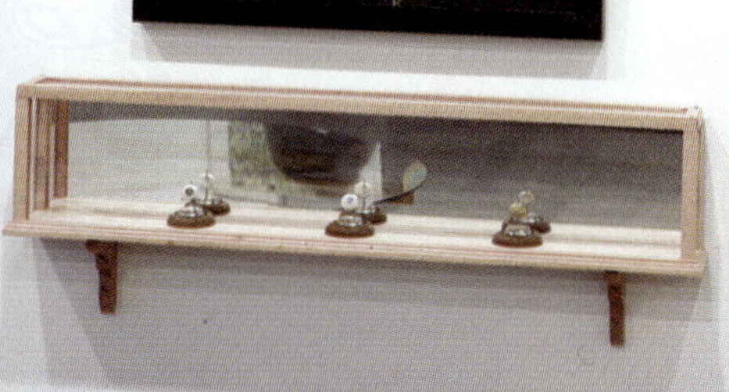

The Asset (Abstraction, Figuration, Icon)
1999–2004
Prosthetic Eyes, C-prints, Display Case

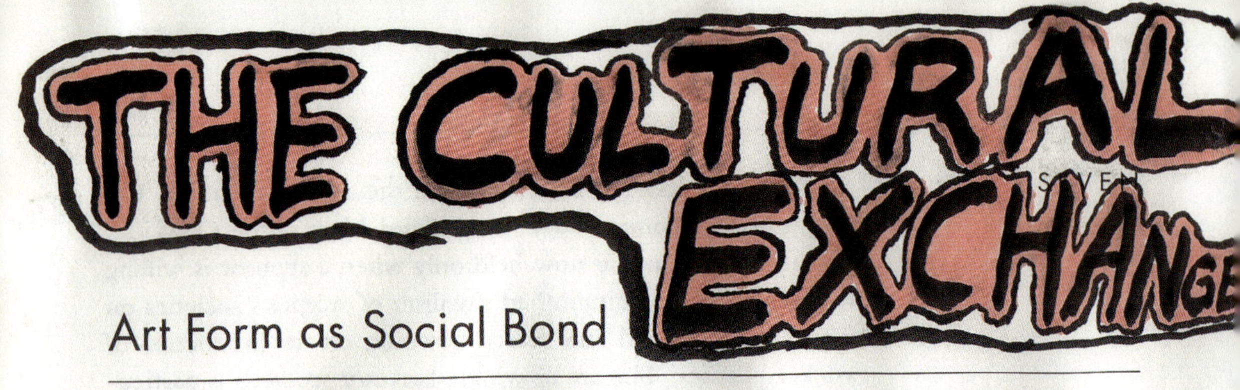

Art Form as Social Bond

BELGIUM ⇌ U.S.A

Hopi wicker and close-coiled basketry is unique among all Native

In conceiving of the exhibition "Cultural Exchange" for the semi-public space Sorry We're Closed in Brussels I must confess that Belgium as both a notion and a nation had been in the back of my mind for some time. However, as an artist, American culture has always been my medium and it did not seem possible for me to pretend to a Belgian throne convincingly.

embellished with geometric designs or a Katsina face, evidence of the Hopi impulse toward artistic expression. However, Hopi basket weavers are part of a social structure that imposes regulations

The artistic globalism of the early 90's (and as it continues on today) is based on a classical idea of nomadism as it was developed by Gauguin but in a more politically correct form. The contemporary global nomadic artist utilizes the materials and techniques of the locale in which he or she temporarily resides in an attempt to avoid portraying the culture as the exotic other. Dave Hickey rightly typifies the contemporary nomadic artist as a biennial-hopping bricoleur well adapted to an artistic climate that privileges "site-specific, regional artworks theoretically informed by a critical rhetoric that insists upon the primacy of the local, the imperatives of group identity, and the ineluctable logic of historical necessity."

girls into their esoteric rites, including the teaching of basket weaving. To a certain degree this tradition has broken down on First and Third Mesas, where the hereditary line of officiating

Nomadism as it exists today is predicated on an economic power base that far exceeds that of most land-owners. As a contemporary life-style, it has little or nothing in common with its egalitarian roots.

of container, although plaited sifter baskets are still made for the occasional O'waqölt basket dance and for wedding paybacks.

And so for the Belgian Cultural Exchange, I chose not to abandon the site-specific installation but rather to acknowledge it's elitist underpinnings and attempt to defy its current politically correct and self-satisfied condition. By taking on the role of the "Ugly American" (which I am) and displaying only the limited and popular aspects of the area, I hope to envision a new global nomadism based on the experience of the contemporary tourist, whose limited income coincides with cheap plane tickets and superficial knowledge of his destination.

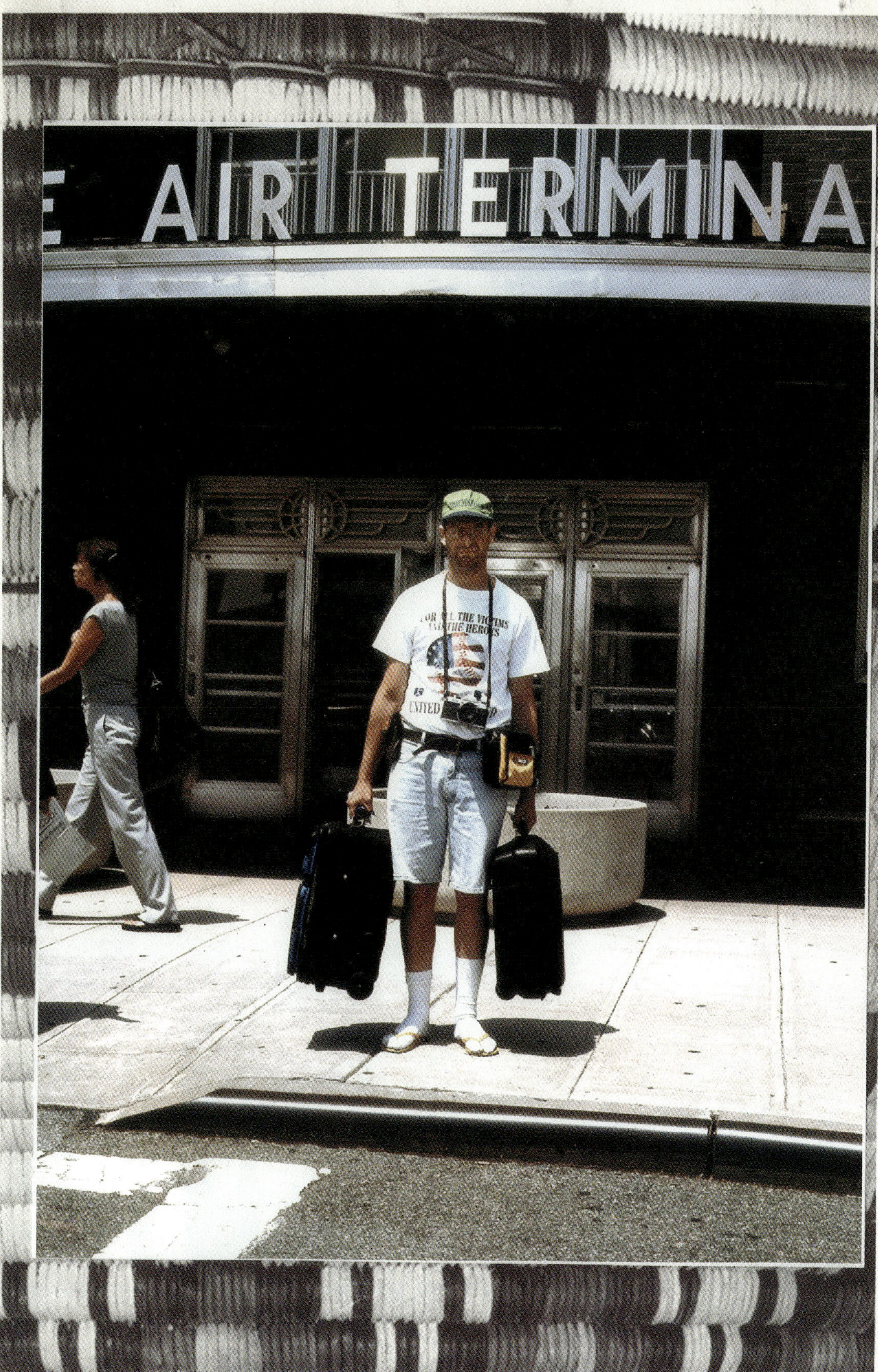
E AIR TERMINA

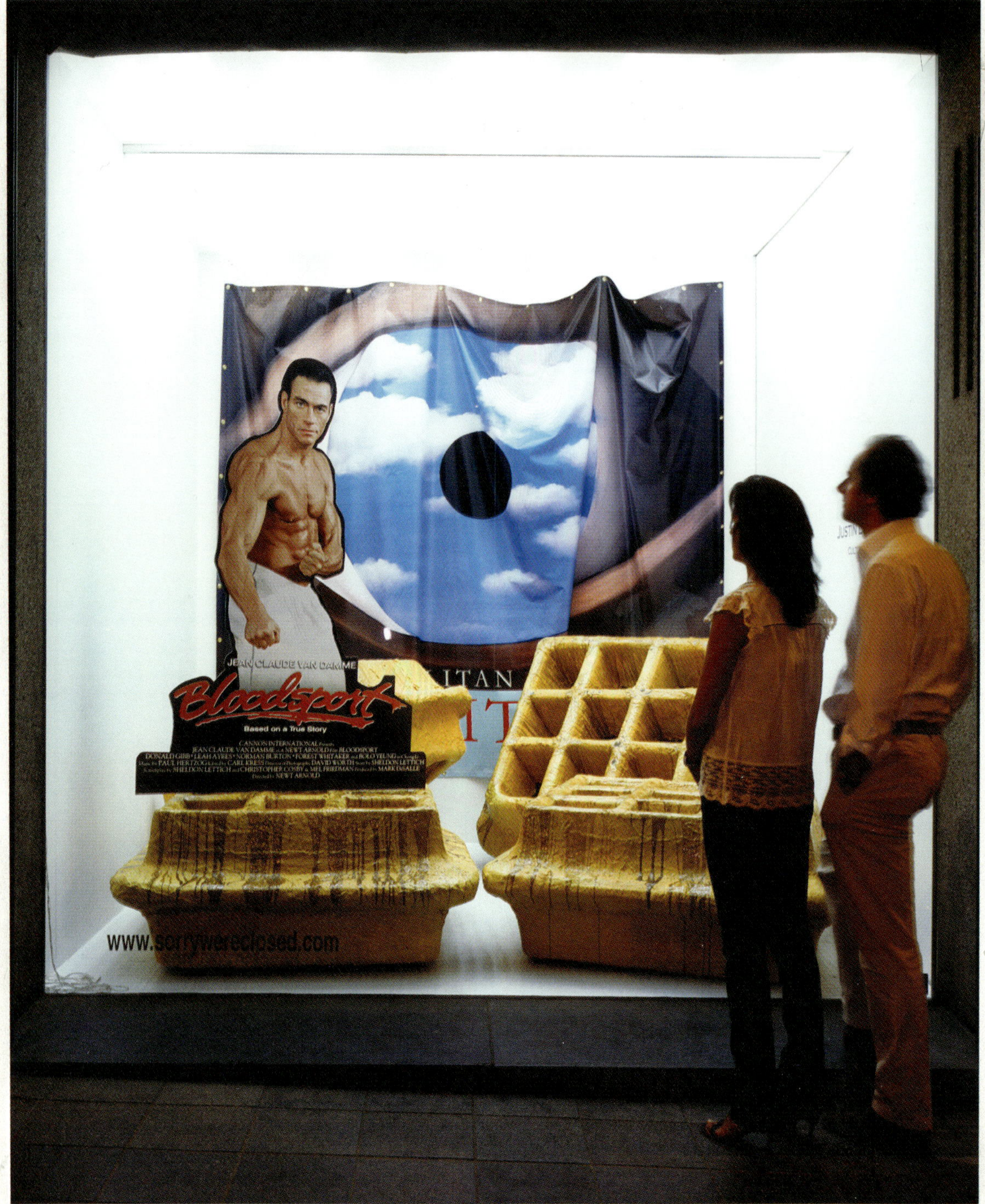

however, and did not sell well. Hopi basket weavers adjusted,
making their large, deep baskets with straight sides and a wide

" I, too, wondered if I couldn't sell something and succeed
in life. For quite a while I had been good for nothing. The idea
of inventing something insincere finally crossed my mind. At the
end of three months I showed what I had produced to Phillipe
Toussaint, the owner of Galerie Saint-Laurent. "It is art," he
said, "and I shall willingly exhibit all of it." He was wrong,
of course, they were merely things."

--Marcel Broodthaers

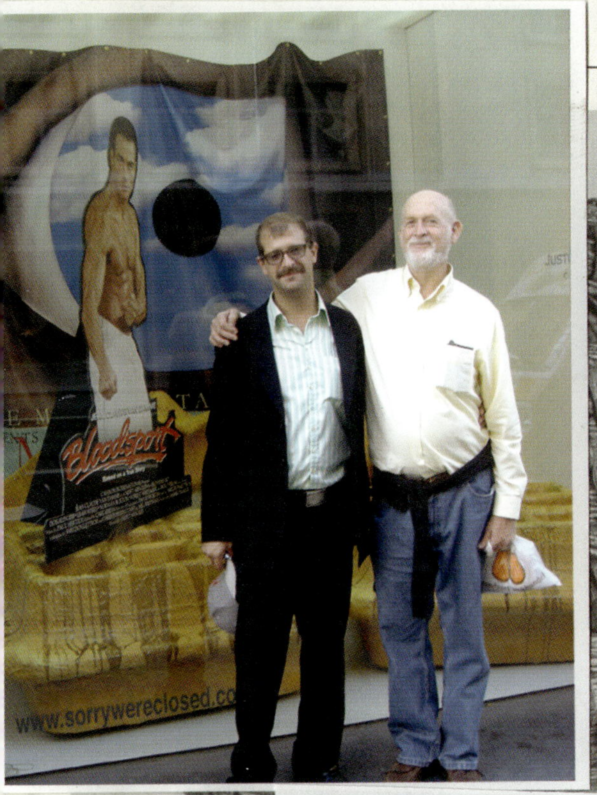

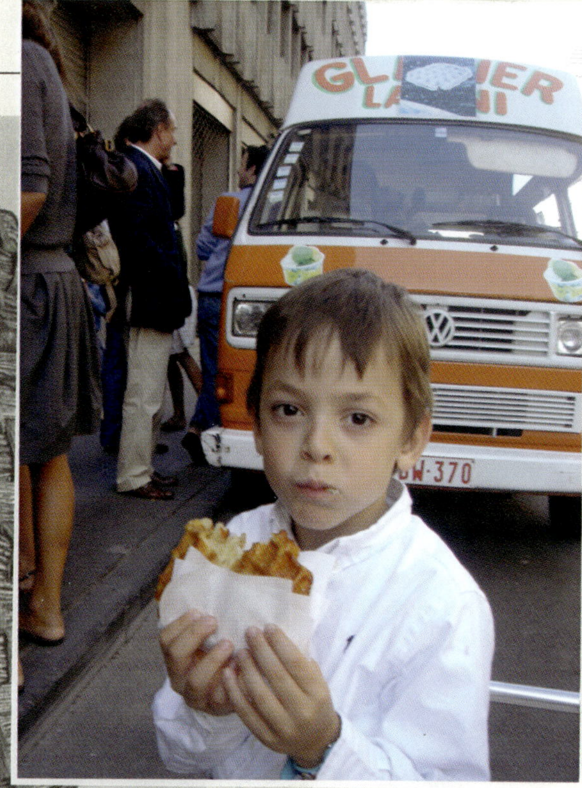

below the Mogollon Rim. ...ndation of the coils ...osed of shredded ...presumably bear- ...1993; height: 7.5"; ...llection no. GP 16975)

plaited and even ... years, nine differe... dation, were usec... raneously. Weav... ing stitches, and ... material for the ... (the plant used b... bundle material. ...

were small, ranging from a quarter to three-eighths of an inch in diameter.

A southern origin for ... possible. Lynn Teague (199... basket weaving techniqu... northern Durango, and v... those of historical norther... archaeological sites in nort... culture because with then...

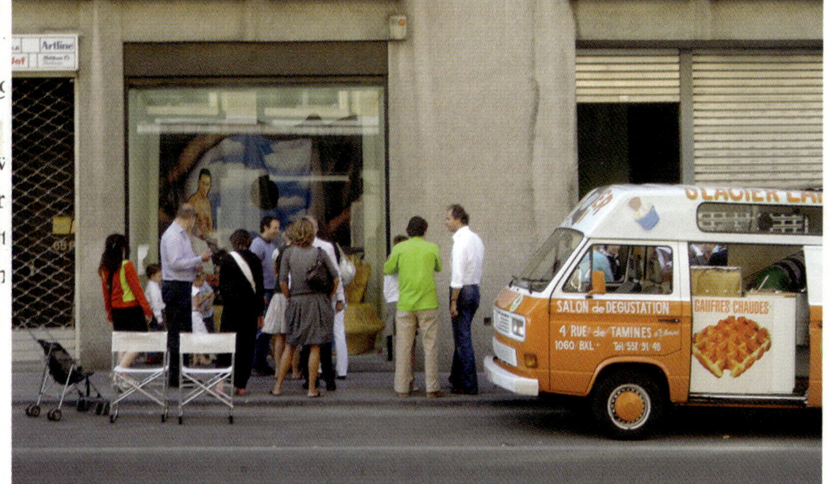

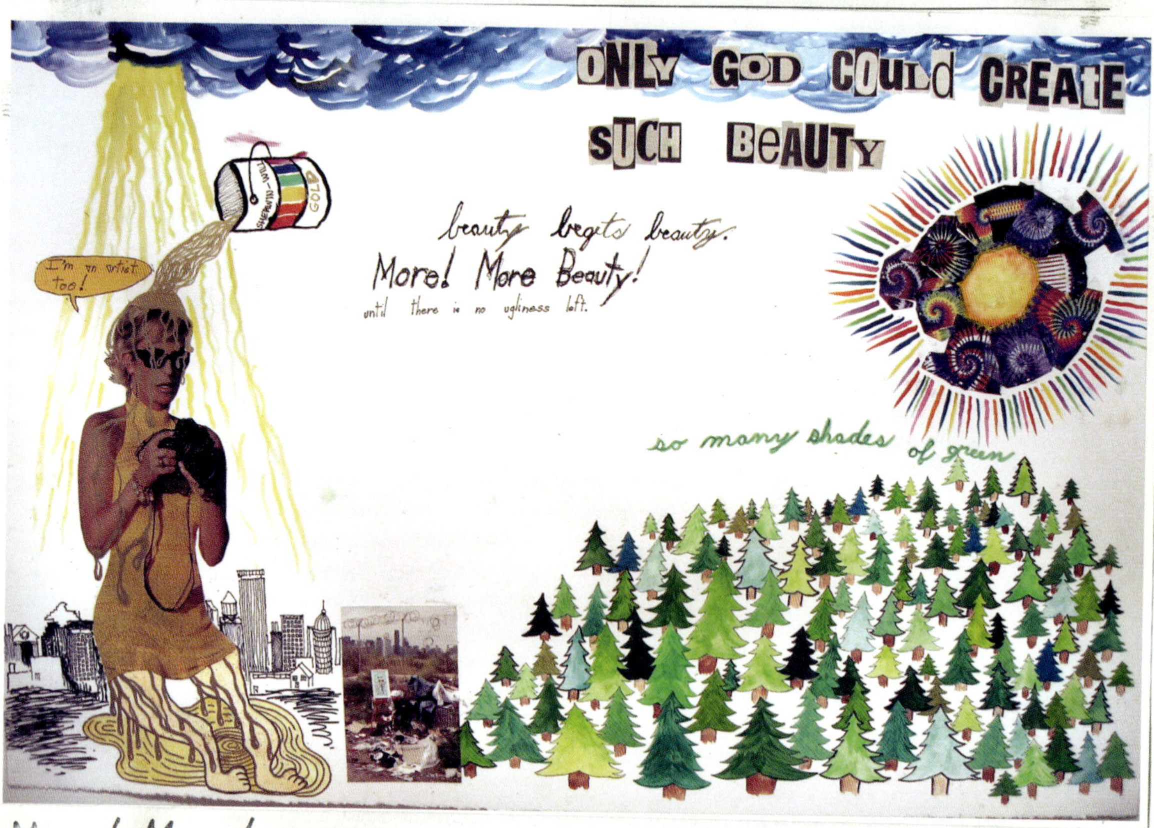

More! More! 2004
collage and ink on paper

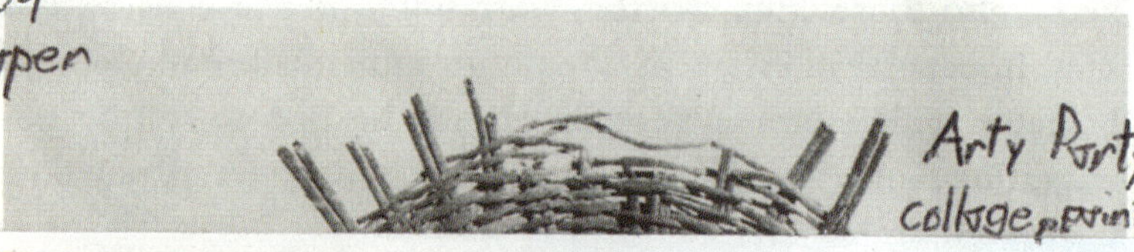

Arty Party 2006
collage, print, sponge on paper

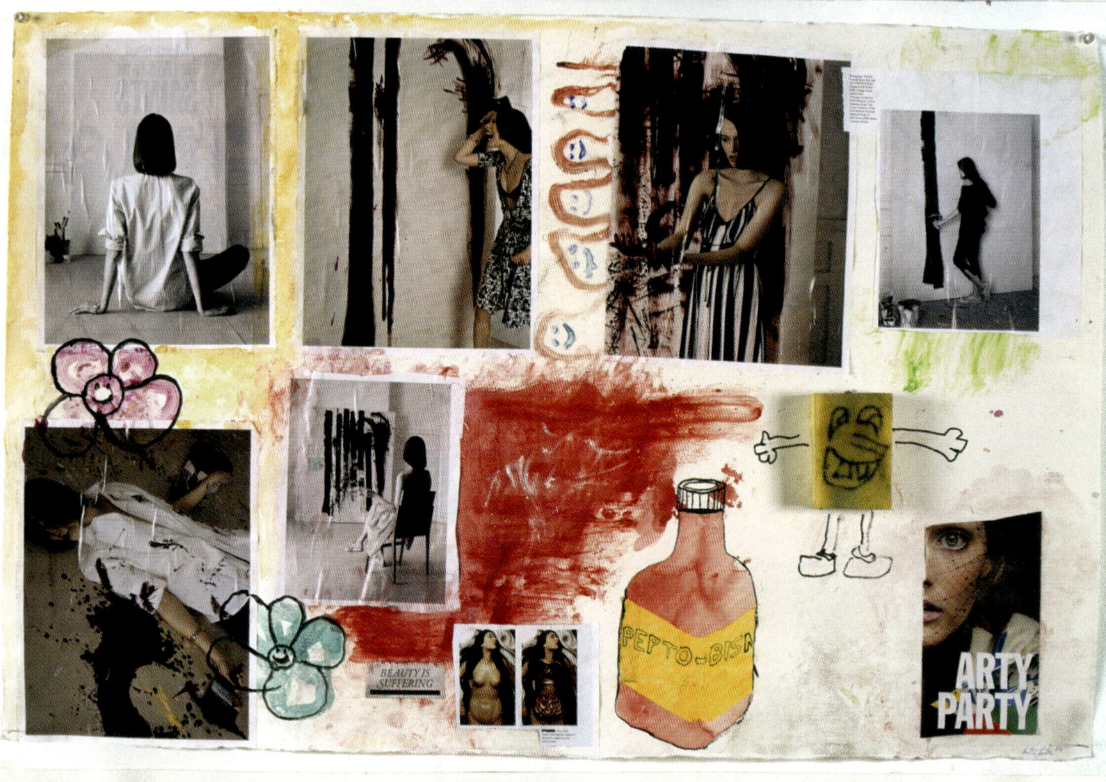

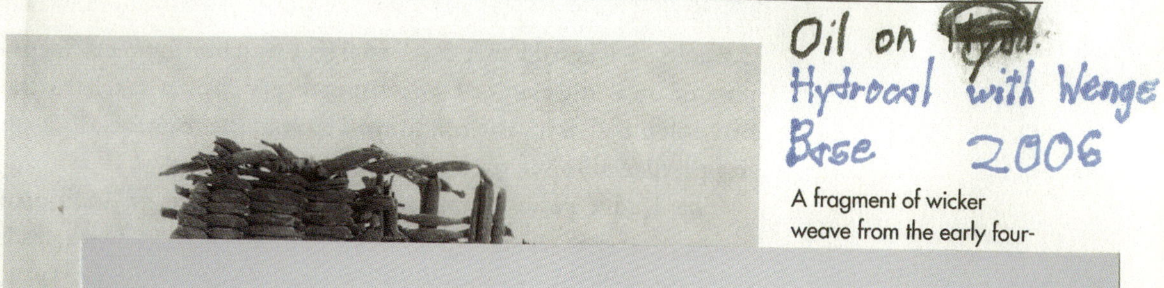

HAMBURGER HELPER

A fragment of wicker
weave from the early four-

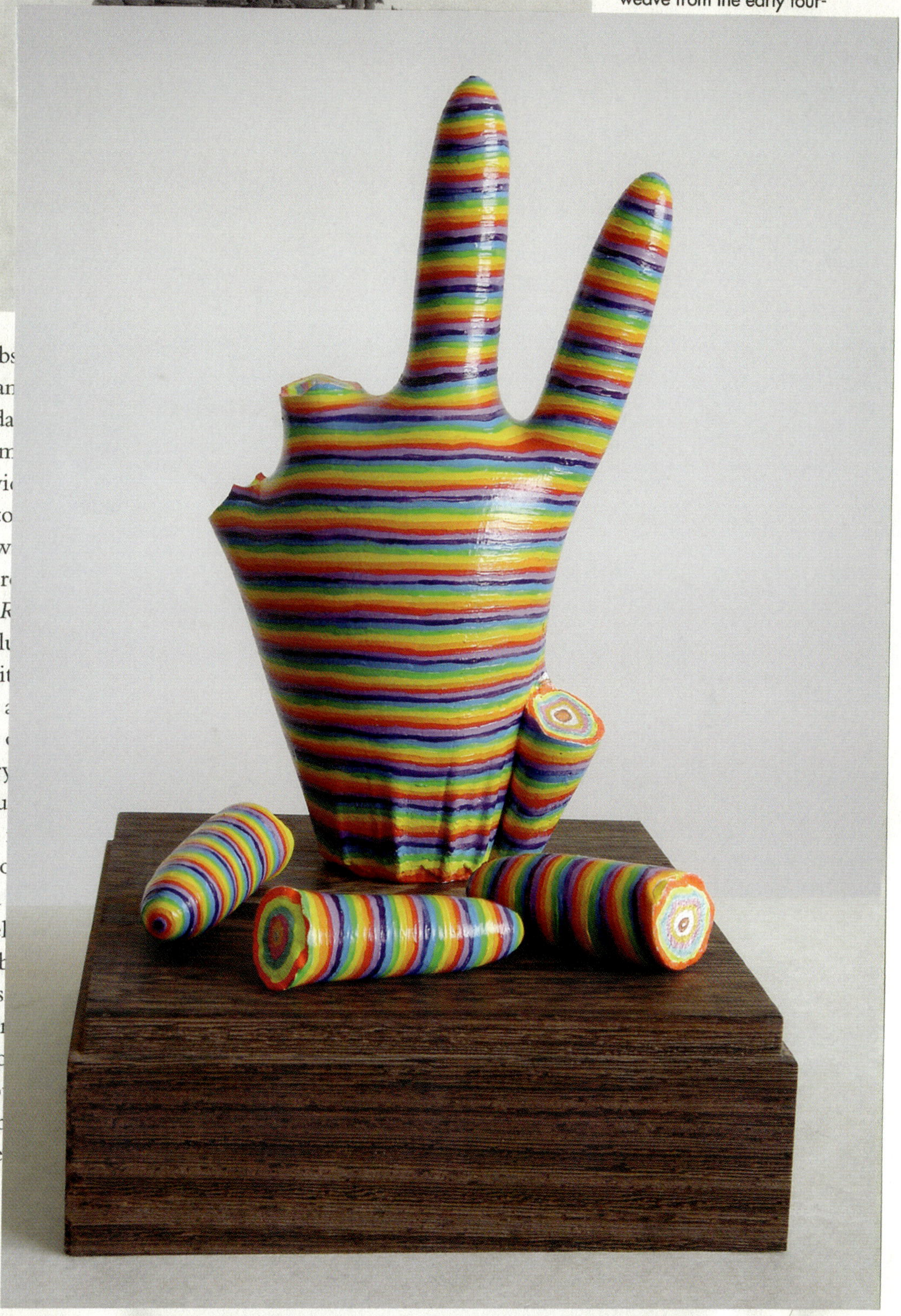

Its subs
unchan
gins da
   Som
the wi
tion to
ture w
1914 r
River R
the Blu
deposit
Hopi a
posits
pottery
a tribu
pahos
Most c
have a
tunatel
these b
becaus
curs or
are loc
previo
describ
for me

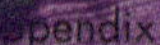

DNA TEST
SHOWS:
CRUISE NOT SURI's
FATHER!!!
SO WHO IS REAL DAD?

Losing the Baby Weight
Holmes is getting back in shape for her wedding
May 28, 2006
June 15, 2005
The first-time mom (nearly six weeks after giving birth) gained an estimated 35 pounds, the top of the recommended range.
Holmes, prepregnancy, stayed fit by running.

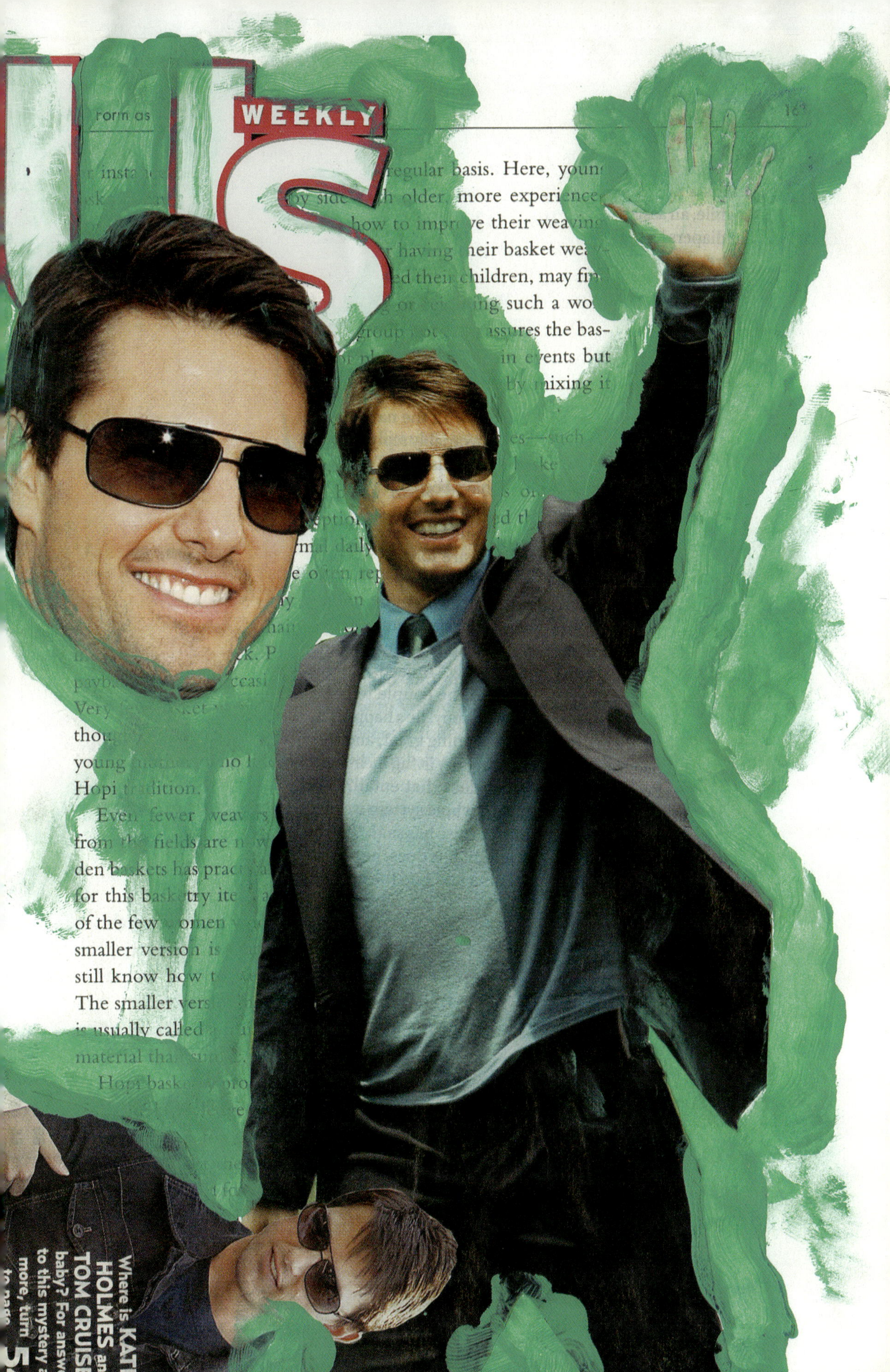
US WEEKLY
regular basis. Here, young
by side with older more experienced
how to improve their weaving
having their basket wea-
their children, may fir
such a wo
assures the bas-
in events but
by mixing it
Hopi tradition.
Even fewer weavers
from the fields are now
den baskets has pract
for this basketry ite
of the few women
smaller version is
still know how t
The smaller vers
is usually called
material that
Hopi basketry
Where is KATIE HOLMES and TOM CRUISE baby? For answer to this mystery a more, turn to page 54

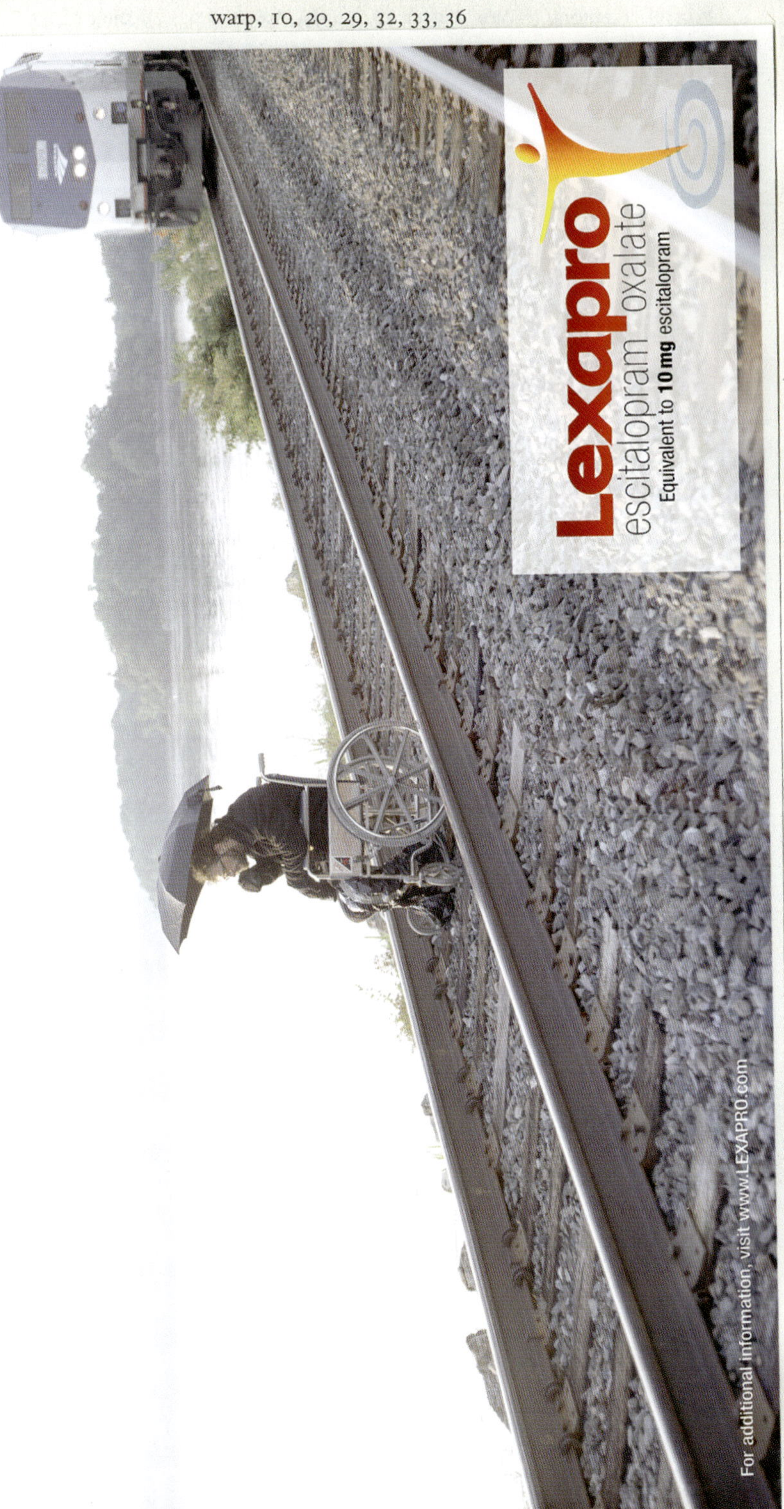
DON'T LET IT COME TO THIS.
Lexapro
escitalopram oxalate
Equivalent to 10 mg escitalopram
For additional information, visit www.LEXAPRO.com

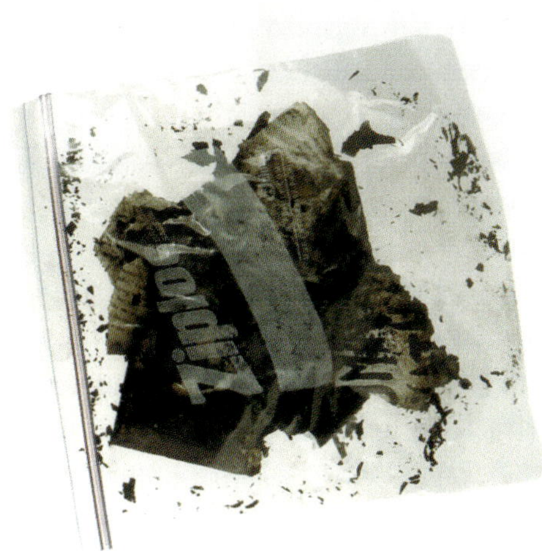

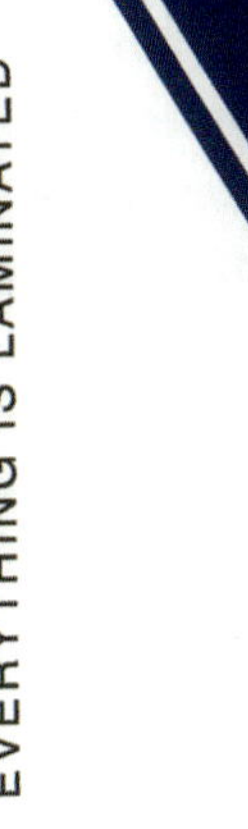

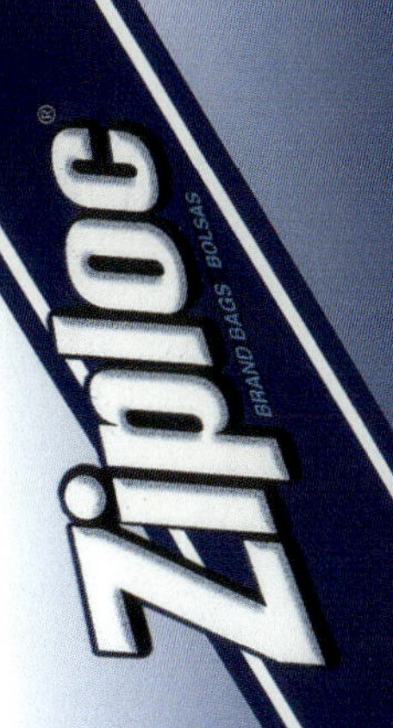

EVERYTHING IS LAMINATED

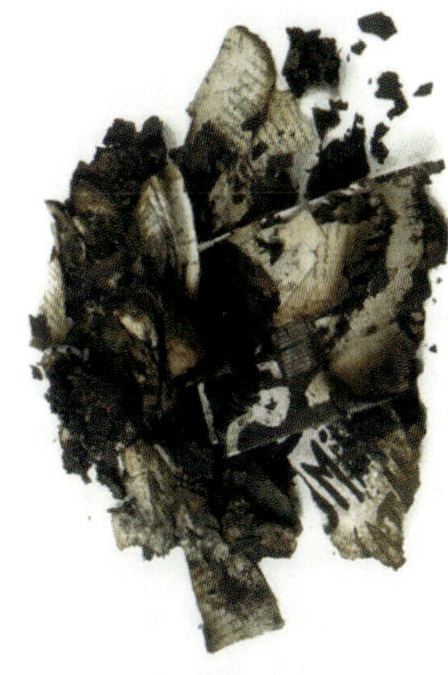

EVERYTHING IS ELIMINATED

EVERYTHING IS ILLUMINATED

About the Author

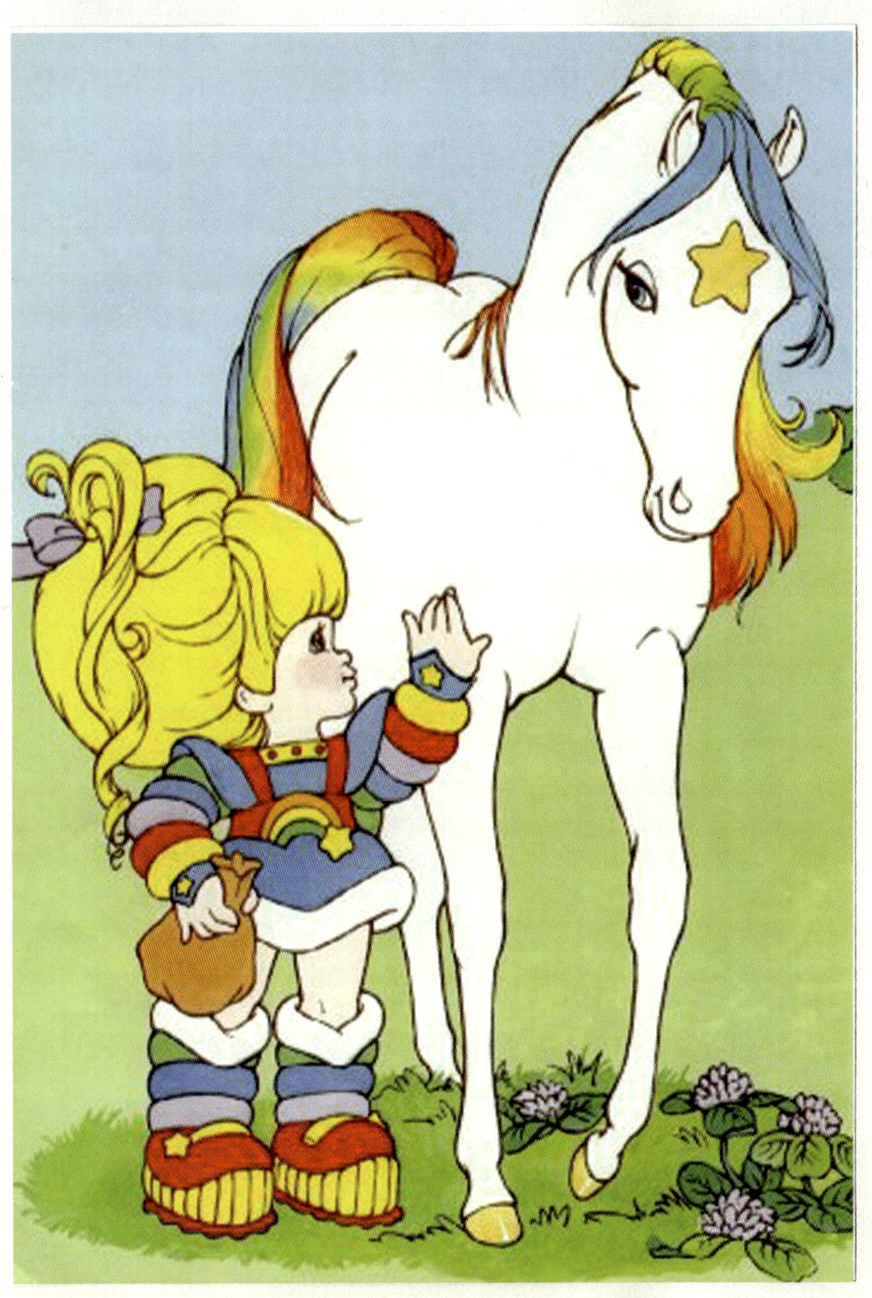